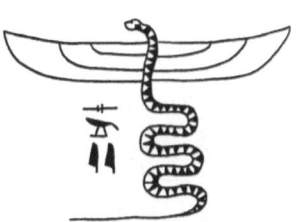

THE COBRA GODDESS
& THE CHAOS SERPENT
in Ancient Egypt

Published by Avalonia

BM Avalonia
London
WC1N 3XX
England, UK

www.avaloniabooks.co.uk

The Cobra Goddess & the Chaos Serpent in Ancient Egypt

Copyright © Lesley Jackson, 2020

ISBN 978-1-910191-24-8
(Paperback)

First published by Avalonia, April 2020
Typeset and design by Satori.

Illustrations by Brian Andrews © 2020

British Library Cataloguing in Publication Data. A catalogue record for this book is available from the British Library.

Every effort has been made to credit material, and to obtain permission from copyright holders for the use of their work. If you notice any error or omission please notify the publisher so that corrections can be incorporated into future editions of this work.

The information provided in this book hopes to inspire and inform. The author and publisher assume no responsibility for the effects, or lack thereof, obtained from the practices described in this book.

All rights reserved. No part of this publication may be reproduced or utilized in any form or by any means, electronic or mechanical, including photocopying, microfilm, recording, or by any information storage and retrieval system, or used in another book, without written permission from the author, with the exception of brief quotations in reviews or articles where appropriate credit is given to the copyright holder.

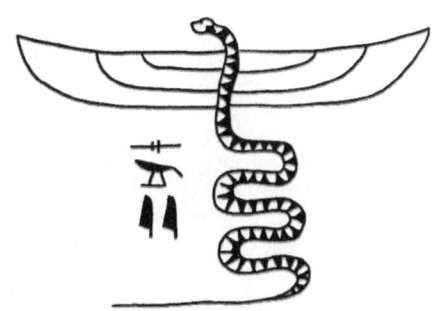

The Cobra Goddess
& the Chaos Serpent
in Ancient Egypt

Lesley Jackson

PUBLISHED BY AVALONIA
WWW.AVALONIABOOKS.CO.UK

Lesley Jackson

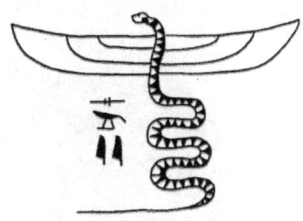

DEDICATION

This book is dedicated to the Cobra Goddess in all her manifestations

"the Uraeus who appeared at the beginning"

and to

Angela, Kate, Susie and Valerie for their enthusiastic support of parties and excursions.

Biography

Lesley Jackson has a lifelong interest in archaeology, ancient history and sacred myth and a fascination with the mysterious geographical, be they lost worlds, otherworlds or the sacred places of this world. She is a devotee of the Egyptian deities and since being blessed with early retirement has devoted much of her time to researching and writing about them.

Lesley is the author of *Thoth: The History of the Ancient Egyptian God of Wisdom*, *Hathor: A Reintroduction to an Ancient Egyptian Goddess*, *Isis: The Eternal Goddess of Egypt and Rome*, and *Sekhmet and Bastet: The Feline Powers of Egypt*, all published by Avalonia. She has written a number of articles about Egyptian religion, some of which have been published in Pagan Dawn and Nile Magazine.

Despite the strong call of Egypt she is a Northerner at heart, preferring cooler climes and wooded landscapes. She lives in the East Riding of Yorkshire, close to the lost world of Doggerland.

ACKNOWLEDGEMENTS

No study of Egyptian religion would be possible without access to their writings. I am indebted to all of those who have studied these ancient languages and have provided translations for the rest of us to use.

I would like to thank the British Library, the Egyptian Exploration Society and the University of Hull for the use of their libraries.

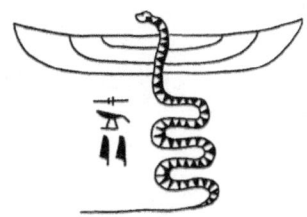

Table of Contents

Introduction 11
The Perfect Symbol 13
The Cosmic Serpent 30
The Great Rebel Serpent 41
The Uraeus Goddess 58
Cobra Goddesses 79
Serpent Gods 106
Serpents of Fire, Earth and Water 122
Magic and Healing 132
Two Serpent Stories 152
Snakes in the Afterlife 162
Serpent Mysteries 189
The Eternal Serpent 218
Bibliography 220
Index 227

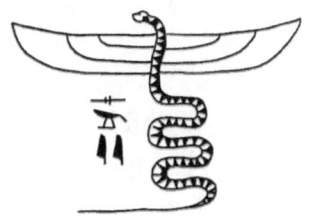

CHAPTER 1

Introduction

"I extended everywhere, in accordance with what was to come into existence."[1]

I have always had a fondness for snakes, more in terms of their elegance and role in mythology rather than their natural history. I have never wanted one as a pet but I always covet gold serpentine jewellery which is imbued with their special powers. You are never far from snakes in Egyptian religion, especially with the Goddesses, so it is perhaps inevitable that my researches should lead me towards the serpentine path. Researching and writing my books about Hathor and then Sekhmet and Bastet deepened my interest in the *Uraeus* Goddess and the strong link between felines and snakes. Forever lurking at the perimeter is the arch-fiend and sun-stealing Chaos Serpent Apophis who cannot be ignored for long. As always I started with questions. Why is there such a strong link between cobras and Goddesses? Where are the Snake Gods and are there any Cobra Gods? Why are Cobra Goddesses essentially good, though not necessarily safe, while the Snake Gods appear to range from good to evil? Why should serpents be considered wise? Amongst this plethora of supernatural serpents are there any dragons in Egypt?

Snakes have simultaneously repulsed and fascinated humans since our earliest origins. Every culture incorporates them in their

---

[1] *Myth and Symbol in Ancient Egypt*, Clark, 1978:51

beliefs. I was initially intending to look at Egypt's neighbouring cultures to see how they compared with the Egyptians' interpretations of snakes. I soon decided that Egypt, including a brief look at its Greco-Roman influences, was sufficient for one book. Here I investigate all aspects of snakes from divine serpents to physical snakes – in the three realms of the cosmic, this world and the afterworld. The words snake and serpent are often used interchangeably. I have tried to be consistent and tend to use serpent when referring to otherworldly or divine snakes, but many times I have chosen the word which sounds best in the context. I appreciate that not everyone shares my fascination for snakes, but to understand Egyptian religion you have to understand snakes. As Ankh-Sheshonk said *"it is better to have a serpent hanging around the house than a fool"*.[2]

---

[2] *The Living Wisdom of Ancient Egypt*, Jacq, 1999:137

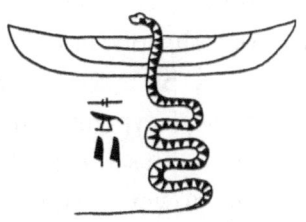

CHAPTER 2

The Perfect Symbol

"The serpent remains the great common denominator, upon which the mind ceaselessly relies." [3]

INTRODUCTION

There are many creatures which are dangerous yet prove alluring for humans. As a predator we admire top predators such as lions yet fear them because we are potential prey. The snake is one such creature and the fear and revulsion of snakes is widespread throughout all cultures, as is the fascination and morbid curiosity they invoke. The Ancient Egyptians were no exception to this. In Western culture the good snake was obliterated by the concept of the evil serpent. This is in stark contrast to Egypt where beneficial and protective snakes abound. Balanced tension is a constant theme in Egyptian myth and religion so where there are good snakes there will be evil ones and vice versa.

THE ESSENTIAL COMPONENTS OF A PERSON

A number of terms occur throughout this book which relate to both humans and deities. The Egyptians believed that a human was made up of a number of components; the physical body and

---

[3] *Snake*, Stutesman, 2005:186

its shadow, the *ba*, *ka* and *akh* and the true name. Deities were similar but usually without the physical body. These terms are difficult to explain and interpretations vary because it is not always clear exactly what the Egyptians understood them to be. The *ba* is sometimes described as the soul but is nearer to our concept of personality and power. Deities usually have multiple *bas*. The *ba* is independent of the body and to emphasise its freedom it is often depicted as the *ba*-bird, a bird with a human head. Jacq describes the *ba* as the power of incarnation.[4] The *ka* can be considered as the life-force or vital energy, but the word is also translated as soul or spirit. The *ka* comes into being at the same time as the person. The *akh* is the form that the vindicated deceased take and is a celestial subtle body. It is a transfigured and imperishable spirit. The true name of the person, or deity, was called the *ren* and was as critical as the other components. Lose your name and you lose your existence. The earthbound *ka* needs to connect with the energy and solidity of earth to recover and replenish its energy, especially when intense or traumatic events have depleted it. Stillness and solitude are essential for the *ka's* recovery. The free-flying *ba* longs for heaven but in life the earthbound serpentine *ka* provides an anchor to reality and stops us drifting off into inner space leaving us unable to cope with the present reality.

A BRIEF NATURAL HISTORY OF SNAKES

Snakes were widespread in Egypt especially in the Delta and along the Nile Valley. Their habitats encompass water, marshes, fields and deserts. During the inundation snakes, and their prey, will have been driven onto higher ground and into close proximity to settlements. They will also have been common around the tombs and temples at the edges of the deserts. The main species that were widespread and symbolic were the cobras and vipers; the Egyptian Cobra (*Naja haje*), the Black-necked Cobra (*Naja nigricollis*), the Horned Viper (*Cerastes cerastes*) and the Sahara Sand Viper (*Cerastes vipera*). The African Rock Python (*Python sebae*) is thought to have been present in Pre-dynastic

---

[4] *Magic and Mystery in Ancient Egypt*, Jacq, 2002:56

Egypt but became extinct there in the Early Dynastic. A few may have been imported from southern counties. Snakes on some Naqada III artefacts have been identified as pythons. Despite being absent for most of the Pharaonic Period pythons certainly weren't forgotten as references to the *"snake who swallowed an ass"* and the fear of being eaten by snakes demonstrates. The cobra is the most distinctive of the snakes with a hood it can expand using its cervical ribs. When it rears up it can elevate the front third of its body. As the black-necked cobra can be 1.5m in length this will create a very threatening posture. The cobra will rear up and extend its hood as a warning when it is frightened or annoyed, but it will keep its mouth closed. Only if it feels threatened will it then lift its head and open its mouth ready to spray venom. All snakes discharge their venom through an opening in their fangs. The angles differ for spitting cobras who can direct their venom horizontally or at an angle of up to 45°. The cobra leans backwards and ejects its venom by muscular pressure. They have a very accurate aim which is always directed at the eyes. Receiving venom in the eyes will paralyse the optic nerve causing burning pain and temporary blindness. In some extreme cases the blindness is permanent. Receiving venom in the eyes will kill small animals such as rats or cats.

All snakes share a number of characteristics. They continually shed their skin as their body grows. As the old skin is rubbed off a new, shiny, skin is revealed. This means that it isn't possible to tell the age of a snake by its appearance. Snakes don't have eyelids, giving them a fixed stare and the suggestion of intense observation. They have a forked tongue which flickers. It is used by the snake to smell with and it is thought that it is forked to allow it to pinpoint the source of the smell as accurately as possible. Snakes have legendary swallowing ability as their lower jaw can be unhinged allowing them to swallow prey larger than themselves, be it an egg or an antelope. Most snakes lay eggs which the female will protect. Some of the characteristics of snakes appear almost otherworldly. They can 'see' in the dark by detecting infrared radiation and vibrations from their prey and surroundings. As humans lose their vision, their primary sense, at night this is particularly significant. Creatures who could apparently see in total darkness were assigned special powers. Part of a snake's fascination and repulsion lies in its shape which appears quite alien, being undifferentiated and totally flexible. They appear to move without an obvious means of propulsion and can tie themselves in knots. Their graceful and sinuous movement is silent and very fast. Snakes appear to flow like water and disappear into cracks in the ground. Some can move through sand as if swimming and can breathe while buried. They can blend perfectly with the vegetation and hang motionless from a branch.

As well as moving quickly, snakes strike very fast. One spell from the *Book of the Dead*, for going against an enemy, alludes to this. "*I have stridden out with the speed of the uraeus.*"[5] Not all snakes are venomous and not all bites are fatal and certain species of snakes are more aggressive than others. Some avoid humans whilst others will readily co-habit as long as they are not disturbed. Cobras in particular are often found near human habitations. While not everyone is happy to share accommodation with a snake some people will have tolerated them as representations of a Goddess or as a protective entity. They can also make effective guards as their known presence is a powerful deterrent.

THE NATURAL ENEMIES OF SNAKES

Despite their powers and venom snakes do have natural as well as human enemies. In Egypt the main predators of snakes are cats, ibis, mongooses and shrews. Both wild and domesticated cats will attack snakes. Archaeologists working in the 1930's commented on cats killing horned vipers and cobras. Cats are considered solar creatures and aligned with the Solar deities especially Ra, Horus and Bastet. Their ability to kill snakes emphasised this link as the Chaos Serpent Apophis is the main enemy of the Sun God. A very popular vignette of spell 17 from the *Book of the Dead* depicts Ra as the Great Cat decapitating a large snake who represents Apophis. Most depictions have a male cat but a female is sometimes shown if the deceased was a

---

[5] *The Ancient Egyptian Book of the Dead*, Faulkner, 1989:37 spell 11

woman. "*The killing of the snake Apophis by the living cat who has come out of the underworld.*"[6] During the Late and Greco-Roman Periods cats were popular depictions on amulets and plaques as they were believed to give protection from snakebite and scorpion stings.

The Sacred Ibis (*Threskiornis aethiopicus*) will kill and eat snakes. It was closely associated with Thoth, the God of magic and wisdom, who has strong afterlife and protective aspects. He is depicted as an ibis, an ibis-headed man or a baboon. The Greeks had plenty to say about the protective aspects of the ibis. Herodotus writes about winged snakes which came into Egypt from Arabia. Fortunately *"the ibises meet them at the entrance to the pass and do not let them through, but kill them. According to the Arabians, this service is the reason for the great reverence with which the ibis is regarded in Egypt, and the Egyptians themselves admit the truth of what they say."* He reports seeing piles of bones from these winged snakes. *"The winged snakes resemble water snakes; their wings are not feathered, but are like a bat's."*[7] Aelian had a similar tale. *"The Black Ibis does not permit the winged serpents from Arabia to cross into Egypt...while the other kind encounters the serpents that come down the Nile when in flood and destroys them."*[8] A spell from the Ptolemaic Period, for an unknown purpose, is written in circles around a drawing of an ibis referred to as *"the one who has swallowed the serpent"*.[9]

The mongoose or ichneumon (*Herpestes ichneumon*) is a small carnivore. They have a slender body, similar to that of a weasel, and are larger than a domestic cat. They are renowned as snake killers and have a natural resistance to snake venom. Aelian comments on mongoose battling snakes describing how they leap at their necks and strangle them. He also records that they eat snake eggs. A mongoose is depicted on a pottery vase from the Naqada II Period. Beneath it are wavy lines which may be snakes but probably represent water. There is a late Dynastic bronze statuette of a mongoose on a shrine who wears a *uraeus* on its forehead. Because of its ability to kill snakes the mongoose was associated with the solar deities, in particular Horus and Atum.

---

[6] *The Cat in Ancient Egypt*, Malek, 1993:83-84
[7] *The Histories*, Herodotus & Selincourt, 2003:124-125
[8] *On the Characteristics of Animals Volume I*, Aelian & Scholfield, 1957:135
[9] *The Greek Magical Papyri in Translation Volume I*, Betz, 1996:124

(Atum is a Sun God and Creator often fused with Ra as Atum-Ra. Amun is also a Creator God and he too was combined with Ra as Amun-Ra.) The Goddess Mafdet was associated with the mongoose as well as with the leopard and cheetah. She is an ancient protective Goddess first attested to in the 1st dynasty. In a number of *Pyramid Texts* spells she kills snakes "*Mafdet leaps at the neck of the in-dif-snake*".[10] She also joins in the fight against Apophis. Given their size (50-60mm) the Egyptian pygmy shrew (Crocidura religiosa) is not an obvious killer of snakes. These tiny nocturnal rodents have a venomous bite and will hunt small snakes, which aligns them with the Solar Gods. Mummified shrews have been found buried with falcon mummies, representing Horus, to protect him from the nightly attacks of Apophis.

SNAKE SYMBOLISM

The varied symbolism of snakes arises from their specific characteristics as well as from the human response to them. It is probably the most symbolic of all creatures across all cultures and all periods of history. The fear of snakes is deeply embedded in humans and is also common in many mammals especially monkeys and primates. Why then does it have a universal presence in all cultures throughout our history? A feared creature would surely be avoided or just associated with negative aspects. Despite our instinctive fear we view snakes with fascination. As a symbol the snake is emotionally loaded and ambivalent. The snake appears alien to us and it seems as if we can't decide whether it is good or evil, beautiful or repulsive. It is because of this intense and ambiguous reaction that snakes have played a major role in the religion and symbolism of most cultures. The Judaeo-Christian tradition has indoctrinated many of us to see the snake as wholly evil, but even they acknowledged its wisdom. The symbol of the pre-Israelite Goddess was a snake on a pole which explains this strong reaction as their religion was particularly Goddess-hating.[11]

---

[10] *The Ancient Egyptian Pyramid Texts*, Faulkner, 2007:88 utterance 295
[11] *Lady of the Beasts*, Johnson, 1988:182

Duality

At first glance the snake is a good symbol of unity as its body is undifferentiated but for the Egyptians, as indeed for many cultures, it was a symbol of duality because of the dual feelings of fear and awe which snakes provoke. The forked tongue emphasises the snake's duality. It is a bringer of death but also a creator and a provider. Snake venom kills but the symbol of a physician is the rod of Asclepius – a snake entwined around a staff. Many species of snakes have bi-coloured skin which will have been interpreted as another reference to its duality. Spells in the *Pyramid Texts* and *Coffin Texts* refer to mottled-snakes. This type of colouring was considered liminal as it contained both light and dark. The *sem*-priests who conducted the funerary rites wore leopard skins. The Celestial Cow is shown spotted and Ruty (the Double Lion) often has spotted skin.

The personification of the ultimate evil and nemesis of creation was the Chaos Serpent Apophis, but the benevolent Goddess Renenutet and the protective *uraeus* is also a snake. "*One acclaims the Uraeus, and spits on the Apophis-serpent.*"[12] Like humans, snakes appear at all points of the good-evil spectrum. Every action has its opposite and the snake is ready to personify them all. Snakes were widespread and common in Egypt and there are numerous spells to prevent and cure snakebite. Despite this the Egyptians never viewed the snake as intrinsically evil just because it was potentially deadly. That was just part of its nature. "*You cannot remove the venom from the crocodile, from the serpent and from the evil man.*"[13] In the *Book of the Dead* every deceased person faces judgment. Should they fail to be worthy of rebirth they face a second and ultimate death. They are thrown to a creature called Ammut, the Devourer of Souls. She is a hybrid of the two most dangerous river creatures, the crocodile and the hippo, combined with a lion or leopard. It is significant that this most feared creature is not a snake, nor does she have any snake parts. Despite being the form taken by Apophis the snake, even in its worst aspect, does not prey on an individual's soul.

---

[12] *The Teachings of Amenophis the Son of Kanakht. Papyrus B.M. 10474*, Griffith, 1926:191-231
[13] *The Living Wisdom of Ancient Egypt*, Jacq, 1999:32

Shapeshifter

Snakes are extremely flexible and they have the ability to take any shape. When straight they can be associated with phallic symbolism, wands, staffs and the masculine in general. Coiled they create circles associated with the feminine; the womb and protective enclosure. What is the true shape of a snake? Does it even have one? As such it is the shape of magic and ambivalence. Its meandering movement suggests the flow of water, linear time and life energy. Coiled, it hints at potential movement, cyclical time and natural cycles. It can be the vibrating energy that flows from the moment of creation through all lives and natural cycles. Its open mouth brings the end; be it the end of an individual's life or the end of creation if Apophis manages to swallow the sun. The coiling snake can also represent life energy flowing through the body. Is this another reason why some deities were depicted with snakes around them?

Rebirth

Snakes are a symbol of rebirth through the periodic shedding of their skin. The snake discards its worn-out form and emerges looking younger in its new skin. This hints at indestructibility as the essential essence of the snake continues only its outer appearance, namely its skin, changes. This dies and is replaced with something similar. Rebirth along with all other symbolism will be covered in detail in the relevant chapters.

Otherworldly

A number of features suggested that snakes were not always of this world. They do not have ears (although the Egyptians may not have known this) suggesting that they were attuned to the divine and otherworld rather than the profane noises of this world. They do not vocalise, apart from hissing, which again suggests communication with a world other than this one. They do not have a smell. Like the elusive deities they are virtually invisible even though you can be in their immediate presence. They do not show emotions, unless it is a clear warning signal. We are not able to 'read' snakes as we can other humans and mammals. We cannot communicate with snakes or develop a true relationship with them. As such they appear superior, mysterious and enigmatic.

WOMEN AND SNAKES

From the Neolithic there has been a strong connection between snakes and women and Goddesses in many cultures. Why should this be? The snake's association with rebirth and fertility is one possibility as is its phallic shape. It also has a similar form to the umbilical cord. Like snakes, women are associated with duality. This can be misogynistic in that men fear women's sexuality but enjoy it. The snake can be associated with the concept of the Earth or Mother Goddess who gives birth to all but also takes everything back at death. There is no evidence of this concept in the Pre-dynastic but it may have been present. In Egypt the cobra has such a strong association with Goddesses that it is virtually interchangeable with any Goddess. Why the cobra has such a strong association with the feminine isn't clear. They are said to be good mothers but so are many female animals. Perhaps the curved shape of the hood hinted at the female form. Cobra Goddesses dominate in the Egyptian pantheon and there tend to be Snake Gods rather than Cobra Gods.

TREES AND SNAKES

Snakes can climb, they hide in trees and bushes and also shelter beneath them, emphasising the link between the two. This presents a danger to any human or animal seeking shade, refuge or fruit. Snakes are thus associated with trees in myth. Many cultures have a snake and tree association where the snake acts as the guardian protecting the tree, its fruit or the gateway marked by the tree. The tree can represent stability and the snake energy. A tree easily becomes a staff or wand that the snake can wrap itself around, such as in the Asclepian wand and the *caduceus*. This is the traditional symbol of Hermes (whom the Greeks associated with Thoth) and consists of two snakes entwined around a staff which often has wings.[14] In the *Book of the Dead* Apophis is slain under a sacred tree.

ROPE AND SPINES

A rope is similar in shape and flexibility to a snake so the rope and snake can be used interchangeably in text and illustrations. The link is further emphasised by the fact that the word for 'twisted rope' puns with that for 'double snake'. The *Greenfield* papyrus shows the Solar Barque being pulled by six men using cobras as ropes.[15] In the *Book of Gates* twelve Gods carry the Snake of Time who is referred to as the Double Rope.[16] A ferryboat spell in the *Coffin Texts* assigns the boat's cable with the *n'w*-snake. The shape and flexibility of snakes also find a visual parallel in knots. As well as being essential for practical work knots had an important function in religion, magic and healing. Specific knots were used for different purposes in magic as well as in practical usage. Each type of knot has specific positive and negative values in the tying and untying. As with magic in general knots are neutral and it is the intent which makes them good or bad. They are used to block or release, bind or free, protect or restrain and to connect or disconnect. A net is made by utilising a pattern of knotwork. As well as practical trapping abilities the net can represent a magical force field. The spine was associated with life-giving energy and the snake. The snake is primarily a spine and the articulate spine of a butchered animal has a similar shape and form to a snake. The vertebrae form a distinct knob aligning them with knots which further enhance the spine's energy symbolism. Aelian reports that *"the spine of a dead man, they say, transforms the putrefying marrow into a snake"*.[17]

SNAKES IN THE PRE-DYNASTIC

Egyptians in the Pre-dynastic would have encountered plenty

---

[14] *Snake*, Stutesman, 2005:70
[15] *Journey Through the Afterlife: Ancient Egyptian Book of the Dead*, Taylor, 2010:309
[16] *The Egyptian Book of Gates*, Abt & Hornung, 2014:175
[17] *On the Characteristics of Animals volume I*, Aelian & Scholfield, 1957:71

of snakes but we do not know what symbolism was ascribed to them. Although there is less material surviving from the Pre-dynastic than from later periods we still have a wide variety of decorated material. Certain themes dominate, such as ships and ostriches. Painted pottery from the Naqada I Period is often decorated with long wavy lines. It can be argued that these represent snakes, equally they could represent water. Only if the head is present do we know for certain that a snake is depicted. There are a number of depictions of snakes on various objects from this period. One bowl depicts a snake with multiple coils stretched out in a V-shape.[18] The horned viper appears as a decorative motif in the Naqada III Period.[19] There is a Naqada pottery vessel stand from a tomb in Qustul, Lower Nubia (now the border with Sudan) on which three serpents are shown in relief crawling up the sides of the pot.[20] A knife handle from Gebel Tarif depicts large snakes with curving bodies. They are thick and heavy like pythons and many have interpreted them as such.[21] Without any accompanying text it is impossible to determine if the snake is representing a deity or power and of which gender.

Snakes are also shown with other animals such as elephants, otters and giraffes. We don't know if these represent deities, tribal totems and important symbols or are primarily a depiction of the wildlife at the time. The earliest depictions of elephants and snakes appear on a Naqada I palette but it isn't clear if this is a cobra or another type of snake. The earliest definite depiction of cobras and elephants occurs on a Pre-dynastic knife handle.[22] An ivory comb dating to the late Pre-dynastic shows animals in processions including elephants standing on the top of snakes. The snakes' heads rise to the same height as the elephants' heads. The snakes seem to lead or protect the elephants rather than being trampled on or chased by them as some earlier commentators have suggested. Whatever the relationship is between the animals it doesn't appear to be a hostile one. Did the

---

[18] *The Cobra Goddesses of Ancient Egypt*, Johnson, 1990:36
[19] *The Animal World of the Pharaohs*, Houlihan, 1996:171
[20] *Before the Pyramids*, Teeter 2011:85
[21] *The Cobra Goddesses of Ancient Egypt*, Johnson, 1990:38
[22] *The Cobra Goddesses of Ancient Egypt*, Johnson, 1990:20

similarity between the shape of the elephant's trunk and the snake suggest an underlying link to the people who produced the art? Bastaway says that there are some African myths which associate elephants and snakes with creation so this depiction may do the same.[23] Bowls from a Naqada cemetery in the south of the country depict various birds and animals including three birds attacking large snakes with their beaks. Teeter suggests that they are vultures with the possible interpretation of the Vulture Goddess of the south, Nekhbet, defeating the Cobra Goddess of the north, Wadjet. My suggestion is that the birds might be Secretary Birds (*Sagittarius serpentarius*) given the shape of the body and their long legs and necks. These birds do prey on snakes in this manner. It is thought that the bowls were imported and painted in Nubia so the scenes are likely to represent local mythology and wildlife.[24]

In the early Old Kingdom the symbolism changes. The snake, lion, hawk and baboon become the dominant divine symbols replacing those of the Pre-dynastic. This is probably due to the rise of the monarchy and the centralised state of Egypt. New symbols were needed that weren't encumbered with meanings from a decentralised, tribal period. Whatever the reason, as soon as the state of Egypt was established serpent symbolism becomes important and the Cobra Goddess as the *Uraeus* became a critical component of both the monarchy and the state religion.

GREEK AND ROMAN SNAKE SYMBOLISM

The Greeks and Romans used a lot of snake symbolism in their mythology and decoration, even before they were influenced by the Egyptians. Snake jewellery was very popular as were serpents in their mythology. When still a young child Hercules strangled two snakes. A serpent guarded the tree bearing the apples of immortality which he later had to retrieve. Many Greek and Roman deities were associated with snakes. Athena (Minerva) is depicted with serpents on her helmet and clothes. Hermes (Mercury) carries a wand entwined by two snakes. It was easy for

---

[23] *The Snake who was God*, Bastaway, 2018:35-39
[24] *Before the Pyramids*, Teeter 2011:89

the Greeks and Romans to appreciate the snake symbolism of the Egyptians and to incorporate it into their own iconography even if they didn't fully understand the nuances.

SNAKES IN EGYPTIAN ART

Hieroglyphs depicting dangerous creatures, such as snakes, sometimes show the creature cut in two or mutilated in some way to destroy their power. The cobra sign is used phonetically for *d* or the feminine *dt*. The sign for a cobra is drawn as a cobra in a resting position, similar in form to a flattened S, which differentiates it from the *uraeus* which is always depicted rearing with its hood extended.[25] The cobra hieroglyph was used at the start of the name of the 1st dynasty king Djet. He is often referred to as the Serpent King because of the way his name is written.[26] The horned viper hieroglyph is used phonetically for *f*.[27] One suggestion is that the name for viper was onomatopoeic with the *f* sound imitating the hiss of the viper.[28] This hieroglyph was used when referring to the viper species, *fy*.

Some depictions of snakes are very realistic, others are not. The afterlife is infested with snakes including many with multiple heads. Snakes with two heads can occur in nature as a result of the incomplete splitting of an embryo. Such sightings may have originally inspired these depictions. It isn't clear exactly what is meant when snakes are shown with multiple heads. Do two heads indicate duality or unity? A two-headed snake can allude to the Two Kingdoms and the unification of Egypt. The *Bakenmu* papyrus depicts the Solar Barque being pulled by an undulating snake with two heads, one wearing the White Crown the other wearing the Red Crown.[29] Do multiple heads hint at multiple aspects or indicate movement? The latter is a device used in modern cartoons. In the *Amduat* there is a three-headed snake near a path. She is called the One who Moves. Her three heads

---

[25] *Hieroglyphics: The writings of Ancient Egypt*, Betro, 1996:113
[26] *Snakes*, Wilson, 2010:46-47
[27] *Hieroglyphics: The writings of Ancient Egypt*, Betro, 1996:113
[28] *Fy 'Cerastes'*, Newberry, 1971:118
[29] *And Each Staff Transformed into a Snake: The Serpent Wand in Ancient Egypt*, Ritner, 2006:214

may indicate the swaying of her body. Some snakes are shown with a second head at the tail. I refer to these as double-headed to distinguish them from the ones with two heads at the head end which I refer to as two-headed. In nature there are some snakes which have a flattened tail which is similar in appearance to its head. This may have helped to develop this concept.

Snakes can also have the head of another creature, such as a human or a lion. The head is the most important distinguishing feature of any creature and so a head of a different species informs the viewer of the chief characteristic or aspect that is being portrayed. When depicting deities this device is also used to emphasise a particular aspect as well as to identify them. The presence of a hawk head points to a connection with Horus and a baboon head with Thoth and communication. One snake amulet from the Saite Period has a cow's head aligning it with Hathor.[30] Lion-headed snakes are found on the healing *cippi* (see chapter 9) which probably allude to the healing powers of Sekhmet. Sometimes the non-snake head appears at the tail or even on top of the snake's own head. Does a human head suggest a distinct personality that distinguishes this snake from others? In the illustrations for the Netherworld Books a number of cobras are shown human-headed. Here they are not just snakes but have the human characteristics of personality, thought and reasoning. A serpent form is the best to adopt whilst traversing this barren part of the underworld but they need to retain their human senses to act as competent guides. Sometimes it is better to go with gut reaction or animal instinct but this must be balanced by common sense and reflection. There doesn't appear to be any correlation with the number of heads, or the non-snake heads, and the roles or aspects of the snakes depicted in the Netherworld texts. For example; snakes with hawk and human heads appear in guardian and rejuvenation roles, but the majority of snakes in these roles are depicted as natural-looking snakes. Snakes with two or more heads appear confined to a similar role but again this depiction doesn't predominate. It may relate to something in the text or to their names but I haven't been able to find the link. No doubt an Egyptian priestess or priest could tell us otherwise.

---

[30] *Amulets of Ancient Egypt*, Andrews, 1994:35

Afterlife snakes can be shown with multiple pairs of legs. These are not the legs of a dragon, being part of the creature's body. The legs appear human in form and are used to indicate movement. There are also many depictions of winged snakes. The wings are not intended to form part of the body. Wings are used to denote protection, the symbolism arising from the way a bird will use its wings to protect or shelter its young. Snakes are shown in all positions. In the funerary texts they are often shown standing straight on their tails. This is to emphasise their length or importance. Lying on the ground will make the snake appear subservient as all other creatures will be higher than it, despite its length, importance and ferocity. A standing posture may also hint at the powerful snake energy rising from the earth to heal or protect. In this form the snake looks like a snake wand or staff which emphasises at its magical powers. Many of these snakes appear in a protective aspect, either as a gate guardian or as the protector of a person of deity. A tall imposing posture emphasises a creature's ability to protect.

Artists took full advantage at the flexibility of snakes. A very long snake can be coiled like a net. This is seen in the 4th hour of the *Book of Gates* where a snake called the Removing One depicts time. This emphasises both the great length of her body as well as hinting at the constraints that passing time places on all life and natural cycles. The Egyptians used staircases to show a transition between states and places as well as gates. Stairs were associated with the underworld from the earliest periods as the tombs had stairs descending into them. Flexible snakes can easily mimic the basic outline of a flight of stairs and with the head pointing upwards they can indicate the direction of movement. This is seen in a vignette from the papyrus of Padiamun where Osiris sits enthroned at the top of a staircase with Isis, Nephthys and Horus in attendance. A long snake splits the staircase from the throne in imitation of a step, his head near that of Horus. The upward movement of the snake depicts the progression of Osiris from death to rebirth.[31]

---

[31] *Reading Egyptian Art*, Wilkinson, 2011:151

SACRED SNAKES

The Egyptians didn't practise zoolatry, the worship of animals. In theory, the creature itself wasn't as important as the divine power it contained. Some animals held the *ba* of a particular deity or were particularly loved by that deity so were chosen to serve as their divine representation on earth. In the *Amduat* there is a snake who is referred to as the *ba*-soul of Osiris. The *Book of the Heavenly Cow* explains that the *"ba of each god and each goddess is in the snakes"* but the *ba* of Apophis is *"in the Eastern Mountain"*.[32] Apophis doesn't belong to the created world so his *ba* isn't stable enough to be contained within a living creature. Only the liminal Eastern Mountain, the horizon where the sun rose, was able to bear such chaotic power.

Sacred animals were kept in temples. *"Near Thebes a species of snake is found said to be sacred to Zeus; these snakes are small and quite harmless, and have two horns growing from the top of their heads. Such as are found dead are buried in the temple of Zeus."*[33] (Zeus was equated with Amun by the Greeks.) Aelian mentions a town in the Delta, Metelis, where a sacred serpent was kept in a tower. The priests used to soak barley in honey and wine for this snake. One priest decided to remain in the temple to view the sacred serpent and having seen it suffered the usual fate of those who spy on the divine. *"He went out of his mind…and shortly afterwards fell down dead."*[34] During the Late and Greco-Roman Periods the offering of mummies to various deities rapidly increased in popularity. Large numbers of bronze boxes with images of snakes on top have been found from the Late Period. These might be votive offerings or coffins for sacred snakes. An X-ray of a supposed cat mummy belonging to the Liverpool Museum showed that it was in fact a bundle of snakes. It is believed to be a votive offering for Amun in his role as Creator or to Atum of Heliopolis as snakes were sacred to him.[35] The Egyptians were always practical, recognising that despite their cosmic and divine significance, all snakes were potentially dangerous. *"Even the smallest serpent is*

---

[32] The Literature of Ancient Egypt, Simpson, 2003:296
[33] The Histories, Herodotus & Selincourt, 2003:124
[34] On the Characteristics of Animals Volume III, Aelian & Scholfield, 1957:383
[35] The Snake who was God, Bastaway, 2018:35-39

venomous."[36] Despite that, they managed to convince Aelian otherwise. He reported that cobras were treated with great respect and as a result *"become extremely gentle and tame"*.[37] Not many would be entirely convinced about the latter statement.

CONCLUSION

The snake's natural characteristics can easily be used to represent a wide variety of complex concepts. Its lack of signs of ageing and the ability to slough its skin shows immortality and rebirth. The fact that it appears and disappears into the ground shows mobility between worlds and secret knowledge of the afterlife. Its venom suggests a supernatural power and evil but also protection and healing. Its limbless mobility emphasises a mysterious spirit-like ability. A snake swallowing its prey whole summarised the mouth of damnation, resurrection and transmutation. With its speed and fast strikes and coiling and uncoiling movements the snakes depicts energy in action or being transferred. Life means movement, especially upward, and a rearing snake could be used to depict the vital life forces. The deceased are frequently exhorted to *"raise yourself"*. With the species' ability to live in all environments the snake can represent universal power and control. All in all it is the perfect symbol of the mysterious twists, changes and renewals of our lives. With such heavyweight symbolism the link between snakes and the divine is strong. The snake and its duality is present at all three levels of creation; the cosmic and the divine, this world and the afterlife.

---

[36] *The Living Wisdom of Ancient Egypt*, Jacq, 1999:32
[37] *On the Characteristics of Animals Volume III*, Aelian & Scholfield, 1957:327

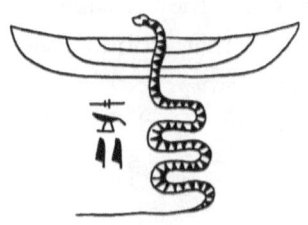

CHAPTER 3

The Cosmic Serpent

"When the first snake makes heaven through its desire...the sky will spit forth an egg, like the egg of a falcon."[38]

THE SERPENT OF ORIGINS

Before creation there was only the *nun* which consisted solely of undifferentiated potential and chaos. The Egyptians envisaged this pre-creation state as a primeval ocean, without form or boundary, because it is impossible to understand or imagine absolute nonbeing and nothingness. Some texts describe it as being *"before two things had developed"*[39] that is before the duality of light and dark, male and female and life and death. In the magical instant of creation the consciousness of the Creator emerged in the *nun*. *"I come into being in my own shape; do not enquire about my creation from the Abyss."*[40] The deities associated with creation vary over time and location but the Cosmic Serpent is prominent in what is known as the Khonsu cosmogony. This is named after the Ptolemaic temple of the Lunar God Khonsu at Karnak where it is inscribed on the precinct walls. It appears to be an attempt to unify the three prominent cosmogonies of Memphis, Heliopolis and Hermopolis.

---

[38] *The Khonsu Cosmogony*, Cruz-Uribe, 1994:169-189
[39] *Egyptian Mythology*, Pinch, 2002:58
[40] *The Ancient Egyptian Coffin Texts Volume I*, Faulkner, 2007:72 spell 75

In the Khonsu cosmogony the original Creator is the serpent Kematef who is the primeval form of Amun. *"Amun-Re…august ba of Kematef, father of the offspring, mother of the egg, who engendered all living things…father of the fathers of the Ogdoad…the one who created this place out of Nun."*[41] Kematef means *"he who has completed his moment"*[42] and alludes to his transformation or rebirth from Primeval Serpent to the God Amun. Like the snake shedding its skin Kematef moves through the various stages of creation. A snake is a good symbol for a Creator due to its undivided body and its flowing movement suggesting the flowing waters of the *nun*. Kematef is also associated with Ptah, the Creator God of Memphis. Scenes from the temple of Khonsu describe how Ptah created the world. It refers to him as *"He of the twisted rope, he is this god and his father, the companion of the double snake throughout the year"*. Having come into being in a mysterious and incomprehensible act Kematef *"created his body form as Irta"* and so *"the second snake came into being"*. Through this act he created the second generation of deities. The texts say that Irta had the face of a beetle. The name Irta means *"creator of the land"*[43] and it is believed that the reference to the beetle is a pun as well as alluding to Khepri (the Sun God in his dawn aspect) who takes the form of a scarab. From this point the text becomes confusing as the various creation theologies are woven together in an attempt to produce an all-embracing account.

Kematef, or Irta, generates the Ogdoad, the eight primitive deities who continue the work of creation. The Ogdoad (a group of eight deities) was found in Middle Egypt with a cult centre at Hermopolis where they were associated with Thoth. The Ogdoad consists of four snake-headed Goddesses and four frog-headed Gods. In a depiction at the temple of Hathor at Dendera the Goddesses have blue heads, symbolising both heaven and the cosmic waters of the *nun*.[44] At this stage the act of creation was still ongoing and the frogs and snakes represented creatures who could live in the unconsolidated muddy water – the primeval slime. Depicting the Gods as frogs rather than snakes might have

---

[41] *The Khonsu Cosmogony*, Cruz-Uribe, 1994:169-189
[42] *The Routledge Dictionary of Egyptian Gods and Goddesses*, Hart, 2005:20
[43] *The Khonsu Cosmogony*, Cruz-Uribe, 1994:169-189
[44] *The Ten Dead Deities of the Temple of Dendera*, Gaber, 2017:239-262

alluded to their powerful fertilising aspect; as seen in the huge amounts of frog spawn and tadpoles produced. Or it could reflect the more female divine powers of snakes. More likely, we do not fully understand the symbolism. The pairs of the Ogdoad are Nun and Naunet who represent the primeval waters, Heh and Hauhet who represent its infinite space, Keh and Kauket who represent its darkness and Amun and Amaunet representing its hidden power. Like their progenitor snakes they belong to a pre-creation stage where everything was still unformed. The powerful primeval energy released by Kematef, Irta and the Ogdoad interacted and the resulting reaction destroyed them but completed the work of creation. They enabled the process of creation to progress past its initial state but they could not be part of it for they could not cross the barrier formed by creation. This is unlike the other inhabitant of the *nun*, the Chaos Serpent Apophis, for whom it is no obstacle. Having created the first land and the lotus which gave birth to the sun Kematef, Irta and the Ogdoad died and were buried in the mound of Djamet at Medinet Habu, which was said to have been the mound of creation. The *Feast of the Decade* was held every ten days in which the God Amenopet (a son of Amun) travelled to the west bank of the Nile to offer libations to his forefathers. *"You will behold Amenopet when he ferries across to Djeme in order to present offerings to Kematef."*[45] The world is built on the sacrifice and bodies of these serpents.

In texts from the Greco-Roman temple of Hathor at Dendera Harsomtus (Horus of the Two Lands) can be equated with Irta. This is also referenced in the much earlier *Coffin Texts*. Horus, to emphasise his antiquity and importance, says that he was one of the original snakes created by Atum. This appears in a similar form in the *Book of the Dead*. *"I am one of those snakes that the eye of the sole lord created before Isis came into being."*[46] Irta appears in epithets of Ptah and it is possible that this theology might have originated at Ptah's cult centre of Memphis. At the temple of Khonsu at Karnak there is reference to a ram-headed snake who fertilised

---

[45] *Traversing Eternity*, Smith, 2009:412
[46] *An Ancient Egyptian Book of the Dead*, O'Rourke, 2016:171 spell 78

the cosmic egg.[47]

The Dendera texts also allude to Hathor as the primeval creator. Here she is depicted enthroned in front of the Ogdoad as the *"Daughter of Irta…who came into being at the beginning with her father Nun"*.[48] Hathor is usually seen as the daughter of Ra and his Eye but there are texts which refer to the Divine Eye of Irta which emits light as he emerges from the *nun*. The Eye of the Sun is also the *Uraeus* Goddess. This suggests that Irta has an androgynous nature, which is not unusual for a Creator. Some other Greco-Roman texts refer to Kematef creating Irta as the Earth Serpent demiurge (creator) and Mut as the primeval *Uraeus* Goddess. Hathor and Mut both have epithets alluding to their form as the primeval *uraeus*. Two examples are *"uraeus of the first primordial god"* and *"who burst forth from Nun together with Irta"*. Having created these two serpents of fire and earth Kematef returns to the *nun* while the process of creation continues. Texts from the Greco-Roman temples of Kom Ombo and Esna describe creation by the *Uraeus* Goddess by *"melting"* the waters of the *nun* and *"baking"* the earth *"with the fire of her eyes and the breath of flame which came forth from her mouth"*.[49]

Neith the Great was an ancient Creator Goddess from the Delta with a cult centre at Sais. She was associated with war and textiles and was one of the protector Goddesses of the sarcophagus together with Isis, Nephthys and the Scorpion Goddess Selket. Neith created herself and then created the land as she needed somewhere to stand. Neith was considered the mother of snakes and crocodiles. In one *Coffin Texts* spell there is reference to the snakes of Neith in a spell for having power over water and for being with Neith. She was also considered the mother of the Chaos Serpent Apophis (see chapter 4). Neith is closely associated with the primeval snakes in her litany at the temple of Khnum at Esna. The writing makes strong use of wordplay to emphasise the meaning of the text. *"To Neith, the creative water, which made the earth"* is written using a lot of hieroglyphs for water. The next invocation uses snake

---

[47] *Egyptian Myth: A Very Short Introduction*, Pinch, 2004:52
[48] *The Theology of Hathor of Dendera*, Richter, 2016:169
[49] *The Theology of Hathor of Dendera*, Richter, 2016:172

hieroglyphs. *"To Neith who made the raising earth. To Neith, the Raising One who made the One who made the earth."*[50] The word raising is suggestive of the rearing cobra. This is also emphasised by the choice of the words – *tnn* for raising earth then *ir-t3* for earth. These are also the names of the primeval divine serpents who form the intermediate steps of creation; Irta and Tenen. (In the Khonsu cosmography Ptah as the Creator is sometimes referred to as Ptah-Tenen) This is alluded to in a later invocation. *"To Neith, the living female ancestor, who appears in the nun together with Irta...the uraeus who appeared at the beginning."*[51]

The serpent Mehen is usually associated with the nightly regeneration of the Sun God and is discussed in later chapters. One spell in the *Book of Two Ways* hints at a role in creation. In this the Lord of All recounts the good deeds he did *"within the Coiled One"*. These include two to silence evil as well as four relating to humans. He made the winds so people could breathe and created the inundation so everyone could grow crops. The other two don't appear to have been very successful as these were to make all men equal and to command them not to do evil.[52]

TEMPORAL SNAKES

The Egyptians had two concepts of time and eternity. *Neheh* is perpetual cyclical time; the ever-renewing and returning cycles of nature seen daily with the sun's journey and annually with the seasons and inundation. It is time which results in continuous transformation such as the process of birth, life and death. *Neheh* is considered a masculine concept, it can be depicted as the sun and is closely linked to Ra. *Djet* is time viewed as continuous and linear, time which remains and endures. It is the apparently eternal presence of the land, in particular Egypt, which underlies all the cyclical changes. Usually considered a female concept it was linked to an image of the earth. Despite the gender difference, Osiris belongs more to the domain of *djet*, especially when mummified, as he represents a more static or completed

---

[50] *Magic in the Sign*, Ciampini, 2016:17
[51] *Magic in the Sign*, Ciampini, 2016:19
[52] *The Ancient Egyptian Book of Two Ways*, Lesko, 1977:130 spell 1130

state and is a chthonic God. The children of Atum, Shu and Tefnut, can be equated with the Twin Lions or Ruty. Shu represents eternal recurrence and Tefnut eternal sameness. Snake symbolism is also used to show both forms of time providing another link with feline and serpentine symbolism.

THE SNAKE AS CIRCULAR TIME

The *ouroboros* is an Egyptian symbol adopted by the Greeks, and later cultures, as an ideal method of symbolising eternity. It is a snake which swallows its own tail forming a circle. One is depicted on the shrine of Tutankhamun (18th dynasty) where it is labelled *"tail-in-the-mouth"*. The Greeks called it *"tail eater"* – *ouroboros*.[53] In the funerary papyrus of Herweben the newborn Sun Child is shown inside the *ouroboros* which is supported by Ruty who symbolises yesterday and tomorrow.[54] It illustrates how the universe and nature can perpetually be renewed and the optimistic view that every end is also a beginning. The *ouroboros* can also be a metaphor for the end of time where time catches up with and runs into the beginning of time. One Classical author describes a serpent which was said to surround the cavern which was the source of the Nile. *"A serpent surrounds this cave, engulfing everything with slow but all-devouring jaws...his mouth devours the back-bending tail as with silent movement he traces his own beginning."*[55]

THE SNAKE AS LINEAR TIME

Linear time, apparently continuous and endless, can be represented by the long snake or by the inanimate but serpentine length of rope. The passing of time can be depicted in a number of ways but the concept of the lifespan of an individual as a predetermined length of thread or rope is common in many cultures. The measuring out, or reeling in, of the rope suggests time and an individual's life passing. The Egyptians used water clocks to measure the hours of the night. These are V-shaped

---

[53] *Images of Time in Ancient Egyptian Art*, Bochi, 1994:55-62
[54] *Egyptian Mythology*, Pinch, 2002:90
[55] *Daily Life of Egyptian Gods*, Meeks & Meeks, 1999:19

vessels and images of them can be seen on some tomb paintings. One example comes from the tomb of Rameses VI (20th dynasty) as part of an illustration for the *Book of Earth*. Here an ithyphallic God, the One Who Hides the Hours, stands in a V-shaped funnel. On either side are six small Goddesses, representing the hours, who hold discs. The funnel is in the centre of a very long draped snake who is referred to as the Great Serpent and the Enveloper.

TIME SERPENTS OF THE NETHERWORLD

The majority of images depicting time come from the New Kingdom books of the Netherworld. These books will be covered in more detail in later chapters. Here the snake not only represents time; it *is* time in that it controls or renews time and allocates an individual's lifespan. In the *Amduat* the 11th hour of the night deals with the mysteries of time – what happens to the hours, those short periods of time that we can understand and feel passing? A mummified Goddess squats on the back of a rearing serpent. She is called *"Time"* (*dt*) which is written phonetically using the cobra hieroglyph. The serpent is *"He who takes away the hours"*. In front of the Goddess are eleven stars. These represent the hours of the night which have passed. The individual hours are born out of the Serpent of Time who swallows them when the hour is spent. Text next to the Goddess explains that *"She swallows her images again at this place"*.[56] Schweizer suggests that the Goddess represents *djet* time and that she is shown mummified, like Osiris, to emphasise the duration of time.[57]

Although there are plenty of snakes in the *Book of Gates* there is less emphasis on their regenerative power and more on time. In the 4th hour of the *Book of Gates* time is shown as a very long snake, called the *"Removing One"*. The snake has a large number of coils and sits in a pit. On either side stand six hour Goddesses who represent the twelve hours of the night. The text explains

---

[56] *The Egyptian Amduat*, Abt & Hornung, 2007:332
[57] *The Sungod's Journey Through the Netherworld*, Schweizer, 2010:176

that the snake gives birth to each hour then swallows it.[58] In this text both the hours and the Time Serpent are female. The *Book of Gates* also deals with time allotted to individuals, albeit the deceased. In the 5th hour twelve Gods carry the Serpent of Time. In between each God are hieroglyphs for *"lifetime"*. The Gods are described as carrying *"the lifetime in the West"*.[59] With the serpent they determine the lifetimes of the deceased. The afterlife is often viewed as eternal but in fact it could only last as long as creation because the end of creation means the end of time and the annihilation of everything.

The interplay of rope and snake symbolism relating to time is seen in this text. When Ra speaks to the Gods carrying the Serpent of Time he refers to it as the Double Rope. In the 6th hour twelve Gods carry a double twisted rope which comes out of the mouth of a mummiform God called Aqen. Around them are stars representing the hours. As a coil appears an hour emerges and when the hour is passed it is swallowed by Aqen. In some versions of the *Book of Gates* the Serpent of Time is referred to as Metui or Metuty – the *"doubly twisted one"*.[60] A single rope can represent the measurement of time and place so why is a double rope needed? The double, twisted rope combines opposing powers which are essential as nothing can manifest without duality and opposites. The single rope measures time but the double rope creates it. In the 8th hour twelve Gods carry a rope which has the head and tail of a snake. There is a coil in between each God and above each coil is a star representing the hours. The Gods are described as carrying the rope Devourer which gives birth to each hour. They say *"Open your coil, that your mysteries can emerge"*.[61] Ra is *"waiting till he is provided with his hour"*.[62] Even the deities are subject to time. It is needed so that change and movement can occur. Without it the Sun God cannot traverse the hours of darkness and be reborn with the dawn. Without time the alchemical transformations necessary for rebirth cannot take place.

---

[58] *The Egyptian Book of Gates*, Abt & Hornung, 2014:120
[59] *The Egyptian Book of Gates*, Abt & Hornung, 2014:174
[60] *Images of Time in Ancient Egyptian Art*, Bochi, 1994:55-62
[61] *The Egyptian Book of Gates*, Abt & Hornung, 2014:279
[62] *The Egyptian Book of Gates*, Abt & Hornung, 2014:280

THREATS TO TIME AND CREATION

The created world is encircled by the chaotic waters of the *nun* which forever threatens its existence. It is the duty of everyone from the deities and the king down to the ordinary people to safeguard creation from annihilation. Time and order (*maat*) must be safely separated from the timelessness and chaos of the *nun*. In the minds of the Egyptians the easiest way to stop time was to halt the Solar Barque which carries Ra across the sky, or to destroy him, for if the sun is suspended or destroyed then so will time be. If time is stopped creation will end. By using the secret name of Ra, Isis herself suspended time and held the world at the brink of destruction when she halted the Solar Barque to force Ra to act when the Horus child had been poisoned. The greatest threat to creation though is another serpent, Apophis. Should he ever succeed in stopping the Solar Barque the world will be destroyed.

THE END OF THE WORLD

"The beginning is light, the end is Unified Darkness."[63] As well as being a symbol of time the snake can also be associated with the cosmic collapse of the universe which will bring about the end or suspension of time. One suggestion is that the imagery came from the way the snake periodically sheds its skin. The dead, empty skin alludes to the apparent destruction of the snake which lives on in its new form, or skin. Nothing created will survive forever but the creative principle can endure. In the *Book of the Dead* Atum explains that *"I shall destroy everything I created; this land earth will return to the state of Nun, to the state of flood, as was its original condition. I am what will remain, with Osiris, when I have been transformed anew into a serpent that men cannot know and that gods cannot see."*[64] A text from the temple of Opet at Karnak says *"there is no god, there is no goddess, who will make themselves into another snake"*.[65] The serpent is the enduring and original form of conscious existence before creation and it will endure after the created world has sunk back

---

[63] *The Sungod's Journey Through the Netherworld*, Schweizer, 2010:24
[64] *Gods and Men in Egypt 3000 BCE to 395 CE*, Dunand & Zivie-Coche, 2004:67
[65] *Conceptions of God in Ancient Egypt*, Hornung, 1996:163

into the *nun*. A rock inscription from Hatnub refers to a previous cycle of creation where the only survivor was a *"kerhet-snake which alone remained in this land, while all the rest of men had perished."*[66]

In a reversal of the process of creation everything created will collapse back into the form of the original Cosmic Serpent. Only the Cosmic Serpent can endure in its formless state in the *nun*. Paradoxically this is precisely the form that the Chaos Serpent Apophis takes. Despite the daily battles with Apophis to stop him from destroying creation, in the end the Creator will perform the act himself and sink back into the *nun*. Exhausted by the maintenance of creation, and ready to begin another cycle of regeneration, the Cosmic Serpent will suspend time and dissolve himself so that the world can be made anew. Apophis tries to destroy creation and with it all differentiation and individuality. This will return all of creation back to its primeval state of oneness. Ironically many spiritual aspirations are to 'be at one' with the Creator or the universe – which can be viewed as a voluntary release of individuality with the aim of returning to the undifferentiated *nun*. Eventually Atum will choose to destroy all he has created so why is this different from Apophis doing the same? Is it about owning your power? The end result is the same but Atum decides when it happens. This voluntary destruction may be needed to ensure his survival.

SNAKE ENERGY

"I follow the Great God, who has created himself. Who is He? Energy. The ocean of primordial energy, the father of the Gods."[67]

But what is energy? Its scientific definition is the ability to do work. Energy makes change happen. It exists in a number of states such as heat, light, motion and potential and can be transferred from one object or state to another. It cannot be destroyed. The cosmic snake has two basic functions, to channel energy and to block it. In channelling it causes something to occur – be it the creation of the universe, the regular cycles of nature or birth and rebirth. The blocking snake prevents change,

---

[66] *The Litany of Re*, Piankoff, 1964:49
[67] *The Living Wisdom of Ancient Egypt*, Jacq, 1999:51

it obstructs progress but in doing so creates stability and continuity. At the extreme it tries to stop life and rebirth, to halt the sun and destroy creation. The Cosmic Snake acts as a conduit which bridges the worlds of the sacred and the secular, of the potential and the manifest as well as the living and the dead. Thus it permits energy to traverse the different states. The Cosmic Snake provides the time and the space for transformations to occur. It holds a protected space for order and life within the endless disorder of the *nun*.

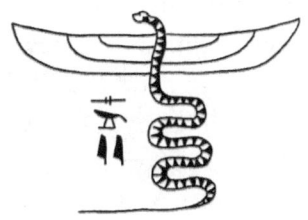

CHAPTER 4

The Great Rebel Serpent

"As for that mountain of Bakhu on which the sky rests...a serpent is on the top of that mountain...it is thirty cubits long, eight cubits of its foreparts are flint, and its teeth gleam."[68]

INTRODUCTION

Apophis is the most dangerous of all the chaos creatures. Each night he attacks the Sun God and tries to destroy the sun. It is impossible to annihilate him, despite what the texts confidently state, he melts back into the *nun* only to reappear another time. Apophis is always a malevolent force, unlike the other cosmic snakes, and he has no redeeming features. He is the ultimate destructive force in the universe and represents total disorder. He wasn't acknowledged as divine as this would have given him too much power and status. His name is written with the snake determinative never that of a deity. A determinative is a sign which gives the meaning of the word but which isn't part of the pronunciation.

NAMING THE ENEMY

Apophis is the Greek version of his name. To the Egyptians he was Apep (*'3pp*). The word is often written in red ink with

---

[68] *The Ancient Egyptian Book of the Dead*, Faulkner, 1989:101 spell 108

black knives drawn over it in an attempt to nullify the power of his name. He has many epithets. A few of them are: Rebel Serpent, Great Rebel, Evil One and the Ill-disposed One. He can be Fierce Faced, Devourer, Enemy, Dark One, Potent of Glance and Evil Minded. In the *Leiden* hymns he is the Dark Adversary. Many epithets are abusive or derogatory such as Bowel of Ra and Intestine of Viscera. Some allude to his desired situation such as Retreater, Fallen or Mangled. He is also called the Fallen One. This refers to the injunctions to fall to the ground, or even die as fallen was a euphemism for death, rather than fallen from divine favour as it is in the Old Testament. The serpent Wamemty is sometimes equated to Apophis. He may just be one of Apophis' cohorts though. With so many names and epithets it was wise to make sure that "*Apep is crushed in all his names*".[69]

APPEARANCE

At first glance the ultimate predator of the universe is depicted in quite a tame manner; as a giant snake. In modern culture we prefer such creatures to look melodramatically scary – from the safety of our armchairs. Actually confronting a giant python in the flesh might be a different matter. To emphasise his length Apophis is sometimes shown tightly coiled. Some texts describe him as 30 cubits in length (15.5m) although one describes him as 120 cubits, about 63m.[70] The largest fossil snake (*Gigantophis garstini*) found to date is over 15 meters in length, twice that of the longest snakes alive today.[71] As this snake lived in Egypt over 40 million years ago it wasn't the inspiration for Apophis. Was Apophis inspired by the African Rock Pythons who swallow their prey whole? They usually reach a length of 3-5m; by comparison the cobra is usually 1-2m in length with a maximum of 3m. The python was present in Egypt during the Pre-dynastic so it is feasible that Apophis was a Great Python deity, totem or demon from these times. Apophis is most active at dusk and dawn, like the python. Alternatively, he could have been partly inspired by a snake swallowing a whole egg. As well as

---

[69] *The Bremner-Rhind Papyrus IV*, Faulkner, 1938:41-53
[70] *The Egyptian Myths*, Shaw, 2014:37
[71] *Snakes in Myth, Magic and History*, Morgan, 2008:104

trying to catch the Solar Barque Apophis was viewed as a water snake who drinks the waters of the celestial ocean leaving the Solar Barque stranded on a sandbank. This is the cosmic equivalent of the failed inundation. His coils become the sandbanks which block the passage of the Solar Barque. This will have been a well-known hazard for boats as the water levels fell.

Snakes are usually silent, not so Apophis. His Egyptian name means Great Babbler. This implies that he was unable to speak properly and gives an onomatopoeic name mimicking the sound a giant water snake could be imagined as making. In the *Book of Gates* he is described as *"one without its eyes...without its nose and without its ears: it breathes on its screaming, it lives on its own shouting"*. As Apophis belongs in the uncreated *nun* he cannot take any energy from the created world. The texts infer that he needs no food except the sound of his own voice. In the *Amduat* we are told that *"it is his voice that leads the gods to him"*.[72] Apophis has a loud roar which echoes through the underworld. Was this sound inspired by the noise of an earthquake? He was associated with frightening events such as unexplained darkness, storms and earthquakes. One epithet of his was Earth Shaker suggesting that he was held responsible for earthquakes. These are a potent symbol of chaos which can reduce an ordered temple, the house of the deities, to rubble in a few minutes. The accompanying noise sounds like the roar of Apophis echoing through the underworld. He also has the epithet Roarer or Roaring Serpent. The other natural events which could have inspired or developed the Apophis mythology were a comet or meteor. The comet appears as a bright streak in the sky. Its tail always points away from the sun giving the impression that it is forever heading towards it. Although a comet is probably a better inspiration and symbol for the fire-breathing *uraeus*. A meteor can produce fast-moving lights, sometimes followed by an air blast producing sound and shock waves if large enough. Whether such events were observed by the Egyptians isn't known but they will certainly have observed comets.

The evil eye of Apophis is his most lethal weapon. It has the power to paralyse the crew of the Solar Barque. *"He will turn his*

---

[72] *Apophis: On the Origin, Name and Nature of an Ancient Egyptian Anti-god*, Morenz, 2004:201-205

eye toward Re. A standstill comes about among the crew." If this happens it will suspend time and if Apophis can destroy the barque it will result in the annihilation of creation. Only the Chaos God Seth seems immune to his dreadful stare, perhaps it is because he too has an evil eye. Seth gives the crew wise advice. "*You who see from afar, just close your eye.*"[73] Snakes in general are connected with the evil eye. The *Pyramid Texts* refer to the dangerous gaze of a snake. "*Direct the face to the road – eye of N, don't look at him.*" A sensible precaution against a spitting cobra. Some of the names of snakes reflect this fear such Starer and Whose Eyes are Destroying. The unblinking stare of the snake will have reinforced this perception, as well as the fact that fear can cause temporary paralysis. One spell in the *Book of the Dead* refers to Apophis who "*lames with his eyes*".[74] His epithet He with the Bad Head may refer to his evil eye rather than his general repulsiveness. It is logical then to blind Apophis to render this weapon ineffective. A fragment of a *stele* from Deir el-Medina refers to blinding him, as does a spell on a statue of Ramesses III (20th dynasty).

OTHER FORMS OF APOPHIS

In some texts Apophis is called the turtle, some translations give it as tortoise which is less likely. The turtle referred to is the African, or Nile, soft-shelled turtle (*Trionyx triunguiss*). They are large, growing up to 95cm in length, and have a very long neck. They are ambush predators lying submerged in the mud with their head protruding, this gives them a very snake-like appearance. They are aggressive and have a strong bite. From at least the Middle Kingdom the turtle was considered an enemy of the Sun God. "*Ra lives, the turtle dies.*"[75] By the late New Kingdom the turtle was linked with Apophis. His name was written with the turtle hieroglyph despite being depicted as a snake. The turtle lives in mud which was associated with negative feelings such as choking and being held fast. Wetlands were often used as symbols of creation with the emerging land, vegetation and

---

[73] *The Evil Eye of Apophis*, Borghouts, 1972:114-150
[74] *The Evil Eye of Apophis*, Borghouts, 1972:114-150
[75] *Devil in Disguise – On the Stellar Mythology of Apophis*, Stemmler-Harding, 2016:111

abundance of animals representing the created universe and the dark, muddy waters representing the *nun*. As an inhabitant of muddy environments the turtle could easily be considered an inhabitant of the *nun* and therefore hostile to the Sun God.

WHERE DOES APOPHIS COME FROM?

His origin is not referred to in the early texts, and he was probably considered a pre-existing inhabitant of the *nun*. Could he have arisen when Kematef created himself? - after all, all the disorder that Kematef rejected had to go somewhere. Did creation create its own enemy and antithesis as a by-product? As soon as matter, or the universe, is created there are some forces acting to keep it together and others acting to rip it apart. Creation endures because the forces are in balance. This is physics but to it we apply the value judgements of good and bad. Greco-Roman inscriptions from the temple of Khnum at Esna state that the Goddess Neith is the mother of Apophis. *"They (the anterior gods) repelled a drop of spittle from her mouth…it was transformed into a serpent of 100 cubits, which was named Apophis. Its heart conceived revolt against Re, with its associates that issued from its eye."*[76] Neith created the world using seven magical words so her saliva would be very magical and potent. The Greek name Apophis is interpreted as *"he who was spat out"* which refers to his creation from the saliva of Neith.[77]

The existence of evil is the Achilles heel of all religions proclaiming all-powerful and all-loving deities. If creation is of divine origin, how did evil and division arise? The Egyptian answer might have been that evil, in the form of Apophis, exists outside of creation and it is his malevolence seeping into creation that creates evil in all human forms. However, this argument is somewhat nullified by the fact that Ra orders the destruction of mankind in one of the myths. The *Book of the Heavenly Cow* explains that Ra became fed up with the rebellious humans and ordered the Sky Goddess to lift him into the heavens far away from their discord. It is only after the separation of heaven and

---

[76] *Gods and Men in Egypt 3000 BCE to 395 CE*, Dunand & Zivie-Coche, 2004:64
[77] *The Routledge Dictionary of Egyptian Gods and Goddesses*, Hart, 2005:31

earth and the withdrawal of Ra to heaven that Apophis emerges. This splitting created a power vacuum in need of filling, and the world became an ambivalent, dualistic place. Apophis doesn't appear in the *Pyramid Texts*. This may be because they don't deal with the journey of the Sun God through the underworld. Once established, the Old Kingdom was a prosperous and stable time so the divine order was never questioned, in state religion at least. There might have been a local tradition of a demon that threatened the sun, perhaps as part of a myth explaining solar eclipses. The first mention of Apophis found so far is in the 9th Dynasty tomb of Ankhtifi at Mo'alla. It depicts a turtle who inhabits the *nun* and is an enemy of the sun. "*The sky is cloudy, but the earth is dried, everyone dies through famine on this sandbank of Apophis.*"[78] In the chaotic and frightening 1st Intermediate Period it was obvious that the king had lost control and was unable to maintain order and repulse evil. As the king was partly divine and what happened in Egypt was a reflection of events in heaven, it was clear that the deities had a powerful enemy who appeared to be gaining the upper hand. One suggestion is that Apophis was originally present in domestic religion but was incorporated into the state religion as he was ideally suited to explain the problems of these times. He is particularly prominent in the New Kingdom funerary texts, and the chaotic 2nd Intermediate Period will have acted to increase his prominence.

WHAT DOES HE WANT?

In the *nun* Apophis "*goes marauding, so that the seasons are no longer differentiated, and the contours of the shadows can no longer be discerned*".[79] This is the uncreated, unlit state of pre-creation and Apophis wants it back everywhere. He represents everything chaotic and formless which seeps into our world from the *nun*. His only desire is the obliteration of the Solar Barque and with it time and space. Alternatively, being generous towards the Chaos Serpent, the *nun* threatens creation like the Mediterranean threatened the low-lying Delta region, like a sandcastle on the beach. Is there any

---

[78] *Apophis: On the Origin, Name and Nature of an Ancient Egyptian Anti-god*, Morenz, 2004:201-205
[79] *Daily Life of Egyptian Gods*, Meeks & Meeks, 1999:17

malevolence behind it or, like the ocean waves, does it just happen because it is in the nature of waves to destroy? The Egyptians certainly wouldn't have taken that view. They held life and creation to be of the utmost value. For them Apophis represented the powers of dissolution, darkness and non-being. They knew he was eternal. The texts may call him dead, defeated and non-existent but to no avail. He returns exactly the same the following sunset and is permanently hostile to Ra and creation. The red sky at dawn could be seen as the blood of Apophis, reassuring everyone that the Chaos Serpent had been defeated once again. Apophis normally limits his attention to the Solar Barque but a different variation of the myth comes from the Greco-Roman temple of Khnum at Esna. (Khnum is a ram-headed God associated with the inundation, he created humans and animals on his potter's wheel). This myth tells how Apophis plotted a rebellion against Ra and was helped by some rebellious humans.[80]

THE FIGHT AGAINST APOPHIS

The perpetual battle against Apophis takes place on two levels, the cosmic or divine and the earthly. As well as being the enemy of Ra, and through him all of creation, he is also the enemy of the state of Egypt, which was virtually the same thing as creation as far as the Egyptians were concerned. His target is Ra but it is not personal, rather a consequence of his nihilistic nature. The Chaos God Seth wants to disturb things for his own ends but Apophis just wants to abolish everything. He doesn't want disorder so much as the end of everything which could be ordered or disordered. He can never be destroyed as you can't destroy what isn't there. He is a void, a black hole which can never be filled or closed. Apophis isn't the equivalent of the Christian devil, he has no interest whatsoever in chasing after an individual's soul. As mentioned previously, it is Ammut not Apophis who devours individual souls. Sometimes Ra fights Apophis on his own. A very popular vignette to spell 17 in the *Book of the Dead* depicts Ra as the Great Cat decapitating a giant

---

[80] *The Egyptian Myths*, Shaw, 2014:52

snake under a tree. The text tells the story of how the Great Cat fights Apophis on *"the night of making war and driving off the rebels"*.[81] The tree is the sacred *ished*-tree known to the Greeks as the *persea*. This is *Mimusops laurifolia* and was associated with Hathor, the inundation and the Solar Deities. At Heliopolis it was sacred to Ra. The sun was believed to rise at the tree of the eastern horizon making it an easy place for Apophis to lie in wait.

Most of the time it is the joint forces of deities who rally to save the Solar Barque. Some are more active and effective than others, Seth in particular. Seth is the violent son of the Sky Goddess Nut and the Earth God Geb and the jealous younger brother of Osiris. Despite being a Chaos God, the murderer of Osiris and the usurper of the throne, Ra supports Seth in the lengthy battles with Isis and Horus. Seth sails in the Solar Barque with the other members of the Ennead. (This is the term for the group of nine deities who were worshipped at Heliopolis consisting of the Sun God and his descendants.) Seth is the strongest of the Gods and so is an essential member of the crew of the Solar Barque. Seth's chief attribute here is his brute strength but he also appears immune to Apophis' trickery and magic – probably he was just more devious. Apophis himself seems immune to trickery or negotiation. Many other divine problems were sorted out using these methods but it appears that the only way to deal with Apophis is to destroy him before he destroys you. Despite Seth's importance in the fight against Apophis he is increasingly vilified in later periods. Assmann (2002) suggests that Seth is needed in the Solar Barque as Apophis represents those forces which cannot be dealt with using the application of *maat*. Seth represents the chaos which is the opposite of civilization and the rule of law, but he is also the aggressive force which sometimes has to be used in the service of good and *maat*. The Egyptians allied Seth with the planet Mercury. This planet can be seen on either side of the sun rather than moving across the sky and so was interpreted as Seth staying close to the Solar Barque as its protector. Horus, the son of Isis and Osiris, has endless battles with Seth but Seth is never totally defeated. At one point in their battles Isis intervenes and refuses

---

[81] *Egyptian Mythology*, Pinch, 2002:108

to kill Seth despite Horus' anger towards her. She has every reason to hate her brother but her wisdom overrides her desire for vengeance. Seth is the only God strong enough to overcome Apophis.

Apophis swallows the waters of the *nun*, all 7 cubits (3.7m), leaving the Solar Barque stranded on the dry celestial riverbed. This seems surprisingly shallow for a celestial river but is comparable to a terrestrial river especially during low water levels. Spell 108 in the *Book of the Dead* explains how Seth stabs Apophis with an iron spear forcing him to regurgitate all the water he has swallowed. In New Kingdom vignettes Sekhmet is often in the Solar Barque driving off Apophis. She "*strikes her spear in him who tries to drink Nun dry forcing the serpent-demon to cough up all he swallowed*".[82] Texts from the temple of Horus at Edfu tell how the temple is sited in "*the Place of Stabbing of the one who stabs the Wamemti Snake*".[83] Apophis is often attacked with knives. Flint knives had traditional and sacred status, enhanced by the fact that they were in continual use since the Pre-dynastic Period. (The connection between flint and snakes is discussed in chapter 8). Apophis is hacked to pieces – but these pieces can reassemble themselves and even grow into clones of him. The Earth God Aker drains away his strength. Aker is an ancient God and guardian of the gates of the horizon. He imprisons the coils of Apophis after he has been hacked to pieces, but the solid energy of earth cannot hold such nebulous chaotic energy for long. Apophis is frequently attacked with fire. The Egyptians used a number of words for fire. *Khet* is terrestrial fire. It is associated with the desert and was considered a natural force. The *Books of Overthrowing Apophis* use the word *khet* to describe the fire sent against him by the Cobra Goddess Wadjet, the God Ha of the western desert and the God Soped of the eastern desert. *Sedjet* comes from the *nun* and has a strong link with water. It was associated with Elephantine and the source of the inundation. (The connection between snakes and the inundation is also covered in chapter 8.) *Sedjet* is sent against Apophis by Sothis (the Goddess personifying the star Sirius who heralds the inundation)

---

[82] *Hymns, Prayers and Songs*, Foster, 1995:60
[83] *The Temple of Edfu*, Kurth, 2004:46

and also Anukis (the Goddess of the Nile cataracts who is also a Daughter of Ra).[84] "*Fire is in thee in the north, and it has power over thee; it is Wadjet, Lady of Pe and Dep, who has commanded what is done against thee.*"[85]

Magic is still the weapon of choice. "*Those in Re's bark destroy you with the spells of their utterances, with the magic in their bodies.*"[86] Ra explains how the Ennead "*created the magic spells for felling Apep. He is imprisoned in the arms of Aker, he has neither arms nor legs, and is confined in one place.*" Which isn't quite true. A magical force field is used to deflect any magical spells coming from Apophis. "*Thine utterance shall not exist.*"[87] In the *Book of Gates* the deities are shown holding up nets as they face Apophis to illustrate the magical force field they have created. "*May you not be, may Thoth make conjuration against you with his magic.*"[88] Thoth frequently fights Apophis using his great magical powers. "*Thoth…may you sacrifice that Rebel Serpent, cut his head off, annihilate his soul, and throw his body on the fire, for you are the god who slaughters him.*"[89] Despite Thoth's great magic and the vindictive curses, Apophis lives on unscathed and probably uncaring. "*Be thou brought to naught, be utterly fallen. The fingers of Thoth are in thine eyes, his magic lays hold on thee, and thy form is annihilated, thy shape destroyed, thy body annihilated, thy shade and thy magic crushed, for he takes away thy life.*"[90] In the *Book of Thoth* the disciple of Thoth says "*I have seen the baboon who punishes the snake*" referring to his role in the fight against Apophis.[91] "*Isis fells thee with her magic.*"[92] Like Thoth, Isis is Great of Magic and "*slays Apophis in an instant*".[93] Reference to Isis and her cosmic battle with Apophis is depicted in the 7th hour of the *Amduat*. The hymns at Philae hold her as the only deity battling Apophis, ignoring the rest of the crew in the Solar Barque. Here she is held as the All-Goddess. "*Beloved of Re, you are in his barque repelling*

---

[84] *Playing with Fire*, Smethills, 2014:12-16
[85] *The Bremner-Rhind Papyrus IV*, Faulkner, 1938:41-53
[86] *The Mechanics of Ancient Egyptian Magical Practice*, Ritner, 1993:33
[87] *The Bremner-Rhind Papyrus IV*, Faulkner, 1938:41-53
[88] *The Bremner-Rhind Papyrus III: The Book of Overthrowing Apep*, Faulkner, 1937:166-185
[89] *Hymns, Prayers and Songs*, Foster, 1995:111-112
[90] *The Bremner-Rhind Papyrus IV*, Faulkner, 1938:41-53
[91] *The Ancient Egyptian Book of Thoth*, Jaznow & Zauzich, 2005:49
[92] *The Bremner-Rhind Papyrus IV*, Faulkner, 1938:41-53
[93] *Hymns to Isis in Her Temple at Philae*, Zabkar, 1988:58

Apophis with the potency of your utterances."[94] In the *Amduat* Apophis is defeated by the magic of Isis and the Elder Magician (the God Heka who personifies the power of magic). *"Their magic enters into you, their spells come against you."*[95] In another ritual it is the Eye of Ra who *"shall have power over you in this its name of Sakhmet".*[96]

The Tilapia and Abydos fish acted as pilots for the Solar Barque during its voyage through the underworld and warned of the approach of Apophis. Size is not always important in the fight against chaos. It is inevitably a joint effort as Apophis is so powerful. The deceased join the crew of the Solar Barque and they too have to assist in the fight against Apophis, hence the spells stating that the deceased can defeat Apophis and heal the wounds he has inflicted. Mehen, the serpent protecting Ra, is the only member of the Solar Barque who doesn't get involved in this battle. He cannot risk leaving Ra unprotected for an instant neither can he risk getting injured.

FIGHTING APOPHIS ON EARTH

The daily fight against Apophis was also carried out on earth as a formal temple ritual. A number of copies of these rituals have survived from at least the New Kingdom. The best-preserved one is in the Ptolemaic *Bremner-Rhind* papyrus which contains a large number of spells against Apophis. Faulkner (1937) gives a translation of these. Some of the titles are the *Book of Smiting Down Apophis* and the *Names of Apophis Which Shall Not Exist*.

The purpose of these books was to ensure the magical protection of the Sun God and the daily cycle of the sun. We know that it was performed twice a day in the temple of Amun-Ra at Karnak. The *Bremner-Rhind* papyrus lists the times when Apophis was most likely to attack; sunrise, noon, sunset, the first hour of the day, the first three hours of the night, at the festival of the new moon, the 6th day festival, the 15th day festival and the full moon festival. The much earlier *Coffin Texts* and the *Book of the Dead* also suggest the likely times of such an attack; at the Eastern

---

[94] Hymns to Isis in Her Temple at Philae, Zabkar, 1988:90
[95] The Mechanics of Ancient Egyptian Magical Practice, Ritner, 1993:33
[96] The Bremner-Rhind Papyrus III: The Book of Overthrowing Apep, Faulkner, 1937:166-185

Mountain as the sun rises, *"just after midday"* and *"at the time of evening"*.[97] Spells against Apophis were said at regular intervals during the day but were also recommended *"during storms, cloud formations, or thunder, when the eastern sky turned red, or when bad weather in the offing"*.[98] The names of Apophis, and Seth, are written in red ink. Harm can be directed towards those named in red ink. Even Seth, despite being essential to the Sun God, is not trusted. The book has a huge number of spells against Apophis. Each spell includes various methods of attack such as; spitting upon him, trampling him with the left foot, smiting him with a spear, smiting him with a knife, setting him on fire and binding him. Apophis is described as the foe of Ra and of the king. There is also reference to the rebels and the confederacy of Apophis who are the demons, and probably the king and Egypt's enemies as well. Some spells concentrate on attack by fire from the *uraeus* others in chopping Apophis into pieces. The object is always to obliterate Apophis, but they knew it was only temporary as the ritual was repeated daily. *"Thy name is destroyed, thy magic is crushed, and thou art destroyed...thou shalt nevermore come forth from this thine hell."*[99] The phrase *"be ye annihilated"*, and similar variations, is repeated endlessly. It is easy to imagine a chorus of priests and priestesses shouting and screaming these ritual words of abuse rising to a crescendo. The repetition of stock hate phrases and the lists of what will be done to the enemy is depressingly familiar throughout history. Variations on the phrase *"thy shalt not exist"* occurs a large number of times throughout one of the spells.[100]

Parts of the spells go into detail about how the body of Apophis is mutilated and destroyed. In this litany there is reference to breaking his arms and cutting off his legs – a clear reference to the human enemies the spell is aimed at. Late Period texts describe wax figurines used to kill enemies of state. A similar spell was probably used for enemies in general. It was said over a figure of Apophis drawn on new papyrus with fresh ink which

---

[97] *Devil in Disguise – On the Stellar Mythology of Apophis*, Stemmler-Harding, 2016:106
[98] *The Mind of Egypt*, Assmann, 2003:405
[99] *The Bremner-Rhind Papyrus III: The Book of Overthrowing Apep*, Faulkner, 1937:166-185
[100] *The Bremner-Rhind Papyrus IV*, Faulkner, 1938:41-53

was then placed in a coffin made of wax. A list of the enemies to be targeted, including their parents and children, was then added to the coffin. This was *"to be placed on the fire after the name of Apep"*. The spell then gives instructions for making a *"serpent with its tail in its mouth"*[101] which is inscribed as Apep the Fallen. A variety of snakes are to be modelled with the faces of a lion, a crocodile and a bird and inscribed with various epithets of Apophis. Symbolic violence became an increasingly important part of the ritual in the later periods. This is a reflection of the weakness and lack of confidence of the Egyptian state and the ever-increasing threat of Persian invasion. It was also a time of decline of the main religions and increasing superstition – as witnessed by the rapid rise in the mummification of animals for votive offerings and the use of anti-social magic. Did the Egyptians think that their deities had deserted them? Rather than admit to such a dreadful thought perhaps they created a frightening cosmic enemy who was impeding the deities who had previously helped them and who would do so in the future once the demon had been annihilated.

One interesting ritual was *Hitting the Eye of Apophis*. Not only is the evil eye of Apophis his most powerful weapon, it counterbalances the Eyes of Ra and Horus, the sun and moon. Temple reliefs depict this ritual where the king hits a ball representing the evil eye of Apophis. The club was made of *moringa*-wood (*b3k*-wood). This tree was believed to have sprung from the Eye of Ra and was of divine origin and for those reasons was a powerful weapon to use against the eye of Apophis. Some have suggested it was the olive tree. This ritual probably originated in the New Kingdom and the king and priests carried out rituals to *"bend down the one whose eye is aggressive"*. At the temple of Horus at Edfu Ptolemy IV (221-205 BCE) carries out the ritual in front of Hathor. "*I have bent down the pupil of the rebel, I have stricken it with the b3k-staff before you. The iris of the Sound Eye is safe in its place.*" He states that he has "*hit it in order to make your heart rejoice*". The same action is performed by Ptolemy VII (145 BCE) before Hathor. "*I come to you Hathor…I bring you the ball as the eye…crushed through my handling the club. You are the uraeus, the iris of the Sound Eye, the Eye of Re.*" The king is quick to point out that it

---

[101] *The Bremner-Rhind Papyrus IV*, Faulkner, 1938:41-53

is the eye of Apophis he has attacked not the Solar Eye. At Dendera the Emperor Augustus (30 BCE- 14 CE) is shown performing this ritual for Hathor who *"has driven away the One whose Character is Evil…with her spells"*.[102] The Emperor Trajan (98-117 CE) also performs this ritual at Dendera where the text references hitting the eye and blinding it. At Philae, Augustus performs the ritual before Sekhmet telling her that he has battered the pupil and cut out the eyes of Apophis. All the Goddesses watching the ritual are the Solar Eye Goddesses. Hathor is referred to as the Eye of Ra to underline the emphasis on the symbolism and importance of eyes to the ritual. Apophis is mocked by playing a game with his eye in front of the Solar Eye which is the source of light, life and order.

APOPHIS IN THE CELESTIAL SPHERE

In the *Book of Gates* Apophis makes his last attack on the sun just before sunrise. He is shown in chains, as well as preventing him from attacking the new-born sun it also ensures that he isn't able to follow the rising sun into the sky. But Apophis isn't confined to the underworld and the *nun*. One *Coffin Texts* spell describes the journey of the Solar Barque as it ascends to the upper sky and traverses the middle sky. The deceased asks that their vision be clear *"so that I may not fear Apophis, the Wanderer"*. [103] In the *Book of Day* the deceased says *"prepare the safe ways of heaven and detour from Apophis"*.[104] In the *Coffin Texts* the deceased boards the Solar Barque and joins the deities in the northern sky where they continue to battle Apophis. The Netherworld texts also refer to Apophis in the sky. In the *Amduat* we are told that the attack against Apophis takes place in the Netherworld but that his home is in the sky. There is reference to the deceased attacking Apophis in the sky when he threatens the Day Barque. In the *Book of Gates* Apophis is later shown chained to his sandbank in the sky. The text describes how the captors of Apophis *"grasp him, when they*

---

[102] *The Evil Eye of Apophis*, Borghouts, 1972:114-150
[103] *Devil in Disguise – On the Stellar Mythology of Apophis*, Stemmler-Harding, 2016:106
[104] *Devil in Disguise – On the Stellar Mythology of Apophis*, Stemmler-Harding, 2016:98

take a rest in heaven". It adds "*his sandbank is in heaven, but his venom descends in the West*".[105] Despite depicting the nocturnal voyage of the Solar Barque in the underground the texts hint at its parallel course in the sky. The reference to his venom descending alludes to his chaotic influence appearing on earth as night falls and following the Sun God as he descends into the underworld. In the *Book of the Day*, on the ceiling of the tomb of Ramesses VI (20th dynasty), Apophis is shown swimming in the *nun* with the Solar Barque sailing above him. The edges of the sky are also close to the *nun*. The Goddess Nut forms a protective boundary between the earth and heavens and the surrounding *nun*.

Stemmler-Harding (2016) suggests the mythology of Apophis is influenced by, or reflected in, the night skies depicted in the astronomical ceilings of the New Kingdom and Greco-Roman Periods. Here Apophis is associated with the constellation of the Crocodile (*Htp-Rdwy*) "*He on his Two Feet*" which equates to the modern constellation of Hydra. Hydra is the Greek version of the Babylonian Serpent constellation. Its brightest star is Alphard whose name was derived from its Arabic name meaning "*the solitary one in the serpent*". Its alternate Arabic name was "*the backbone of the serpent*".[106] The Crocodile is always shown facing a man with a spear, this constellation isn't named but equates to the modern constellation of Gemini. In the tomb of Petosiris a turtle is shown next to the Crocodile. "*Mshtyw overturns him in the northern sky, those who are in the starry firmament fetter him.*"[107] *Mshtyw* is the modern constellation of Ursa Major seen as the foreleg of a bull by the Egyptians. If Apophis is linked to Hydra then his abode is at the fringes of the northern sky. His epithets of the Wanderer or Retreater could allude to the movement of his constellation during the year. But is Hydra actually Apophis and if so why is he depicted as a crocodile in the astronomical ceilings but as a snake elsewhere? There is some evidence linking Apophis to the crocodile. "*Get back, crocodile of the north, living on Apophis in the midst*

---

[105] *The Egyptian Book of Gates*, Abt & Hornung, 2014:427
[106] *Devil in Disguise – On the Stellar Mythology of Apophis*, Stemmler-Harding, 2016:104
[107] *Devil in Disguise – On the Stellar Mythology of Apophis*, Stemmler-Harding, 2016:106

of the night hours."[108] In the *Book of Gates* Apophis is shown with a crocodile named Shesshes. Like the turtle, the crocodile was associated with the dark waters of the Nile and basking on sandbanks. It is also a very dangerous creature. If the crocodile was fused with the Apophis snake at times it would be understandable. At the Greco-Roman temple of Hathor at Dendera the astronomical ceiling shows the constellation of Hydra as a rearing snake. The constellation of Leo stands above the snake.

Using software to calculate the star positions in Egypt around 2222 BCE, Stemmler-Harding discovered that at the Egyptian New Year the constellation of Hydra parallels the ecliptic. This is the arc of the sun during the day and the visible Milky Way at night. The constellation of the Divine Lion *Mzi*, the modern Leo, closely superimposes the sun whilst that of Gemini opposes Hydra from its rising to setting. The Celestial River (the Milky Way) bisects the sky just as the Nile bisects Egypt. The northern sky, home to the imperishable (circumpolar) stars and the constellations of the northern hemisphere, lies above it. This region was considered the abode of the deities and the deceased who are reborn as stars. Hydra is particularly prominent during the winter. Stemmler-Harding suggests that the rituals against Apophis were related to the positions of Hydra throughout the year as well as at different hours of the night.

APOPHIS IN LATER PERIODS

The image and mythology of Apophis continued to be used in magic spells into the Byzantium Period (the 6th century CE onwards). One Greek spell to produce a vision refers to the battle between Ra and Apophis. *"You who direct night and day…restrain the serpent."*[109] A coin issued in Alexandria by Domitian (81-96 CE) depicts a snake with a spear through its neck on the reverse. Images of Apophis immobilised in this way were a popular apotropaic image in the Greco-Roman Period, taking inspiration from images in vignettes and tomb scenes. The depiction on the

---

[108] *Devil in Disguise – On the Stellar Mythology of Apophis*, Stemmler-Harding, 2016:109
[109] *The Greek Magical Papyri in Translation Volume I*, Betz, 1996:57-58

coin could be to guarantee victory and the safety of the Emperor but was more likely to commemorate a recent victory. One suggestion is that it depicts the crushing of one of many conspiracies against Domitian.[110] During the Roman Period Horus was often depicted as a hawk-headed legionary on horseback fighting Seth in his crocodile or hippo form. A Greco-Roman relief in the temple of Hibis depicts a winged Seth slaying Apophis in a similar fashion. Some have suggested that these are the inspiration for Saint George and the Dragon.[111]

HIS NAME LIVES ON

The Egyptians placed in Apophis the most powerful and destructive forces they could perceive. Devoid of the normal animal senses, he lurks at the edge of the ordered universe, which excludes him. His natural habitat is the primordial ocean which laps at the edges of the sky and the underworld. Apophis can't be destroyed as he doesn't exist. He is the antimatter to the matter of the universe, and he is part of the perpetual battle of good against evil. Apophis threatening the Solar Barque with standstill could also be seen, at an individual level, as a manifestation of death which brings a halt to life. The importance the Egyptians gave to the true name is clearly seen in the spells against Apophis. There are endless references to the obliteration of his name as well as his existence. "*May ye not permit his name to be spread abroad.*"[112] Ironically the name of Apophis has endured and spread around the world thanks to texts such as these. The *Names of Apep* carefully records for prosperity the names of the greatest enemy of Egypt and all of creation. This ensures that the names and consequently Apophis survive. At the end of this cosmic cycle Atum will destroy creation and revert back into serpent form and everything will return to the *nun*. What will happen to Apophis then? Does he stay as a current of destruction within the *nun* contrasting with the current of potential or is he truly dissipated?

---

[110] *The Apophis Snake on a Coin of Domitian from Alexandria (BMC Alexandria 348; RPC 2, 2756)*, Kerkeslager, 2001:287-290
[111] *The Gods of Ancient Egypt*, Watterson, 2003:113
[112] *The Bremner-Rhind Papyrus IV*, Faulkner, 1938:41-53

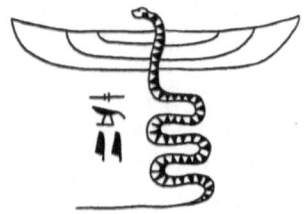

CHAPTER 5

The Uraeus Goddess

"The uraeus which is above us, the great serpent, is mighty for us. As to the living, we give praise, for she puts dread in the faces of those who are under her uraeus." 113

INTRODUCTION

The *uraeus* is always present on the crowns of deities and royals and is frequently draped over depictions of the solar disc. She is their ultimate protector. The Egyptian Cobra is used to depict the *uraeus* and it is always shown rearing with its hood extended. This is the warning pose a cobra assumes when it perceives a threat. The cobra is the ideal symbol for the *uraeus* as it is immediately recognisable and intimidating. It can remain at its position because it attacks by spraying venom and thus is the perfect bodyguard. The *ba*, or divine essence, of the Goddess resided in the *uraeus* in the same way as the spirit of a deity could manifest in a sacred statue or other image once the necessary rituals had been performed. *Uraeus* is the Latin version of the word used by the Greeks, *ouraios*. They derived it from the Egyptian *iaret* which translates as *"risen one"*.[114] The determinative

---

[113] *A Crossword Hymn to Mut*, Stewart, 1971:87-104
[114] *The Cobra Goddesses of Ancient Egypt*, Johnson, 1990:5

for the word *uraeus* is the hieroglyph sign of a rearing cobra with its hood extended. The determinative for the word Goddess was usually a cobra and that hieroglyph alone can represent a Goddess. Any Goddess could take the form of the *uraeus* as it was the symbol of the powerful and protective power of the female divine.

THE DEVELOPMENT OF THE *URAEUS* SYMBOL

Given its importance at the start of the Pharaonic Period, it is safe to assume that the cobra was of importance in the Pre-dynastic Period, but there is little evidence to explain its symbolism and significance. Excavations of a Pre-dynastic centre at Tell el-Farkha in the eastern Delta have produced a number of ivory carvings of *uraei* which were probably attached to a sculpture. The cobra may have been a tribal totem. Johnson (1990) suggests that the *Uraeus* and Cobra Goddesses developed from Pre-dynastic beliefs of a female ancestor who appeared in the form of a snake and was associated with fertility and vitality. Some have suggested it came from the nomadic peoples of what is now Libya but there is no evidence to confirm this. The first image of a *uraeus* on a crown is from an ivory label from the 1st dynasty on which Den is depicted smiting his enemies. He wears a crown with a wavy line protruding at the front which is interpreted as the *uraeus*. There is some debate as to whether this is a *uraeus* or not. The earliest undisputed depiction of a *uraeus* is in a rock-cut relief from Wadi Maghareh in Sinai depicting Djoser (3rd dynasty) with a *uraeus* on his crown.

THE ORIGIN OF THE *URAEUS*

The origin of the *Uraeus* Goddess is told in the myth of the *Angry Eye*. Our version comes from the *Bremner-Rhind* papyrus but is thought to be a retelling of an older myth. Eyes are of major significance in all cultures, a reflection of the fact that sight is our primary sense and because eyes are an important part of the face in terms of identification and non-verbal communication. The eye was one of the most important and symbolically rich symbols in Egypt. The sun, and at times the moon, was the main provider of light enabling sight. Both were of similar shape to an eye and were considered the eyes of the Creator or the Solar and Sky Gods. The Solar Eye, the visible sun disc, is normally considered the right eye of the Sun God. The Lunar Eye, the moon, is thus the left eye. It is also referred to as the Eye of Horus (the son of Isis and Osiris). There is also Horus the Elder who is a Sky God and both the sun and moon can be referred to as his eyes. The symbolism is fluid and contradictory at times. The word for eye is *irt* which is similar to that of *uraeus* which is *iaret*. It was also similar to the word for 'doing' and as such was linked with the active power of the divine, namely divine intervention. As the word was feminine the Eye was considered female and the Solar Eye was a Goddess and considered the Daughter of the Sun God. The Eye Goddess could be viewed as the visible manifestation of the sun. The sun and moon were referred to as the *"fiery eyes who came forth from Sekhem"*[115] which links them back to Sekhmet and her personification of the original power of creation. Having a Sun God whose Eye is a Goddess was also a method of expressing the initial androgyny of the Creator who must have contained both male and female elements before they separated out at the moment of creation. The Eye myths are of major significance in Egyptian religion but it is that of the *Angry Eye* which is of most importance in the serpent's story.

After the first phase of creation Ra created Shu, the God of air and sunlight, and Tefnut, the Goddess of moisture. For reasons not stated Shu and Tefnut did not remain with Ra on the primeval mound but drifted away into the endless chaotic waters of the *nun*. The created universe might not have been strong enough to contain or nurture them, or possibly they needed to develop as individuals and had to be separated from Ra in order to do this. *"I came into being in this land and Shu and Tefnut rejoiced in the nun."* Ra sent his Sole Eye to look after them. *"Mine Eye following after them since the aeons when they were far from me."*[116] Serpent and solar energy are critical in growth and development so the Eye also provided a source of energy otherwise unavailable in the

---

[115] *An Ancient Egyptian Book of Hours*, Faulkner, 1958:24
[116] *The Bremner-Rhind Papyrus III: The Book of Overthrowing Apep*, Faulkner, 1937:166-185

nun. Without it Shu and Tefnut might have been too unformed in their early stages of development to remain distinct entities in the all-absorbing *nun*. While his Sole Eye was absent Ra found himself unable to function without her, so he replaced her with the Glorious Eye. The Glorious Eye is the Akhet Eye which was the shining sun disc. It was this that became the Aten as worshipped by the heretic Akhenaten (18th dynasty). When they were fully developed Shu and Tefnut were brought back by the Sole Eye. She was furious to find that she had been replaced. Ra said that she "*was wroth with me when it returned and found that I had made another in its place*".[117] Ra's act was a major pivotal point in evolution. His was the first act of betrayal resulting in the first separation and anger. The Eye Goddess can never be fully pacified, reassured or completely reconciled with Ra. Her tears of anger and distress fell to the ground and, imbued with her creative energy, gave rise to the equally ambivalent humans. If humanity is a by-product of the tears of the Eye Goddess then we are children of the Serpent Goddess.

To pacify the furious Goddess, and possibly as an act of atonement, Ra "*advanced its place onto my brow, and when it was exercising rule over this entire land, its wrath fell away completely, for I had replaced that which had been taken from it*".[118] The Eye was transformed into the *uraeus*, the most powerful of the deities. Ra tells her "*Great will be your power and mighty your majesty over the bodies of your enemies...all mankind will cringe beneath you and your might, they will respect you when they behold you in that vigorous form*".[119] In other versions of the myth, such as in the *Book of the Dead*, it was Thoth who "*returned the sacred eye, he has pacified it after being sent out by Re...it was enraged, but it was Thoth who satisfied the eye after it had given vent to its wrath*".[120] The Sun God now has two solar eyes, the permanent shining sun disc and the restless and aggressive Eye who can detach herself from the Sun God. Because of this the Eye Goddess is associated with cycles of renewal.

Why was the Sole Eye turned into a cobra? Perhaps she had

---

117 *The Bremner-Rhind Papyrus III*, Faulkner, 1938:41-53
118 *The Wisdom of Ancient Egypt*, Kaster, 1993:56
119 *Myth and Symbol in Ancient Egypt*, Clark, 1978:222
120 *Hathor and Thoth: Two Key Figures of the Ancient Egyptian Religion*, Bleeker, 1973:121

always had this form. As discussed earlier some creation theologies considered Hathor and Mut to be the primeval *uraeus*. The *uraeus* can be considered a representation of the heat and light emitted by the solar disc. Reference is made to the *uraeus* of Horus which *"pervades the whole land"*.[121] The fact that the cobra aims for its victim's eyes provided another link to the Eye Goddess. The burning sensation caused by its venom also linked the cobra to the fiery Eye of the Sun. The *uraeus'* means of attack is fire, an appropriate method for such a solar creature. *"The uraeus, which is on your head, punishes them…it burns by its flame."*[122] She is referred to as *"Mistress of the Flame"* and *"Mistress of the Fire"*.[123] The ambiguous symbolism of the cobra reflects the two contradictory aspects of the solar disc and Eye Goddess. The flowing movement of snakes can be aligned with the rays of the sun. On the positive side the sun's rays have creative power as they are an agent of life and renewal powering life on earth. They provide warmth and light to see by and also enable the growth of vegetation. On the other hand there is a dangerous aspect to the sun's heat and this was an ever-present threat in Egypt. It desiccates vegetation, dries up water sources and turns fertile land into barren desert bringing drought and famine.

Depicting the Uraeus

The *uraeus* is a ubiquitous symbol in Egypt, ranging in scale from jewellery to monumental architecture. All-pervasive, the *uraeus* provides an effective, if dangerous, protection. As mentioned earlier the *uraeus* is a rearing cobra with its hood extended. The earliest examples of the *uraeus* can be very naturalistic and well-executed. The best are considered to be the king's *nbty* name *uraei* of the early 4th dynasty which formed the basic style for *uraeus* cobras from then on.[124] From the Pre-dynastic throughout the Old Kingdom there are no depictions of a *uraeus* with its mouth open, caught at its moment of striking. This emphasised its beneficial aspects, it would attack only to

---

[121] *The Egyptian Book of the Dead*, Faulkner & Goelet, 2008:134 spell 183
[122] *Death as an Enemy*, Zandee, 1960:133
[123] *Death as an Enemy*, Zandee, 1960:136-137
[124] *The Cobra Goddesses of Ancient Egypt*, Johnson, 1990:90

protect those it guarded and only when provoked. By the New Kingdom this had changed and vignettes from the *Books of the Netherworld* depict fire-spitting cobras. If the *uraeus* is coloured it is usually gold with a blue and red head. Blue is associated with the heavens, the *nun* and water. Red is associated with fire and anger. Together these reflect the origins of the *uraeus*. Gold was considered a solar colour and regarded as a divine substance. As it didn't tarnish it was associated with eternal life.

Numbering the *Uraei*

Numbers contain powerful magic and symbolism. Duality was of great significance to the Egyptians. The geography of their country emphasised duality with the Nile Valley and the Delta, the desert and the fertile land and the fact that the Nile flowed north bisecting the country into east and west. Egypt itself was formed of two previously separate kingdoms, Upper Egypt in the south and Lower Egypt in the Delta region. It was always referred to as the Two Lands reflecting both its duality and its unity. As a result, depictions of two *uraei* are common and they have multiple meanings. Two *uraei* symbolise dual protection, with one on each side giving all-round protection. It also doubles their attacking powers and can represent the duality of the Eye Goddess.

The *wedjat* eye was a very popular symbol, combining the facial markings of the hawk with a human eye and eyebrow. It represents the whole or healed Eye of Horus and through this all aspects of divine order and was often shown with *uraei* on both sides. The *wedjat* eye is never used to represent the Eye Goddess because of her volatile and wandering nature. Khepri, the form of the Sun God at dawn, was depicted as a scarab beetle. As the newborn sun he was vulnerable and could be depicted with two *uraei*, as could the solar disc. The *Pyramid Texts* refer to the "*two serpent-goddesses who are on your brow*".[125] Two *uraei* wearing the Red and White Crowns symbolise the Two Lands of Upper and Lower Egypt and the Two Ladies (Wadjet and Nekhbet, the tutelary Goddesses of Lower and Upper Egypt). Two *uraei* are often referred to directly as the Two Ladies.

---

[125] *The Ancient Egyptian Pyramid Texts*, Faulkner, 2007:158 utterance 468

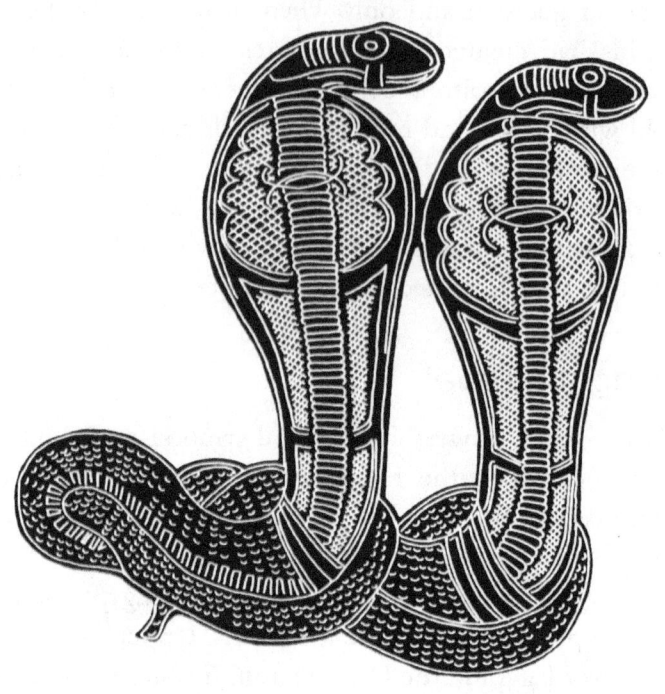

1 - Double Uraei Amulet. Cairo Museum

In the New Kingdom the Goddess Mut frequently wears the double crown of Egypt with a pair of *uraei*. In spell 313 of the *Coffin Texts* Osiris is referred to as having two *uraei*. In later funerary texts, such as the *Amduat*, the two *uraei* often represent Isis and Nephthys who assume the roles of Wadjet and Nekhbet. Unlike Horus, most of the kings normally wore a single *uraeus*. Perhaps two was considered the privilege of the deities. This didn't stop Tiy, the wife of Amenhotep III (18th dynasty), being depicted with three crowned *uraei*.[126] The double *uraeus* was worn by the 25th dynasty Kushite kings and it was especially popular during the reign of Taharqo. Given that they were a foreign dynasty this may have been to emphasise their divine authority to rule.

Four is often used to denote the four cardinal points providing protection in all directions. One *Coffin Texts* spell refers to four *uraei* who dwell in the eastern part of the sky.[127] The deceased associate with the fourth of them saying that they have

---

[126] *Two Wooden Uraei*, Lilleso, 1975:137-146
[127] *The Ancient Egyptian Coffin Texts Volume I*, Faulkner, 2007:228 spell 311

come into being as Khepri. Seven is a number of great magical significance in Egyptian religion and healing and its importance increased over time. There are references to seven *uraei* in the funerary texts and in magic. Deities can also have many *uraei*. One *Coffin Texts* spell refers to a star as *"multitudinous of uraei"*.[128] This is a very good description of a star suggesting solar flares and the way that the rays of the sun can be seen shining through clouds.

THE *URAEUS* GODDESS

The nature of the *Uraeus* Goddess is fire. She is the warming or burning heat of the sun and the searing pain of poison and fever. Like both the sun and the snake she can be life-giving and life-taking, but despite her dangerous powers she was never demonised. Following the precedent of the *Angry Eye* she has to be constantly pacified and reassured but she is beneficial at heart and the ultimate protector. That is assuming that you are the one being protected rather than the one being viewed as the aggressor. Texts sometimes refer to a living *uraeus*. This means one in which the power or presence of the *Uraeus* Goddess dwelt rather than just a depiction of her. There are a number of Goddesses who take the role of the *Uraeus* Goddess and they tend to be those with solar or serpentine aspects. They are usually one of two types, a Cobra Goddess such as Wadjet or one of the Eye Goddesses such as Hathor. Many times though we don't know the name of the *Uraeus* Goddess – she is just herself.

EPITHETS OF THE URAEUS GODDESS

The word *nesret* (*nsrt*) can mean the *Uraeus* Goddess, the Cobra Goddess or her flame. [129] One medicinal papyrus links the word to fevers and the burning sensation associated with bites and stings. During the New Kingdom and Late Period the epithet Lady of Flame (*Nbt Nsrt*) was given to a number of Goddesses. Nesret is synonymous with the phrase *"uraeus of Re, the Coiled One upon his head"*.[130] It can also be translated as the Royal Serpent.

---

[128] *The Ancient Egyptian Coffin Texts Volume III*, Faulkner, 2007:125 spell 1028
[129] *Playing with Fire*, Smethills, 2014:12-16
[130] *Hymns to Isis in Her Temple at Philae*, Zabkar, 1988:73

Johnson has identified at least seven different variations of names for the *Uraeus* Goddesses used in the text on the walls of Unas' pyramid. They are often just translated as *uraeus* or *uraei* but they have subtly different meanings which will have altered the specific emphasis of each phrase. Weret (the Great One) or Weret-Hekau (Great of Magic) is usually the *uraeus* on the head of Horus and kings. *Iaret* is the risen one, the *uraeus* who was the Angry Eye and pacified by being placed on Ra's forehead. It thus refers to a rearing cobra and to its elevation in status. *Iarwet* is plural and used in spells referring to the seven *uraei*. *Akhet* is also a name of the *uraeus*. The root of the word means to become a spirit, glorious or splendid. The guiding serpent is *Sebi* derived from the word for watch over. *Saryet* is from a verb meaning to ascend or rise in rank. The name *Tepet* is derived from the word meaning principal or foremost.[131] Most other epithets refer either to the fire of the *uraeus* or the fear it inspires such as *"Great of dread"*.[132] Mistress or Lady of Flame is a frequent epithet. Many of the fire-spitting cobras of the *Amduat* have these types of names. A few examples are; She with the Hurtful Flame, Fiery One, Burning One and She who Cuts.[133]

THE GODDESSES TAKING THE ROLE OF THE URAEUS

Hathor

Hathor is an ancient Goddess who was much loved and worshipped throughout Egypt for all of its history. As such she has a wide range of aspects but it is her solar one which makes her one of the Daughters of Ra, and so an Eye Goddess and *Uraeus* Goddess. This was an important aspect of Hathor's which was emphasised by the sun disc, draped by the *uraeus*, which she wears between her cow-horn crown. As a Solar Goddess Hathor is at her most volatile, reflecting the ambivalence of the sun and fire as a life-giver and life-taker. The earliest evidence of the *uraeus*

---

[131] *The Cobra Goddesses of Ancient Egypt*, Johnson, 1990:7
[132] *A Crossword Hymn to Mut*, Stewart, 1971:84-104
[133] *The Egyptian Amduat*, Abt & Hornung, 2007:31

worn by Hathor is in a 6ᵗʰ dynasty relief from Tel Basta.¹³⁴ Hathor's epithets include *"the uraeus who shines on the forehead of her father"*.¹³⁵ She is the *uraeus "whose fire is great"*.¹³⁶ On one offering scene, at her temple at Dendera, Hathor is referred to as being in the midst of Dendera and the phrase is written using horizontal signs and the word *k3b* is repeated. This word means folds or coils and the whole phrase alludes to Hathor in her cobra form, both in the spoken and written word.¹³⁷ Puns, both visual and oral, were of great significance they were not just a clever or amusing conceit. A similarity in form or sound signified an underlying connection between two objects or deities and hinted at their true and sacred name and purpose. Another phrase *"Hathor, uraeus of Ra"* is written with three cobra hieroglyphs to emphasise her manifestation as the *Uraeus* Goddess. These are; a cobra encircled by its tail, a *uraeus* wearing Hathor's crown and a sun disc with a *uraeus* which refers to the *uraeus*, Hathor and Ra respectively.¹³⁸

Isis

Originally Isis had no connection with the *Uraeus* Goddess, but once she began to assimilate Hathor she acquired Hathor's solar aspects. During the Middle Kingdom she starts to appear as the *uraeus*. In the 19ᵗʰ dynasty tomb paintings from the Valley of the Kings Isis and Nephthys are depicted as *uraeus* cobras. Nephthys takes on this role because she is twinned with Isis in many texts. The *Bremner-Rhind* papyrus refers to Isis as *"the Noble Serpent which issued from Rē"*.¹³⁹ Hymns to Isis at her temple at Philae align her with various Goddesses including the *Uraeus* Goddess. She is the *"Mistress of flame who assaults the rebels…uraeus of Rē"*.¹⁴⁰ Another hymn describes her as the Goddess who *"shines as the Diadem on his forehead. You are the one who rises and dispels*

---

134 *The Cobra Goddesses of Ancient Egypt*, Johnson, 1990:164
135 *The Theology of Hathor of Dendera*, Richter, 2016:37
136 *The Theology of Hathor of Dendera*, Richter, 2016:172
137 *The Theology of Hathor of Dendera*, Richter, 2016:54
138 *The Theology of Hathor of Dendera*, Richter, 2016:55
139 *The Bremner-Rhind Papyrus I*, Faulkner, 1936:121-140
140 *Hymns to Isis in Her Temple at Philae*, Zabkar, 1988:58

darkness".[141] The *Jumilhac* papyrus from the Greco-Roman Period gives one version of the stories of the battles between Horus and Seth. Isis and Nephthys transform themselves into *uraei* to attack Seth. Something appears to have been lost in the telling as they throw lances at Seth, a strange method of attack for cobras.[142] Perhaps the original meaning was that of throwing flames like spears.

Mut

"Mut, the Great, Eye of Ra"[143] is the Great Goddess of Thebes who was closely associated with kingship. She is usually depicted as a mature woman to emphasise her political authority. Mut does have a very solar character being described as the *"goddess in the sun disc"*.[144] Thus she becomes the *"coiled one"*[145] the *uraeus* who is *"upon the brow of her father"*.[146] In one text there is reference to her as *"Mut, the resplendent serpent who wound herself around Re and gave birth to him as Khonsu"*.[147] In the New Kingdom Amun-Ra, Mut and Khonsu formed a triad. In the *Crossword Hymn to Mut* she is referred to as Lady or Mistress of the *uraeus*, Goddess of the *uraeus* and Noble *uraeus*. As with Hathor the dangerous aspect of Mut is taken by Sekhmet who becomes *"the flame of Mut"*.[148] She has similar epithets to the other *Uraeus* Goddesses. She is the *"Palace Snake"*[149] and *"there is no form which escapes her flame"*. Mut may not be as well-known as she once was but *"Her name endures as the uraeus"*.[150]

Sekhmet

Sekhmet is a Lioness Goddess who can be both a Goddess in

---

[141] *Hymns to Isis in Her Temple at Philae*, Zabkar, 1988:80
[142] *The Egyptian Myths*, Shaw, 2014:134
[143] *Le Role et le Sens du Lion dans L'Egypte Ancienne*, de Witt, 1951:350 (my translation)
[144] *Mut Enthroned*, Troy, 1996:304
[145] *Mut Enthroned*, Troy, 1996:302
[146] *A Crossword Hymn to Mut*, Stewart, 1971:87-104
[147] *The Death of Gods in Ancient Egypt*, Sellers, 1992:167
[148] *The Story of Egypt*, Fletcher, 2015:208
[149] *Hathor Rising*, Roberts, 2001:77
[150] *A Crossword Hymn to Mut*, Stewart, 1971:87-104

her own right or the alter-ego of Hathor and Mut. Her name means Powerful One and she embodies *sekhem*. This was one of the original powers that arose at the moment of creation and which drives creation. On earth its main manifestation is as the life-giving energy of the sun. It is heat, light and fire, and as such has positive and negative forms. Sekhmet is the more aggressive aspect of the Solar Goddess and the destructive aspect of the sun.

Like many Creator Gods, Ra isn't entirely benevolent and it is not just his enemies who suffer from his wrath – as explained in the myth of the *Destruction of Mankind*. This is discussed in more detail in Jackson (2018). Ra discovers that not all humans respect him and a group of rebels start to plot against him. Whilst not such a threat as Apophis, humans can cause chaos and disrupt *maat* and what happens at one level of creation impacts on another. After debate with the other deities it is agreed that Ra's Eye should "*go out so that it might smite them for you, those who have planned evil…It will go down as Hathor*".[151] The phrase "*go down*" refers to the descent of the *uraeus* from Ra's brow and also puns with the word for destroy. There is a phrase in one spell from the *Book of the Dead* which may allude to Ra using his Eye to kill people. "*Do not let the eye swallow its tears.*"[152] It was the tears from the Angry Eye Goddess which created people. As Hathor descends to earth she transforms into the lioness Sekhmet. The anger of Hathor was concentrated and manifested itself in the form of Sekhmet, which is how "*Sakhmet came into being*".[153] Sekhmet kills Ra's enemies as intended but becomes inflamed by the killing and doesn't stop. Only by some clever thinking does Ra get her drunk so she forgets the slaughtering and returns back to him. The divine retribution meted out by Ra justified the king's retribution against his enemies and those of Egypt, both real and perceived. The *Uraeus* became the Lady of Slaughter striking terror into the enemy and the king's subjects.

Of all the Solar Goddesses Sekhmet is the most closely linked with the fire breathing *uraeus* and the Eye of Ra. She is only ever shown as a lioness-headed woman or occasionally as a lioness.

---

[151] *The Destruction of Mankind: A Transitional Literary Text*, Spalinger, 2000:257-282
[152] *An Ancient Egyptian Book of the Dead*, O'Rourke, 2016:165 spell 64B
[153] *The Literature of Ancient Egypt*, Simpson, 2003:291

Despite her ferocity she was never demonised and was a renowned healer, especially of the fevers and infectious diseases which she brought. Like the other Goddesses who take the role of the *Uraeus* Sekhmet is referred to as the Goddess or Lady of the *Uraeus*. She is identified as the *uraeus* in many of the funerary texts. She sometimes replaces the Goddess Nekhbet as one of the Two Ladies. "*Sekhmet is on your head, Wadjet is on your forehead.*"[154] One *Coffin Texts* spell refers to Sekhmet as the White Crown and Wadjet as the Red Crown of Egypt. At the temple of Osiris at Abydos the king is shown offering flowers to Sekhmet and Ptah. She replies "*I place myself before thee as thy uraeus, my protection being thy guardian, my breath is a flame against thy enemies*".[155]

Tayet

Tayet is the Goddess responsible for the production of linen, especially for funerary purposes. At the temple of Hathor at Dendera she can take the form of the *uraeus*. New clothing in the afterlife is often guarded by *uraei* so this is an appropriate form for Tayet to assume.

Tefnut

Tefnut is the sister of Shu and is one of the main Eye Goddesses, which is strange given that it was her and her brother that the Sole Eye went looking for. The myths we have are silent on this transition. Does this suggest that Tefnut was originally two Goddesses who have been merged into one? In one *Pyramid Texts* spell the king's *uraeus* is referred to as Tefnut, his "*Serpent of Praise*".[156] Tefnut also fights Apophis with her flame.

Wadjet

Wadjet is covered in the following chapter.

---

[154] *Sekhmet et la Protection du Monde*, Germond, 1981:214 (My translation)
[155] *Temple Ritual at Abydos*, David, 2016:80
[156] *The Ancient Egyptian Pyramid Texts*, Faulkner, 2007:64 utterance 254

Wepset

Wepset is mentioned in the *Coffin Texts* as the Eye of Ra and her name means "*she who burns*".[157] The spell is "*for becoming Shu*" and in it he lists his actions which include cooling her and silencing her flame. This may align her with the *Distant Goddess* (described below) as Shu was one of the peacemakers sent by Ra to retrieve the estranged Goddess. Wepset appears to have been a local *Uraeus* Goddess. Texts say that she had a cult centre on the island of Biga. She is found in temples here and in Lower Nubia. In the Greco-Roman temples of Nubia she is depicted as a Goddess with a *uraeus* on her head, sometimes wearing a cow-horn sun disc, or as a lioness-headed woman.

Weret-Hekau

As befits a Goddess whose name means Great of Magic or Great Enchantress, the true identity of Weret-Hekau is hard to establish. The epithet Great of Magic is also applied to Isis, Hathor, Sekhmet, Mut and Pakhet. It is also used in connection with the Two Ladies in their form of the Two *Uraei*.[158] Weret-Hekau personifies the magic (*heka*) of both the Egyptian crowns and the *uraeus*. In the *Pyramid Texts* her name was sometimes associated with the *uraeus* and the Red Crown of Lower Egypt and as such was considered a manifestation of Wadjet. Weret-Hekau can be depicted as a cobra, a cobra with a woman's head and torso or as a lioness-headed woman. She has a very close connection with royalty, her main role is to protect the king, and through him Egypt. Tutankhamun (18th dynasty) and his wife Ankhesenamun are called "*beloved of the Great of Magic*" nine times on his golden shrine. Here Weret-Hekau is referred to as "*Lady of the Palace*".[159] Her name appears at the start and end of the inscription on all four corners of the shrine. She is shown embracing Tutankhamun. An amulet depicts her as a Cobra Goddess with a human head and torso nursing the infant Tutankhamun. The amulet is inscribed "*Tutankhamun, beloved of the*

---

[157] *The Complete Gods and Goddesses of Ancient Egypt*, Wilkinson, 2003:228
[158] *The Theology of Hathor of Dendera*, Richter, 2016:214
[159] *Golden Shrine, Golden Queen: Egypt's Anointing Mysteries*, Roberts, 2008:12

goddess Weret-Hekau".[160] In other texts there is reference to Ramesses II (19th dynasty) as the *"nursling of Weret-Hekau"*.[161] Weret-Hekau was present at the coronation and other important royal ceremonies. In the temple of Amun at Karnak Weret-Hekau is depicted as a lioness-headed Goddess when she accompanies Thutmose III (18th dynasty) in procession. She is also in this form in the Great Hypostyle Hall at Karnak where she presents Sety I (19th dynasty) with symbols for his jubilee.

There is reference to an Overseer of Priests in the temple of Sekhmet at Memphis, whose titles included Priest of Weret-Hekau.[162] Her close association with the crown and *uraeus* suggests that Weret-Hekau is a state Goddess only. However there is one interesting New Kingdom *stele* from Deir el-Medina which must have been dedicated by an ordinary person. It shows Amun in front of an offering table with Weret-Hekau in cobra form. She is entwined around a papyrus flower and her crown is the same as Amun's – feathers and a sun disc. It was dedicated by Permennefer to *"Weret-Hekau, the beloved, the august, mistress of the Place of Truth, mistress of heaven, lady of the gods"*.[163] Amun was a God of the ordinary people despite his important state role, so a *stele* dedicated to Amun is not unusual. In this dedication Weret-Hekau is obviously closely connected to Amun. Was she seen as his consort in this locality? Mut was usually the consort of Amun. The people of Deir el-Medina also worshipped the local Cobra Goddess Meretseger at this Period and would have been very familiar with the other Cobra Goddess Renenutet. Is this why Permennefer decided to dedicate his *stele* to another Cobra Goddess?

OTHER GODDESSES ASSUMING THE ROLE OF THE URAEUS

Some Goddesses who take on the role of the *Uraeus* are less

---

[160] *Hieroglyphs & the Afterlife in Ancient Egypt*, Foreman & Quirke, 1996:22
[161] *The Dedicatory and Building Texts of Rameses II in Luxor Temple: II Interpretation*, El-Razik, 1975:125-36
[162] *A Writing Palette of the Chief Steward Amenhotpe and some Notes on its Owner*, Hayes, 1938:9-24
[163] *A Particular Form of Amun at Deir el-Medina*, Toye, 2017:257-263

easy to explain. The *uraeus* can be associated with Maat as she is also a Daughter of Ra. This is used in the rebus of Hatshepsut's name Maatkara. Maat is very different to her volatile fiery sisters, being calm and focused on maintaining order and harmony. In one *Coffin Texts* spell, to become Hathor, the deceased states that they are a *uraeus* who lives on the truth, which does suggest a connection to Maat. In one text in the tomb of Rameses VI (20th dynasty) the king greets Maat as the Eye of Ra and refers to her as the Brilliant Eye, the *Uraeus* and the Ipet-serpent. Here she is called Opener of the Ways as she leads the deceased king to the eastern horizon.[164] Seshat is depicted as the *Uraeus* Serpent in the temple of Hathor at Dendera.[165] She is an ancient Goddess of writing, notation and architecture and is often considered the consort of Thoth. In one statuette (now in the Louvre Museum, Paris) she is depicted with two snakes draped over her headdress, which is a five-pointed star symbol.[166] In reality any Goddess can take on the role of the *Uraeus* Serpent. The nature of the specific Goddess will have an impact on the aspect of the *Uraeus* Goddess they wished to emphasise in that particular context.

THE *URAEUS* GODDESS AND KINGSHIP

The *uraeus* was strongly linked to the monarchy and became the legitimate symbol of kingship. The theory was that only the legitimate heir to the throne would be granted divine protection. As a result the *uraeus* and the White and Red Crowns of Egypt became almost synonymous as the crown was never without its *uraeus*. *"To her belongs the uraeus of the head of every god. There is no god who has seized it for himself on earth."*[167] In one myth from the New Kingdom Geb discovered that Shu had a crown with a living *uraeus* which was hidden near Pi-'Iaret in the Delta. When Geb opened the lid of the box the *uraeus* leapt out breathing fire which badly burnt his head.[168] Geb is usually viewed as the legitimate ruler before his son Osiris inherited his throne. Perhaps he was

---

164 *The Tomb of Rameses VI*, Piankoff, 1954:321
165 *The Theology of Hathor of Dendera*, Richter, 2016:214
166 *The Gods of Ancient Egypt*, Vernus, 1998:59
167 *A Crossword Hymn to Mut*, Stewart, 1971:87-104
168 *The Egyptian Myths*, Shaw, 2014:65

just trying to get power too early. As a consequence the coronation ritual was of supreme importance. "*The Uraeus is distinguished on your head. The white crown and the red crown are united on your head. Your kingship is the kingship of Ra.*"[169] Once the *uraeus* is fixed on the king's forehead his right to rule is established. It was assumed that she would not affix herself to one who was not destined to be king.

There are coronation rituals inscribed in a number of temples where the new king is given his symbols of kingship by various deities. At Abydos Isis presents the *menit, sistrum* and *uraeus* to Sety I. "*Take for thyself upon thy brow the uraeus.*"[170] Thoth recites an offering list to the king which includes "*he adorns thee with the Eye of Horus, the uraeus which is within the uraeus-goddess*".[171] Thoth presents the king with an *ankh*, held to his nose, and two staffs which have two cobras wearing the Red and White crowns entwined around them. They are as important as the breath of life to the king. Weret-Hekau was frequently involved in the coronation rituals. Texts from a statue of Horemheb (18th dynasty) describe how she embraced the king during his coronation and became his *uraeus*. It describes how "*her arms in welcoming attitude, she embraced his beauty and established herself on his forehead*".[172] She was also present at the coronation of Hatshepsut (18th dynasty). Texts from Speos Artemidos depict her as a lioness-headed Goddess. "*Utterance by Weret-Hekau-Pakhet, Lady of Heaven, Mistress of the Two Lands…I rear myself between thine eyebrows, my fiery breath being as a fire against thine enemies and thou art glad through me like Re forever.*"[173] It isn't clear if Weret-Hekau is acting as Wadjet in her role of Goddess of the Coronation or just as Weret-Hekau in her own right.

In one New Year ritual the king was anointed with nine different oils in a ritual invoking the *uraeus*. This oil allowed the life-giving powers of the *uraeus* to enter into the king and protect his health for the year. "*Wosret is on his brow, shielding him with her*

---

[169] *The Theology of Hathor of Dendera*, Richter, 2016:216
[170] *Temple Ritual at Abydos*, David, 2016:65
[171] *Temple Ritual at Abydos*, David, 2016:202
[172] *The Great Enchantress in the Little Golden Shrine of Tutankhamun*, Bosse-Griffiths, 1973:100-108
[173] *Texts of Hatshepsut and Sethos I inside Speos Artemidos*, Fairman & Grdseloff, 1947:12-33

terrible fury, preserving him with her mysterious powers."[174] Wosret (Waset) appears to have been a personification of the city of Thebes. Her name means Powerful One.[175] The *uraeus* was so closely connected with kingship that a rebellion was considered an insurrection against the *Uraeus* Goddess herself. *"Men have fallen into rebellion against the Uraeus...even she who makes the Two Lands content...behold the Serpent is taken from its hole and the secrets of the Kings of Upper and Lower Egypt are divulged."*[176]

PACIFYING THE GODDESS

The volatile nature of the Eye Goddess and *uraeus* is explained in the myth of the *Angry Eye*. Another myth emphasises the continual need for pacification of the Goddess, that of the *Return of the Distant Goddess*. It is considered an ancient myth which we have been able to recreate from Greco-Roman texts in temples of that era and the *Leiden* papyrus. Ra and his daughter quarrel, we are not told what the source of the problem is. The *uraeus* detaches herself from her father and transforms into a lioness and heads to the deserts of Nubia. Ra is powerless without his *uraeus*, she is his protector and his striking power. Only the *Uraeus* Goddess can protect him from the rebellious humans and his nemesis Apophis. Without any counterbalance the separated Eye is dangerous. In the desert her rage increases because this is the domain of chaos, as opposed to the civilised land of Egypt, which only acts to agitate and inflame her further. The Distant Goddess is usually Hathor or Tefnut but at Esna it is Sekhmet. This myth is discussed in detail in Jackson (2018). Ra sends either Thoth, Onuris or Shu to retrieve the Goddess. (Onuris is a warrior and hunter God from the Abydos region.) Thoth eventually *"pacified her who is in in the middle of her rage"*.[177] She is persuaded to return to Egypt and to Ra. As in any worthwhile tale this is not straightforward and she needs constant reassurance and pacification. Finally the Goddess is reconciled with Ra. *"Welcome! Come back upon the head of him you have protected, that head from which*

---

[174] *Golden Shrine, Golden Queen: Egypt's Anointing Mysteries*, Roberts, 2008:33
[175] *The Complete Gods and Goddesses of Ancient Egypt*, Wilkinson, 2003:169
[176] *The Admonitions of an Egyptian Sage*, Faulkner, 1965:53-62
[177] *Egyptian Mythology*, Pinch, 2002:72

you went forth."[178] Cosmic order is restored when Hathor, in the form of both the *uraeus* and the Solar Eye, is reconciled with her father and returns to her proper place on his brow. *"Making the Eye healthy, making the uraeus live."*[179] The *Return of the Distant Goddess* is alluded to in a scene from the temple of Hathor at Dendera. Shu presents the *wedjat* eye to Hathor, behind her Ra-Harakhti raises his arms in adoration. (Harakhti is Horus of the Horizon.) *"I extend my arms around the uraeus in her shrine."*[180] The word used for shrine puns with that for light or bright.

Even when in her place on the brow of Ra the *Uraeus* Goddess retains her volatile character. She is always *"great of rage"*.[181] As her main role was to protect the person on whose head she resided, the *Uraeus* Goddess would view all who approached her as an enemy until proved otherwise. The daily rituals carried out in the temple of Abydos are inscribed on the walls. Part of the ritual for opening the shrine was the recitation of a spell before offering incense to the *Uraeus* Goddess. Before the statue of Ra-Harakhti was dressed each morning a prayer was recited four times to the *Uraeus* Goddess. In another relief the king is shown presenting gifts to Ra-Harakhti but he addresses his fearsome guardian first. *"Oh, great uraeus-goddess...mayest thou be praised and mayest thou be glorified."*[182] Burning incense in front of the statue of a deity was believed to soothe the *uraeus* as well as please the deity. *"Thy Living Eyes which emit fire, thy Healthy Eyes which lighten the darkness, awake in peace, so thy awakening is peaceful."*[183]

In the Old and Middle Kingdom there were hymns to the crowns of Upper and Lower Egypt and also to the diadem of the crown, namely the *uraeus*. It seems strange to us to treat a crown in this way but what is being addressed is the divine power resident in the crown, either that of the *Uraeus* Goddess or the Two Ladies. The following *Morning Hymn* was sung by priestesses to awaken and greet the protective *Uraeus* Goddess. The phrase *'wake in peace'* is common in hymns and prayers to all deities as a

---

[178] *The Apotropaic Goddess in the Eye*, Darnell, 1997:35-48
[179] *The Theology of Hathor of Dendera*, Richter, 2016:25
[180] *The Theology of Hathor of Dendera*, Richter, 2016:29
[181] *Temple Ritual at Abydos*, David, 2016:144
[182] *Temple Ritual at Abydos*, David, 2016:147
[183] *The Litany of Re*, Piankoff, 1964:47

precaution. No one wants to disturb or startle a resting deity especially one as volatile and dangerous as the *Uraeus* Goddess.

> *Awake in peace! Great Queen, awake in peace; thine awakening is peaceful!*
> *Awake in peace! Snake that is on the brow of the king, awake in peace; thine awakening is peaceful!*
> *Awake in peace! Upper Egyptian snake, awake in peace; thine awakening is peaceful!*
> *Awake in peace! Lower Egyptian snake, awake in peace; thine awakening is peaceful!*
> *Awake in peace! Renenutet, awake in peace; thine awakening is peaceful!*
> *Awake in peace! Uto with splendid…awake in peace; thine awakening is peaceful!*
> *Awake in peace! Thou with head erect, with wide neck, awake in peace; thine awakening is peaceful!*[184]

A resting cobra is sometimes used as a decoration on objects, including the *sistrum*. The *sistrum* is a cult object of Hathor and Isis and a musical instrument which was used in pacification ceremonies and to repel evil. Depicting a cobra in this posture may allude to the pacified Goddess, perceiving no threat she has returned to a position of rest. She is still present for protection should the need arise. The *sistrum* has horizontal rods to hold the metal discs which make the sounds when shaken. The ends of the rods are often bent where they project out to mirror the form of the snake hieroglyph, *dt*, by bending one end upwards and the other downwards.[185]

CONCLUSION

This spell from the *Book of the Dead* summarises the critical role of the *uraeus*. "*I am the red flame that is on the forehead of sunlight, that causes the Two Lands and everyone to live by the heat of its mouth, and that saves Re from Apophis.*"[186] The *Uraeus* Goddess is the ultimate protector, protecting the king against his enemies and the deities against theirs especially the annihilating chaos of the *nun* in the

---

[184] *Ancient Egyptian Poetry and Prose*, Erman, 1995:12-13
[185] *Reading Egyptian Art*, Wilkinson, 2011:213
[186] *An Ancient Egyptian Book of the Dead*, O'Rourke, 2016:91 spell 149

form of Apophis. She is the personification of the original feminine energy of *sekhem* and because this is solar energy she has a volatile personality and can be ambivalent and extreme. The *uraeus* has been an important symbol from the start of the Dynastic Period and it continues in use today as the eternal and "*most ancient female of the world*".[187] She is not the only Cobra Goddess though, as can be seen in the following chapter.

---

[187] *Myth and Symbol in Ancient Egypt*, Clark, 1978:224

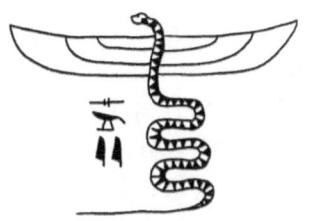

CHAPTER 6

Cobra Goddesses

"I live according to my will, for I am Wadjet, Lady of the Devouring Flame, and few approach me."[188]

INTRODUCTION

Cobra Goddesses are present in Egypt from the Pre-dynastic and continue into the Roman Period. Like the *Uraeus* Goddess they pervade all aspects of life and art. While it isn't always easy or realistic to differentiate a *Uraeus* Goddess from a Cobra Goddess there are some differences. I use the term Cobra Goddess to describe those Goddesses whose main form is that of a cobra but, as to be expected, in the serpentine world nothing is easy to untangle. A Goddess doesn't have to be the Eye of the Sun to take the form of a cobra. The main Eye Goddess such as Hathor, Mut and Sekhmet are not depicted as cobras even though they take the form of a cobra when they manifest as the *Uraeus* Goddess. The *Uraeus* Goddess is focused on kingship and adorning the brow of kings and deities as their protector. On the whole the Cobra Goddesses have a wider range of aspects. Taking this definition, there are three main Cobra Goddesses each associated with the natural habitat of snakes; Wadjet in the marshes, Renenutet in the fields and Meretseger in the desert mountains.

---

[188] *The Ancient Egyptian Book of the Dead*, Faulkner, 1989:49 spell 17

WADJET

Wadjet is the Goddess who encompasses both the Cobra and the *Uraeus* Goddess. She is the tutelary Goddess of Lower Egypt and has been so since the 1st dynasty. It is possible that she was originally a manifestation of a Pre-dynastic Goddess and a symbol of the fertile Delta before she became associated with sovereignty and Lower Egypt. Her name is sometimes translated as Edjo or Uadjt. To the Greeks she was Uto. This name derives from her cult city of Buto, ancient Pe and Dep. Her name means Green One which alludes to the papyrus swamps of her Delta home as well as to the green vegetation of the fertile land. It can also refer to the green colour of some snakes. The word *w3d* means green or fresh, alluding to the growth of vegetation, and forms the basis of her name *W3d.t*.[189]

Iconography and Symbols

Wadjet is normally depicted as a cobra and her hieroglyph symbol is a rearing cobra coiled on a basket. It has two meanings, that of 'lady' and 'all', and can be read either way or with the dual meaning of Lady of All. Sometimes Wadjet is depicted as a lioness-headed cobra. During the Late Period she was increasingly associated with Sekhmet so was often depicted as a lioness-headed Goddess. Lioness Goddesses were particularly popular at this time. It is not easy to distinguish between the lioness-headed Goddesses without an accompanying inscription. A bronze throne (now in the Louvre, Paris) depicts women adoring a lioness-headed Goddess described as Wadjet. A similar throne (now in the Civic Archaeological Museum, Bologna) depicts Apries (26th dynasty) offering a papyrus sceptre to a lioness-headed Wadjet. In coronation scenes she was depicted as a woman wearing the crown of Lower Egypt. It is rare to see her in this form in any other setting. This might have been to emphasise a more peaceful aspect for the safety of the king.

Wadjet does not have specific fertility or agricultural aspects but she does have a strong association with vegetation, which is a

---

[189] *The Theology of Hathor of Dendera*, Richter, 2016:214

reflection of the verdant, fertile Delta. One of her epithets is *"She of the Papyrus"*[190] which is the sacred plant of Lower Egypt. One *Pyramid Texts* spell alludes to her creating the papyrus swamps. *"O papyrus-plant which issued from Wadjet."*[191] As she created the papyrus her creative and protective powers reside within the plant. *"May Wadjet let him flourish by means of her papyrus amulet."*[192] (Him being the deceased.) The phrase forms a pun between her name and the word to make flourish. Another spell from the *Books of Breathing* asks that the torch used by the deceased flourish. A strange term to use for a torch but it provided the all-important pun on her name. It also infers a large and long-lasting flame as the papyrus is both tall and long-lived. The papyrus had strong protective powers. *"The betbet-serpent exults for your ka. Its papyrus will appear as your protection."* The *betbet*-serpent is the name of the serpent who protected Osiris in Pe and Dep. It may be another name of Wadjet's or a special manifestation of her. Wadjet was also associated with the *seneb*-plant. Unfortunately the species of plant hasn't been identified, all we know is that it had apotropaic powers. One spell in the *Books of Breathing* states that Wadjet *"will present you with seneb-plants in Khemmis and destroy all your enemies"*.[193] It is referred to as the divine *seneb*-plant, meaning that it is imbued with divine powers. Amulets of *seneb*-plants were used during mummification of the body. Several are mentioned in the *Books of Breathing*. One describes the plant fashioned into twelve amuletic knots and placed on the right leg of the deceased. Another involves 36 knots, the text explaining this is because there will be 36 deities whom the deceased's *ba* will encounter in the afterlife. Another amulet made from the plant is placed in the hand of the deceased and is described as *"the perfect protection of Horus himself"*.[194] Children wore such amulets for protection, as the Horus child will have done. Other spells refer to the deceased flourishing within the protection of the *seneb*-plant.

Spell 17 in the *Book of the Dead* aligns malachite with Wadjet. Its green colour gives a link to her name and her associated

---

[190] *The Gods of Ancient Egypt*, Watterson, 2003:126
[191] *The Ancient Egyptian Pyramid Texts*, Faulkner, 2007:272 utterance 662
[192] *Traversing Eternity*, Smith, 2009:598
[193] *Traversing Eternity*, Smith, 2009:149
[194] *Traversing Eternity*, Smith, 2009:239

plants. Green is the colour of vegetation and has the ensuing meaning of growth and life. It is also a colour symbolising rebirth with the green shoots appearing from the bare earth and buds growing from formerly bare branches. Wadjet *"makes green the Two Lands and guides the gods in this her name of Wadjet...Wadjet has power over good things in that her name of Lady of Memphis"*.[195]

Relationships

Wadjet is paired with Nekhbet, the Vulture Goddess of Upper Egypt who had a cult centre in Hierakonpolis. From the 1st dynasty she is depicted with Nekhbet as the Two Ladies – a rearing cobra and a vulture sat on baskets. Sometimes their iconography is fused and they can appear as two cobras or two vultures. Nekhbet is shown as a cobra when acting as one of the Two *Uraei*. Two *uraei* surrounding a solar disc are usually Wadjet and Nekhbet.[196] Horus of Edfu *"has placed himself between the two uraeus goddesses...he has taken Nekhbet with him as uraeus goddess...Uto is with him as uraeus goddess"*.[197] They sometimes take on each other's roles. There is a reference to *"Edjo of the South"*.[198]

Wadjet was one of the nurses of the Horus child (the son of Isis and Osiris) when he was being brought up in hiding in the marshes of the Delta. Texts from the temple of Hathor at Dendera describe Wadjet as *"making shelter for her infant amid the marsh plants, bringing up her son Horus in the papyrus-marshes"*. Horus was *"nursed by Edjo in Dep"*.[199] Wadjet was associated with Isis for this reason. In later periods Isis assimilates Wadjet taking the epithet Lady of Pe and Dep and the hymns at Philae refer to her *"Making the Two Lands flourish, and leading the gods, in this her name of Wadjet"*.[200] Wadjet is sometimes referred to as the Eye of Ra in the Marshes. In this particular text she is associated with the lotus, the plant of Upper Egypt, which might be because Philae is in Upper Egypt. She brings both blue and white lotuses to the

---

[195] *The Bremner-Rhind Papyrus II*, Faulkner, 1937:10-16
[196] *The Cobra Goddesses of Ancient Egypt*, Johnson, 1990:5
[197] *The Myth of Horus at Edfu – I*, Fairman, 1935:26-36
[198] *An Ancient Egyptian Book of Hours*, Faulkner, 1958:2
[199] *Horus the Behdetite*, Gardiner, 1944:23-60
[200] *Hymns to Isis in Her Temple at Philae*, Zabkar, 1988:111

deceased which will protect them. *"All protection of life will enter into you."*[201]

Nefertem is the God of the Primeval Lotus which opened and gave birth to the young Sun God. He was also associated with perfume making. He is usually considered the son of Sekhmet and Ptah and occasionally of Bastet. In some regions of the Delta Wadjet takes on the role of his mother. As mentioned previously Wadjet was increasingly associated with Sekhmet which may be one reason why she could be the mother of Nefertem. Purification ceremonies depicted in some of the Greco-Roman temples give a temporal link when they invoke *"Sekhmet of yesterday…Wadjet of today…protect the King with that papyrus of life which is in your hand, in this your name of Wadjet"*.[202] Despite these maternal roles, Wadjet does not have a consort. This may have been a consequence of her representing the state of Lower Egypt as Nekhbet does not have a consort either.

The Greeks associated Wadjet with Leto, the consort of Zeus and the mother of Apollo and Artemis. Leto is a poor fit with Wadjet displaying none of her attributes as Leto was the Goddess of motherhood and depicted as the Greek's ideal woman – modest, demure and largely powerless. They aligned Apollo with Horus and Artemis with Bastet which might have suggested the link to the Greeks because all three deities had temples in Buto.

Wadjet and Kingship

Wadjet was very much a State Goddess and closely linked with kingship – both with the king and with the crown of Egypt. She and Nekhbet are the two protectors and keepers of the crowns of Egypt. Wadjet was closely connected to the crown, in particular the Red Crown of Lower Egypt, and the crown could be considered a manifestation of her. The king was considered to be the living Horus and as Wadjet was one of the mothers of Horus she became one of the mothers of the king. Sety I (19th dynasty) aligned himself with some very powerful Goddesses

---

[201] *Traversing Eternity*, Smith, 2009:234
[202] *A Wooden Figure of Wadjet with Two Painted Representations of Amasis*, James, 1982:156-165

when he described himself as the *"son of Bastet, foster-child of Sekhmet...born of Pakhet, reared by the Sorceress...brought up by Edjo"*.²⁰³ The Sorceress is Weret-Hekau. As well as being a Cobra Goddess in her own right, Wadjet is also the Eye of Ra and through that a *Uraeus* Goddess. The *uraeus* as a symbol might have developed because of the cobra form of Wadjet through her very close association with kingship. It is as the *uraeus* that she protects the king. *"The might of your terror is upon your enemies, O Wadjet, She who renews the Two Lands, your magical power is great against all malevolent things which can harm the pharaoh...more omnipotent than the gods."*²⁰⁴ Inscriptions relating to battles fought by Thutmose III (18th dynasty) and Rameses II (18th dynasty) refer to her slaughtering enemies with her fiery breath.²⁰⁵ She is referred to as *"Edjo who is in her moment"*²⁰⁶ equivalent in meaning to being in the act of striking. This role extends to protecting Ra and the other deities. Wadjet *"who protects the gods...I am Edjo who dwells in the starry sky"*.²⁰⁷

On his ascension to the throne the king took a number of official names. His second was the *nebty* name meaning *"he of the Two Ladies"* which placed him under the protection of Wadjet and Nekhbet as well as symbolising a united Egypt. The oldest *nebty* title of the king is on an ivory plaque from 1st dynasty Naqada which depicts a cobra and a vulture on a basket.²⁰⁸ The Two Ladies, as well as all the other major deities, are depicted participating in the all-important coronation scenes. In these Wadjet and Nekhbet are shown as women wearing the Red and White Crowns respectively. Wadjet crowns the king with the Red Crown and Nekhbet crowns him with the White. At the temple of Hathor at Dendera Wadjet and Nekhbet present the king with the emblems of their realm. These are a *uraeus* wearing the Red Crown entwined around the papyrus of Lower Egypt and a *uraeus* wearing the White Crown entwined around the lotus of Upper Egypt. Together these sceptres form the *w3d.ty*, the two *uraei* who

---

203 *Texts of Hatshepsut and Sethos I inside Speos Artemidos*, Fairman & Grdseloff, 1947:12-33
204 *Golden Shrine, Golden Queen: Egypt's Anointing Mysteries*, Roberts, 2008:41
205 *The Routledge Dictionary of Egyptian Gods and Goddesses*, Hart, 2005:161
206 *The First Two Pages of the Worterbuch*, Gardiner, 1948:12-18
207 *The Ancient Egyptian Coffin Texts Volume III*, Faulkner, 2007:87 spell 952
208 *The Cobra Goddesses of Ancient Egypt*, Johnson, 1990:46

represent the united Two Lands. One of the king's epithets is *"Great One of the two Uraei"*.[209] A similar scene is depicted in Speos Artemidos during the coronation of Hatshepsut (18th dynasty). Wadjet tells Hatshepsut *"I give thee the Two Uraei upon thy brow"*. Wadjet is described as *"Edjo who came forth from the horizon"* while on another scene she is *"Edjo, Lady of Heaven"*.[210] In another inscription Wadjet assures her *"I place your terror in all lands. I rear up between your eyebrows, my flames are fire against your enemies"* and *"I have placed the two cobras on your head"*.[211] In the chapel of Sety I (19th dynasty) the Ennead is depicted endorsing his accession. *"He has united with Great-of-Magic…the Lady of the Crown of Upper Egypt, the Lady of the Crown of Lower Egypt, may they assume their position, abiding upon his brow."*[212] Wadjet then says to the king *"my arms are around thee in life and dominion"*.[213]

Afterlife

Wadjet will be there for the deceased *"in the form of a living uraeus"* appearing on both sides of their head. These *uraei "will not fail to manifest themselves upon your head at any time just as they do for her father Re"*.[214] In some *Coffin Texts* spells the deceased state that either they are Wadjet or that she is their *uraeus*. This will align them with her great power and prestige. In a vignette for spell 17 in the *Book of the Dead* Wadjet and Nekhbet appear as cobras curling around the lotus and the papyrus. Another part of the same illustration shows a lion on a plinth. Overhead the Wadjet cobra climbs the papyrus stems which hang over the lion's head.

Worship

The twin cities of Pe and Dep (modern Tell el-Fara'in) were one of the earliest and most important religious centres in Egypt.

---

[209] *The Theology of Hathor of Dendera*, Richter, 2016:213
[210] *Texts of Hatshepsut and Sethos I inside Speos Artemidos*, Fairman & Grdseloff, 1947:12-33
[211] *Hathor Rising*, Roberts, 2001:46-47
[212] *Temple Ritual at Abydos*, David, 2016:195-196
[213] *Temple Ritual at Abydos*, David, 2016:199
[214] *Traversing Eternity*, Smith, 2009:232

"*While I dwell in Dep of the goddess Wadjet.*"[215] Her shrine in Pe and Dep was called the *per-nu* – the house of fire. Excavations of a Pre-dynastic site in Dep have produced a number of ivory carvings including one of a snake with the head of a woman. This may be an early representation of Wadjet.[216] She was worshipped here in Pre-dynastic times where she took the form of a cobra. It is possible that she was the original Mother Goddess of the Delta, but if she was then most of those attributes were lost as she became increasingly associated with kings and the state of Egypt. The neighbouring city of Pe was the residence (possibly just legendary) of the early kings of Egypt which is why Wadjet was promoted as the tutelary Goddess of Lower Egypt. By the New Kingdom these cities had been merged and renamed as Per Wadjet – the House of Wadjet.[217]

A temple dedicated to Wadjet was found at Tell Nabasha in the Delta. A statue of Wadjet was found and she is depicted as a snake with a woman's head wearing the double crown of Egypt. Ahmose II (26th dynasty) restored and constructed many Delta temples and shrines including this one. The underlying structure is thought to date to the New Kingdom. This is likely to have been the temple referred to by Herodotus as Per-Edjo. "*The temple, which is dedicated to Leto, stands in a great city called...Buto.*"[218] The earliest reference to the Per-Edjo is in the 20th dynasty in connection with a high priest.[219] One inscription on a limestone block refers to a temple scribe of Wadjet. Other Delta temples of Wadjet include one at Qantir which was close to the Great Temple of Ra.[220] A temple was excavated near el-Hosayneya in the north-east Delta which was originally thought to be Wadjet's temple. Later research suggests that it was dedicated to the local triad of Wadjet, Min and Harpokrates during the Ptolemaic Period.[221] There was an arc of fortified sites on the eastern side of the Delta which was designed to control access through Sinai.

---

[215] *The Ancient Egyptian Book of Thoth*, Jaznow & Zauzich, 2005:27
[216] *Before the Pyramids*, Teeter, 2011:60
[217] *The Gods of Ancient Egypt*, Watterson, 2003:126
[218] *The Histories*, Herodotus & Selincourt, 2003:160
[219] *The Tell El-fara'in Expedition, 1968*, Seton-Williams, 1969:5-22
[220] *The Complete Temples of Ancient Egypt*, Wilkinson, 2000:108
[221] *Preliminary Report on the First Season of the Tell Nabasha Project, Autumn 2015*, Neilson, Gasperini & Mamedow, 26:65-74

One of these stations is referred to as the *"tract of Edjo"*. The commander of one of these towns, Sile, was given the title *"prophet of Edjo who sets limits to the Two Lands"*. Wadjet was depicted in lioness form in this site. Another station was referred to as the *"storehouse of the lion"* in battle reliefs at Karnack.[222]

Most of Wadjet's worship was carried out by the king and high priests and priestesses as depicted in temple reliefs. These examples come from the temple of Osiris at Abydos. In one the king kneels and offers incense. *"Be pure and be censed, oh Great Magician Edjo, Mistress of Pr-wr who is residing in the house of flame of Sekhmet."*[223] In another scene the king offers two rolls of green cloth. The spell starts *"may Edjo appear! The Mistress of Nebyt is excellent, whom none can approach in the sky or on earth. She hands over Re-Harakhte…to her powers…he becomes young again like fresh plants"*.[224] Although Wadjet was a state Goddess she appears to have had followers amongst the ordinary people. A 19th dynasty *stele* from Heliopolis was dedicated to Wadjet by *"the Doorkeeper Tety"* whose mother was a *"Chantress of Edjo"*.[225] She is depicted as a lioness-headed Goddess and holds a papyrus flower staff. The deceased and his mother are depicted offering papyrus flowers to her. Amulets of Wadjet were common during the Saite Period. At this time Egypt was ruled from the Delta, Wadjet's stronghold. The first Saite ruler had overthrown both Kushite and Assyrian rule so the rise in popularity of the Goddess of Lower Egypt came with renewed national pride. A Late Period statue depicts a man kneeling and offering to Wadjet who is depicted as a lioness-headed Goddess.[226]

RENENUTET (ERNUTET)

Renenutet is an ancient Goddess and is very much a Cobra Goddess rather than a *Uraeus* Goddess although in the Old Kingdom she was sometimes aligned with the *uraeus* in her role of protector of the king. There is reference to her as the *uraeus* in a

---

[222] *Report on the 1993 and 1997 Seasons at Tell Qedwa*, Redford, 1998:45-60
[223] *Temple Ritual at Abydos*, David, 2016:137
[224] *Temple Ritual at Abydos*, David, 2016:144
[225] *A Stela from Heliopolis Dedicated to Edjo*, Bakry, 1969:177-180
[226] *The Gods of Ancient Egypt*, Vernus, 1998:151

few of the funerary spells. *"The flaming blast of my uraeus is that of Ernutet who is upon me."*[227] This doesn't appear to be her true nature though as she was always seen as friendly and helpful. Her name is derived from the word *rnn* – nourishment. She is *"the snake who nourishes"*.[228] Many of her epithets reflect her role as a Goddess of the Harvest. She is Mistress of the Threshing Floor[229] and Lady of Granaries. In the more general agricultural sphere she is the Lady of the Fertile Field[230] and the Beautiful Mistress of Provisions.[231] *"You are the golden one, the lady of the field, Renenutet."*[232] The Greeks called her Hermouthis or Thermouthis.

Iconography

Although she is attested to from the early Old Kingdom all the surviving images of Renenutet date from the New Kingdom. She can be depicted as a woman, a cobra-headed woman or a cobra. When she is shown as a cobra-headed woman she is often enthroned and nursing a child. As a cobra she wears the cow-horn sun disc often with two plumes surmounting the sun disc. Like the other Cobra Goddesses she can be depicted as a lioness, but this is not a very common form for Renenutet. At Dendera she has a lioness-headed form and the *Fayum* papyrus shows her as a lioness-headed *uraeus*. Any deity could be depicted as feline as a way of emphasising their power or a particular aspect.

Relationships

Renenutet carries the immature grain God Nepri (or Neper) within her. He is the God of grain, representing the prosperity brought by these crops. He was later considered an aspect of Osiris so Renenutet can be his mother, which strengthened her association with Isis. Osiris, as the slain Vegetation God, is reborn as the germinating seed Nepri. According to one *Coffin Texts* spell, Nehebkau (a Snake God discussed in the following

---

[227] The Ancient Egyptian Pyramid Texts, Faulkner, 2007:66 utterance 256
[228] Egyptian Mythology, Pinch, 2002:185
[229] The Routledge Dictionary of Egyptian Gods and Goddesses, Hart, 2005:135-136
[230] The Gods and Symbols of Ancient Egypt, Lurker, 1986:100
[231] Gods of Agriculture and Welfare in Ancient Egypt, Leibovitch, 1953:73-113
[232] Mut Enthroned, Troy, 1996:312

chapter) is the son of Geb and Renenutet. In the Fayum Renenutet was sometimes considered the wife of the Crocodile God Sobek. There is a small temple dedicated to them in Medinet Madi. It was founded by Amenhotep III and IV (18th dynasty) but redeveloped in the Greco-Roman Period. In the Ptolemaic Period Renenutet and Sobek formed a triad with Horus as their son. Renenutet is sometimes equated to Maat. Some tombs in the Valley of the Kings depict Renenutet as a mummified woman with a cobra head and called *"Lady of Justification"*.[233]

In the Greco-Roman Period Renenutet was assimilated by Isis who took her epithets and roles. Sometimes they were combined to form Isermouthis. An inscription from the temple of Hathor at Dendera refers to *"Isis the most great goddess also called Thermouthis"*. Another one refers to *"Isis-Thermouthis the lady who is on the dyke of the avenue of Hathor"*.[234] Renenutet was still worshipped and depicted at this time, usually in the same style as Isis. One Ptolemaic Period statue shows her as a standing woman with her legs merging into the body of a snake. A young boy stands by her side.[235]

The Harvest Goddess

"Renenutet, Lady of Food, Mistress of Nourishment."[236] Agricultural and Harvest deities are to be expected amongst an agricultural people but why did the Egyptians view their Harvest Goddess as a Cobra Goddess? Snakes were associated with the harvest for two reasons. The fertility given by Renenutet came with the annual Nile inundation which brought a layer of fertile silt to the fields as well as water. The floodwaters would have driven snakes and their prey onto higher ground, concentrating them near settlements. This helped reinforce the link between snakes and the life-giving inundation, which is covered in detail in chapter 8. In a granary at Karnak, Hapi is depicted offering to Renenutet. Hapi is the God of the inundation, here he offers the inundation so that Renenutet can bring forth the essential crops. Isis had a

---

[233] *The Routledge Dictionary of Egyptian Gods and Goddesses*, Hart, 2005:136
[234] *Cities and Administration in Roman Egypt*, Bowman & Rathbone, 1992:107-127
[235] *Gods of Agriculture and Welfare in Ancient Egypt*, Leibovitch, 1953:73-113
[236] *Inscriptions from the Palace of Amenhotep III*, Hayes, 1951:35-56

very strong link with the inundation through her connection with Sothis, the Goddess who personified the star Sirius. The inundation had been linked with the heliacal rising of the star Sirius since the early dynastic period. A heliacal rising is when the star reappears in the east just before sunrise, having been invisible for a period of time. The assimilation of Renenutet by Isis strengthened the link between the inundation and Renenutet. The inundation was essential for the food crops so was a logical extension to her aspects. *"Hail! Good Isis-Ermuthis, with thy great name, magnificent, it is on thee that rests every city…thou givest gifts, the year being accomplished at the month of Pakhons for the welfare of everybody…persuading the Nile, in his golden course, thou raisest him on the land of Egypt for the rejoicing of all humanity."*[237] By bringing fertility to the land and crops Renenutet enabled the harvest. *"Plants will grow weighed down by their fruit; with Renutet ordering all."*[238]

No matter how bountiful the land, the harvest would be wasted if it couldn't be protected, and this was another critical role of Renenutet as the Goddess of the Granary. Snakes preyed on the rodents which infested the granaries and on the grain-eating birds. Before the domestication of the cat (about the 18th dynasty) the snake was the main protector of this essential food supply. Following on from this Renenutet was also a Goddess of the household, protecting the food stores in the same way. Food provision, and its safe storage, was never taken for granted. As the proactive link between Egypt and the deities, the king was ultimately responsible for the provision of food for his (or sometimes her) people. An inscription at Karnak for Ramesses IV (20th dynasty) refers to him as *"the beautiful Lord of food of Egypt, and Renenutet who maintains everybody"*.[239] Like all the kings Hatshepsut had a series of official names, the first cartouche one being Maatkara – true one of the *ka* of Ra. A cryptographic writing of this name appears on a number of statues of her official Senenmut where he presents a group of hieroglyphs of a rearing cobra crowned with the cow-horn sun disc and enclosed by the arms of the *ka* hieroglyph. Robins suggests that the cobra refers

---

[237] *Gods of Agriculture and Welfare in Ancient Egypt*, Leibovitch, 1953:73-113
[238] *Ancient Egyptian Literature Volume III*, Lichtheim, 2006:99
[239] *Gods of Agriculture and Welfare in Ancient Egypt*, Leibovitch, 1953:73-113

to Renenutet.[240] Hatshepsut was linked with Renenutet because the king was responsible for ensuring the prosperity of Egypt, especially in terms of the food supply. Although her titles refer to her in the masculine form of the king, using some feminine grammar allowed her first name to be written cryptically to link her directly to Renenutet.

Renenutet was considered to be a gracious and beautiful Goddess and she does not appear to have had any dangerous aspects, despite her cobra form. This makes it surprising that she is a Cobra Goddess given her lack of aggressive attributes. Possibly this dates back to the Pre-dynastic and an ancestor Mother Goddess perceived as a Cobra who later lost her negative aspects to another Goddess. It seems unlikely that people weren't bitten while working in the fields or when they encountered the resident snake of the granary. Perhaps the noise of the labour-intensive activity in the fields frightened the snakes away before someone accidentally disturbed one. Renenutet may have been seen to intervene to protect the workforce. In any case, if the workers were bitten it doesn't appear to have been seen as retribution from Renenutet.

Mother of the King

Renenutet was also associated with the nourishment provided by a nursing mother, hence her depiction as a nursing Goddess. As the mother of Nepri she could also be one of the divine mothers who nourished the king's *ka* (his vital energy). She is involved in childbirth through her protective and fertility roles as well as that of fate.

Allocator of Fate

Renenutet became associated with fate and destiny because she was responsible for the success of the harvest, thus determining a good or disastrous year for people. In the Middle Kingdom *Satire on the Trades* she is deemed responsible for an individual's destiny. "*A scribe's Renenet is on his shoulder on the day he*

---

[240] *The Names of Hatshepsut as King*, Robins, 1999:103-112

*is born."*²⁴¹ Not only does she determine that he will become a scribe she oversees his upbringing and education, determining how successful he will be. The other two deities associated with fate are Meskhenet and Shay (or Shai). The God Shay determines the life-span and prosperity of an individual. *"There are none who ignore Shai and Renutet."*²⁴² Meskhenet was one of the Goddesses presiding at the birth and she determined the fate and life-span of the new-born child. In the judgement scene on the papyrus of Ani both Goddesses are depicted as personified birthing bricks. This suggests that the circumstances a person was born into is taken into account when their actions are judged.²⁴³

The Afterlife

Although principally a Goddess of this life Renenutet did have some afterlife aspects. In parallel with her role as Harvest Goddess for the living, she provides nourishment for the *ka* of the deceased. As the nursemaid and protector of the king she will look after the deceased in the same way. In the *Book of the Dead* a spell for assembling a bier states that *"Renenutet will raise you up"*.²⁴⁴ This alludes to both the reborn deceased standing up as well as the rearing cobra. Renenutet doesn't have a connection with textiles in life but she does in the afterlife. This aligns her with Tayet and the *uraei* guarding the funerary linen. New funerary clothing was essential because it symbolised rebirth. Renenutet is associated with linen offered to the deceased, one spell gives her the epithet of Linen.²⁴⁵ *"The vestment of Renenutet is yours."*²⁴⁶ She is referred to as *"Mistress of Robes"* at the temple of Horus at Edfu.²⁴⁷ One *Pyramid Texts* spell refers to the king wearing *"this Ernutet-garment of which the gods are afraid"*.²⁴⁸ Here she is either embodying the royal robe or has imbued it with magical protection. Many cultures considered there to be a link between spinning and fate

---

[241] *Ancient Egyptian Literature Volume I*, Lichtheim, 2006:191
[242] *Gods of Agriculture and Welfare in Ancient Egypt*, Leibovitch, 1953:73-113
[243] *Magical Bricks and the Bricks of Birth*, Roth & Roehrig, 2002:121-139
[244] *The Egyptian Book of the Dead*, Faulkner & Goelet, 2008:128 spell 170
[245] *The Ancient Egyptian Coffin Texts Volume III*, Faulkner, 2007:40 spell 862
[246] *Traversing Eternity*, Smith, 2009:497
[247] *The Routledge Dictionary of Egyptian Gods and Goddesses*, Hart, 2005:136
[248] *The Ancient Egyptian Pyramid Texts*, Faulkner, 2007:258 utterance 622

which may have added to Renenutet's role in determining the fate of individuals.

Worshipping Renenutet

Despite being mainly a Goddess of the ordinary people, Renenutet was also worshipped at the state level. No agricultural deity would be overlooked. There is reference to Amenhotep III dedicating a shrine to Renenutet. *"The king is introduced to the sanctuary of Renenutet, the living one of Dja."*[249] There was a chapel to her at the national granaries of the New Kingdom temple of Amun-Ra at Karnak. One inscription refers to Senenmut the steward of Amun who *"carries Renenutet of the granary of the god's offering of Montu, Lord of Armant. He causes her to appear and he lifts up her splendour on behalf of the life, prosperity and health of the king of Upper and Lower Egypt (Maatkara) living enduringly."*[250] In the 4th dynasty there is reference to Mari who was a priest of Renenutet. There is evidence of her worship in the New Kingdom in Giza, Abydos, Thebes and Kom Abu Billo in the Delta. A papyrus from the Roman Period contains information from an unknown temple to the Roman authorities. Included among the items listed is *"Thermouthis – a diadem"*.[251]

There is reference to a festival of Renenutet in the Greco-Roman funerary texts. Her festivals were held twice a year; when the sowing had been completed and when the harvest was ready. In the tomb chapel of Nebamun there is a black shrine which has an image of *"Renenutet, Lady of the Granary"*.[252] In front of it are two large libation vessels and a large bouquet of lotus flowers. She was also associated with vineyards and winemaking. *"Renenutet, she will give you wine."*[253] Private Theban tombs from the New Kingdom depict scenes of viticulture and winemaking with shrines dedicated to her. One shows the offering of grapes. Pa-wah was the overseer of all the granaries. In his tomb he is shown giving an offering of *"all good and pure things"* to Renenutet on the

---

[249] *Gods of Agriculture and Welfare in Ancient Egypt*, Leibovitch, 1953:73-113
[250] *The Names of Hatshepsut as King*, Robins, 1999:103-112
[251] *A Temple Declaration from Early Roman Egypt*, Eckerman, 2012:55-62
[252] *The Painted Tomb-Chapel of Nebamun*, Parkinson, 2008:118
[253] *Traversing Eternity*, Smith, 2009:658

first day of the harvest, the day considered to be the birthday of Nepri. He offers a *"supply of all good and pure plants for thy ka, Renenutet, Lady of the Granary. Mayest thou cause that the Chief of the Granary be every day in thy favour"*.[254] The relief shows an enthroned Renenutet nursing a child. She looks much like Isis apart from her cobra head. Renenutet appears in a similar form in statuettes. In one funerary text there is reference to a festival of Renenutet celebrated in the temple of Mut. *"The weaving women in the act of loosening the knot on the day of robing Renenutet."*[255] This will have been one of many rituals involved in removing the old clothing before cleaning and anointing the statue prior to dressing it in new clothes. In one Theban tomb the deceased offers to Amun and the *"revered Ernutet, lady of granaries"* who is depicted as a cobra sat on a basket. Another tomb depicts the deceased offering *"all things good and pure to Ernutet, lady of the granary...this day of the birth of Nepy"*.[256]

Renenutet was most widely revered by farmers and ordinary people, especially in agricultural areas. From at least the Middle Kingdom she had a cult based at Dja in the Faynum region. This was a very fertile area about 60km south-west of Cairo so her popularity is not surprising. The villages in agricultural areas had chapels dedicated to her. There was a strong domestic cult of Renenutet because she was identified with the household and family life – centred on her role as protector of the harvest and as a nursing Goddess. Amulets of her were popular as she was seen as a protective Goddess as well as being a fertility Goddess. Many cobra-shaped bowls and figurines have been found in houses and these probably represent the Mistress of Provisions and Lady of the Granaries. There are *stele* offered to Renenutet by individuals. An *ostracon* fragment from Deir el-Medina (19th dynasty) depicts Renenutet seated on a throne as a snake-headed woman nursing a child. A man holds out a loaf of bread to her. The missing fragments probably had a prayer or request written on.[257] A statue, dating to the 18th dynasty, depicts a kneeling figure holding

---

[254] *Gods of Agriculture and Welfare in Ancient Egypt*, Leibovitch, 1953:73-113
[255] *Traversing Eternity*, Smith, 2009:411
[256] *Some Occurrences of the Corn-'Aruseh in Ancient Egyptian Tomb Paintings*, Blackman, 1922:235-240
[257] *Ancient Egypt and Nubia*, Whitehouse, 2009:96

a statue of a cobra in front of him. The inscription reads "*adoration of Ernutet by the standard-bearer of the Lord of the Two Lands, Nakht*".[258]

The Bountiful Renenutet

Most cultures have an Earth Goddess but the Egyptians had the Earth God Geb who, along with Osiris, was responsible for the fertility of the Earth and crops. It is in the Cobra Goddess Renenutet that we have the closest equivalent to the concept of the earth as the providing, nurturing mother. "*The field that brings forth everything.*" [259] Renenutet was seen as helpful and friendly and displayed only the positive aspects of snakes. Like Isis, although not quite as great, she was a much-loved Goddess.

MERETSEGER

Meretseger is very much a Cobra Goddess, albeit a very local one. She is the guardian Goddess of the Theban necropolis. Her names translates as the "*one who loves silence*" an appropriate name for a Goddess who lives in the empty, mountainous desert.[260] Like all Goddesses she can be addressed as Lady of Heaven and Mistress of the Two Lands but her main epithet is Peak of the West which refers to the mountain of el-Qurn which rose above the village of Deir el-Medina. It had a shape which could be seen as a pyramid or a coiled snake. This was the abode and presence of Meretseger. As it overlooked the Valley of the Kings el-Qurn was considered one of the entrances to the afterworld.

Iconography

Meretseger is depicted as a coiled cobra or as a snake with a woman's head and arms. She is shown as a human-headed snake in an 18th dynasty sandstone sculpture and on the sarcophagus lid of Ramesses III (20th dynasty). On *stele* and ostracon from Deir el-

---

[258] *Statue of a Serpent Worshiper*, Faulkner, 1934:154-156
[259] *A Roman Period Demotic Manual of Hymns to Rattawy and Other Deities*, Kockelmann, 2003:217-229
[260] *Soulful Creatures. Animal Mummies in Ancient Egypt*, Bleiberg et al, 2013:55

Medina she can be depicted both as a coiled snake and as a human-headed snake. The Turin *stele* of Nefer'abu shows an altar table and offerings to a Snake Goddess with three heads dedicated to Meretseger.

Her Nature

Unlike many other Goddesses Meretseger doesn't appear to have any particular aspects and she has no known relationships with any other deities. She is just herself, by herself. As her name suggests she did not appreciate being disturbed. Like all snakes she prefers to be left in peace and will attack if provoked. She would strike at wrongdoers causing blindness or send snakes and scorpions to attack them. Swearing a false oath also provoked her. She cured the victim if they repented. It is an almost automatic reflex to say *"what have I done to deserve this?"* when things go wrong. For most people there is usually a duty neglected or an inappropriate action that can be blamed. In some ways it does give you a sense of control, if you know what you did wrong then perhaps you can prevent the disaster from recurring.

On his *stele* Nefer'abu offers praise to Meretseger and a warning to others. *"I was an ignorant man and foolish, who knew neither good nor evil. I wrought the transgression against the Peak and she chastised me."* He warns *"Be ye ware of the Peak…She smites with the smiting of a savage lion: she pursues him that transgresses against her"*. Exactly what he had done he isn't admitting to, unless the workmen knew what was meant by a transgression. Perhaps he didn't know what he had done to offend her. Suffering from a disease, or perhaps the effects of poisoning, Nefer'abu begged her forgiveness. *"I called upon my Mistress: I found that she came to me with sweet airs; She was merciful to me, after she had made me behold her hand. She turned again to me in mercy: She caused me to forget the sickness that had been upon me. Lo, the Peak of the West is merciful, if one call upon her."* Equating Meretseger's method of attack to that of a lion is unusual, but the feline and serpent link is always strong. Perhaps it was a way of emphasising how dangerous she could be if provoked. On another *stele* a man called Nekhtamun calls on her to cure his blindness. *"Praised be thou in peace, O Lady of the West, the Mistress* *that turns herself toward mercy! Thou causest me to see darkness by day. I will declare thy might to all people. Be merciful to me in thy mercy!"*²⁶¹ Eye diseases and blindness were unfortunately very common. Dangerous working conditions, dusty air, flies and poor hygiene were the main causes. An attack by a spitting cobra might only result in temporary blindness, providing that the victim received proper treatment.

Meretseger was invoked for protection by the local residents of the area along with the other deities. *"The great Peak of the West, who gives her hand to him that she loves, and gives protection to him that sets her in his heart."*²⁶² In the 20th dynasty a carpenter, Maanakhtef, writes *"I am calling upon Meretseger, mistress of the West, and all the gods of Thebes to look after you"*.²⁶³ Although she was a local Goddess she was called upon by her followers when they were travelling. The scribe Dhutmose writes *"please call upon Amon of the Thrones of the Two Lands and Meretseger to bring me back alive from the wilds of Namekhay"*. Later he writes from Nubia *"please call upon Amon of the Beautiful Encounter and Meretseger to bring me back alive"*.²⁶⁴ Hopefully she did.

Worship

The New Kingdom tomb workers in the Valley of the Kings and Valley of the Queens lived with their families in Deir el-Medina and it is here that Meretseger was worshipped. A number of *stele* have been found dedicated to this dangerous but merciful Goddess. They were designed both to propitiate her and to beg for forgiveness. Hers was not an official cult and she would have been worshipped at home, in the workplace and in small shrines and chapels cut into the hillside. One such shrine is located on an outcrop of limestone near the path to the Valley of the Queens. Reliefs in the form of *stele* have been carved into the rocks. Individuals are depicted worshipping Meretseger. People would come here to pray and leave small *stele* dedicated to her. These show the person kneeling and worshipping Meretseger in her

---

261 *The Religion of the Poor in Ancient Egypt*, Gunn, 1916:81-94
262 *The Religion of the Poor in Ancient Egypt*, Gunn, 1916:81-94
263 *Letters from Ancient Egypt*, Wente, 1990:167
264 *Letters from Ancient Egypt*, Wente, 1990:178 & 189

snake form and were probably votive offerings to thank her for assistance. Similar votive offerings have been found at Deir el-Medina. One depicts Lady Tarekhanou kneeling before a large undulating cobra wearing a crown. On a grid on the lower part of the *stele* are nine rows with two snakes in each. These may be further representations of Meretseger or of Cobra Goddesses in general.[265]

Meretseger's statues do appear in the nearby temples of Hathor and Ptah. There is also reference to a man called Pasen who *"has been appointed as the singer of Meretseger"*.[266] Meretseger is depicted on the tomb decorations of Rameses VI and Ramesses IX (20th dynasty). Amenhotep II (18th dynasty) is depicted with Meretseger in a statue from Karnak. Her rearing head rests upon his head and her body is coiled behind him for protection. She wears the cow-horn sun disc often associated with Hathor.[267] It is possible that these kings learnt about the local cult of Meretseger and wanted to ensure her protection. Acknowledging the Goddess who would preside over their tombs was a wise precaution.

Meretseger Retired

Meretseger's worship was restricted to the Theban necropolis and when the tomb builders left, her cult disappeared, allowing Meretseger to enjoy her silence once more. She is a true *genius loci*, a guardian Goddess of a specific location. There would have been many similar places in the Egyptian deserts and mountains where workers would have encountered both snakes and Goddesses. There may have been other Cobra Goddess cults similar to that of Meretseger's, but if there were we have no record of them.

KEBEHWET

Virtually nothing is known about the Goddess Kebehwet, the

---

[265] *Religion and Ritual in Ancient Egypt*, Teeter, 2011:87
[266] *Friendship and Frustration: A Study in Papyri Deir El-Medina IV-VI*, Sweeney, 1998:101-122
[267] *The Treasures of Ancient Egypt from the Egyptian Museum in Cairo*, Bomgioanni & Croce, 2003:144

Celestial Serpent. Her name is thought to derive from the word *kbhw* meaning 'firmament'. *"The starry sky serves your celestial serpent whom you love."*[268] Could the Celestial Serpent be associated with the Milky Way? Although it is usually referred to as the Winding Waterway it does have a serpentine shape. It is possible that the Milky Way was originally conceived as a serpent with the concept being superseded by that of the Sky Goddess Nut and the Celestial Cow. One resurrection spell states that the *"Celestial Serpent has placed him at her side."*[269] The king was thought to be resurrected as a star, so this will have been an appropriate position. Kebehwet is mentioned a number of times in the *Pyramid Texts*. Part of an ascension text calls her the *"Daughter of Anubis, the companion of Thoth, who is at the uprights of the ladder"*.[270] One of the ways of ascending to heaven was to climb a ladder. *"Your sister the Celestial Serpent has cleansed you."*[271] She is associated with purification, possibly through her link with Anubis who oversaw the mummification process which included purification rites. *"I am bound for the Field of Life, the abode of Re in his firmament, I have found the Celestial Serpent, the daughter of Anubis, who met me with these four nmst-jars of hers…she refreshes therewith my heart for me…she cleanses me, she censes me."*[272] That is all we know about Kebehwet, but her inclusion in the *Pyramid Texts* suggests that she was a Pre-dynastic Goddess, or at least the memory of one.

THE GRECO-ROMAN ISIS AND HER SNAKES

During the Pharaonic Period Isis was depicted as the *uraeus* in many afterlife scenes. Although Isis is very much an Egyptian Goddess a lot of her character was developed during the Greco-Roman Period and during this time she can have a very serpentine aspect. Isis was associated with Renenutet in the early Ptolemaic Period. The earliest known reference is from the 1st century BCE where Isis is invoked as Thermouthis. This name is not attested to before the Ptolemaic but the joint Isis-Renenutet

---

268 *The Ancient Egyptian Pyramid Texts*, Faulkner, 2007:203 utterance 535
269 *The Ancient Egyptian Pyramid Texts*, Faulkner, 2007:211 utterance 548
270 *The Ascension-Myth in the Pyramid Texts*, Davis, 1977:161-176
271 *The Ancient Egyptian Pyramid Texts*, Faulkner, 2007:299 utterance 690
272 *The Ancient Egyptian Pyramid Texts*, Faulkner, 2007:190 utterance 515

may have appeared in the New Kingdom. When she assimilated Renenutet Isis took on her aspects of fate and harvest and so became an obvious consort to the Gods of fate, in particular the Greek-influenced Gods Agathos Daimon and Shay (see chapter 7). Isis was depicted as a *uraeus* cobra in the Pharaonic Period and her association with the Cobra Goddess Renenutet further added to her Greco-Roman cobra form.

The Ptolemies gave Isis a new consort, Serapis. He was later merged with the serpentine Agathos Daimon. Isis and Serapis began to be portrayed as a pair of snakes. There are a number of statues of Isis and Serapis in the form of snakes, with the Horus child.

2 - Isis & Serapis as Snakes

One example is a marble statue from Alexandria which shows him seated between Isis-Thermouthis, who is depicted as a snake-headed woman with the cow-horn sun disc, and Serapis-Agathos Daimon who has a snake-head and the double crown of Egypt.[273] Another limestone relief from the Roman Period shows Isis and Serapis as snakes with human faces shown in the Greco-Roman fashion. They turn slightly towards each other. Their tails intertwine as another sign of their union. Both of them have the *kalathos* – a fruit basket in the stylised form of a lily. This is a fertility symbol which emphasises their agricultural aspects.[274] A small sandstone statue from Dendera, dating to the Roman Period, depicts two naked children (a boy and a girl) standing in the coils of two snakes. The snakes are thought to be Isis-Thermouthis and Serapis-Agathos Daimon. There was a shrine to Isis outside the enclosure wall of the temple of Hathor of Dendera and this is believed to be a votive statue from the shrine. The children may be Shu and Tefnut as they wear solar and lunar crowns. There is reference to Dendera as *"the palace of the lion pair"* and to a *"prophet of Shu and Tefnut"*. The *Ebers* papyrus refers to Shu and Tefnut as the *"children of Isis of Chemmis"*. [275] Isis is normally the mother of Horus but there is never mention of a sister to Horus. If the statue depicts Horus then his sister is a Greek invention. When shown in serpent form Isis takes on the role of Agathe Tyche, the Goddess responsible for the good fortune of the city. An analysis of the Agathos Daimon and Agathe Tyche figures on the reverse of coins from Alexandria shows that the Agathos Daimon is depicted as the non-venomous Asclepian Snake (*Elaphe longissimi*) while the Agathe Tyche and Isis are depicted as cobras.[276] The cult of Isis was extremely popular in Greco-Roman Egypt and later spread across the Roman Empire. It was a mystery religion and like all similar religions incorporated the snake as an important symbol. In the Isis cult the snake was seen as an emblem of sovereignty, life and chthonic power.

A tomb in Alexandria dating to the reign of Hadrian was

---

[273] *A Graeco-Roman Group Statue of Unusual Character from Dendera*, Abdalla, 1991:189-193
[274] *Beyond the Nile: Egypt and the Classical World*, Spier et al, 2018:245
[275] *A Graeco-Roman Group Statue of Unusual Character from Dendera*, Abdalla, 1991:189-193
[276] *A Snake-Legged Dionysus from Egypt, and Other Divine Snakes*, Bailey, 2007:263-270

excavated in Tigrane Pasha Street. It was decorated in a combination of Egyptian and Classical styles and it is believed to belong to a member of the cult of Isis. The walls flanking the entrance are decorated with a rearing snake on each side facing the entrance to protect it, these are probably Isis and Serapis in serpent form. The one on the right has a beard and wears a composite crown. Its mouth is open and its tongue protrudes. The scales on his back are green with a black outline, the tip of his beard is green and the rest of the body is yellow. The second snake, believed to be Isis, also has its tongue protruding. The crown looks like a cow-horn sun disc. The crown is yellow and the rest of the snake is green with detailing in black. Venit says this snake is similar to one of Renenutet in the 12th dynasty shrine at Medinet Madi and suggests that Renenutet may have had her own mystery cult. Both snakes and vegetation deities have mysteries associated with them through their life-death-rebirth aspects. On the other hand, the decoration could have just been copied from the Medinet Madi shrine. Inside the tomb is a pair of niches. One is decorated with two snakes, it is thought the other was the same but its decoration has been destroyed. The remaining decoration shows the lower part of a large cobra and below that a smaller one. Other surviving tomb decorations show sphinxes, with the face of a woman, standing above snakes.[277]

A fresco from the temple of Isis at Pompeii (62-79 CE) depicts Io arriving in Egypt. Isis is seated and behind her stand her priestesses and priests. She extends one hand to Io, in the other she holds a rearing cobra with its tail wrapped twice around her wrist.[278] In another relief the priestess leading the procession has a *uraeus* coiled around her wrist.[279] Depictions of Goddesses and priestesses wearing snakes around their wrists may have inspired the snake bracelets worn to ward off evil spirits and bring good fortune. They were often worn as a pair hinting at double protection, the double *uraeus* and the two snakes entwined around a staff. These bracelets remained popular until the 4th century CE. In the Pharaonic Period Isis and Nephthys were

---

[277] *The Tomb from Tigrane Pasha Street and the Iconography of Death in Roman Alexandria*, Venit, 1997:701-729
[278] *Beyond the Nile: Egypt and the Classical World*, Spier et al, 2018:255
[279] *Apuleius of Madauros – The Isis Book*, Griffiths, 1975:232

depicted as *Uraeus* Goddesses but for the Isis cult of the Greco-Roman Period two snakes may have represented Isis and Serapis or Isis and Osiris.

Snake decorations were added to many items of the Isis cult such as *situla* (a jug in the form of a breast used to hold offerings of milk) and jugs used in ceremonies. The handles are sometimes in the form of snakes or *uraei*. The *cista mystica* was a basket used to hold sacred snakes during initiation ceremonies. It was used in the cult of Dionysus and is a Greek tradition rather than an Egyptian one but was adopted by the Isis cult. In *the Golden Ass*, Apuleius gives a description of a procession in honour of Isis. One priest carries a vase with a broad handle *"above it was an asp coiled in a knot, the striped swelling of its scaly neck rearing high"*.[280] When Isis appears to him her *"crown was held in place by coils of rearing snakes…From her left hand dangled a boat-shaped vessel, on the handle of which was the figure of a serpent in relief, rearing high its head and swelling its broad neck."*[281]

Within Egypt the *uraeus* retained its original form but it was exported around the Roman Empire, probably in conjunction with the cult of Isis, where its form changed. In Salford Museum is a carved marble fragment with a *uraeus*. It was found somewhere in Rome. The *uraeus* is similar to the Egyptian one, but below the hood it has a circle with a scalloped edge and a vertical line descending from this circle. Is this an interpretation of the *ankh*? It appears to have been part of a frieze of *uraei* possibly from a temple. On Roman coins which show the temple of Isis there is often a frieze of *uraei* decorating the architrave. Other Roman examples are less Egyptian in style. The pattern on Egyptian *uraei* is derived from the cobra's hood but it is likely that the Roman sculptors hadn't seen either a cobra or an Egyptian *uraeus*. The Roman ones all emphasis the horizontal scales on the hood and some detail small semi-circular scales.[282] Many of the depictions are similar to those of Renenutet. This suggests that the craftsmen weren't able to, or didn't need to, differentiate between Cobra Goddesses.

---

[280] *The Golden Ass*, Apuleius & Walsh, 1994:225
[281] *The Golden Ass*, Apuleius & Walsh, 1994:219-220
[282] *The Roman Uraeus*, Hardwick, 2017:254-257

NEITH THE MOTHER OF SNAKES

"Each cobra is marked by her name." Many *uraei* or cobras are depicted with Neith's sign at the centre of their hood. This is a shield with crossed arrows and dates from the Pre-dynastic. These cobras are not associated with her in either the text or the scene and so may allude to her role as the creator of snakes. One example is found in the tomb of Horemheb (18th dynasty) from the *Book of Gates*. She does not normally take the role of a *Uraeus* Goddess but the *Litany of Neith*, from the Greco-Roman temple at Esna, does call her *"the great uraeus"*.[283] Neith is usually depicted as a woman but like any Goddess she could take the form of a cobra. This is seen in vignettes from spell 185 of the *Book of the Dead* and she appears as a gilded wooden cobra in Tutankhamun's tomb. *"Neith will come to you as the coiled one."*[284]

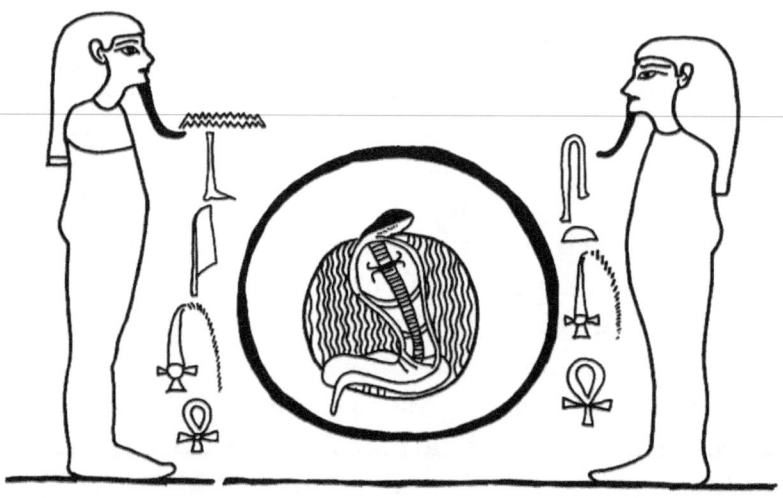

3 - URAEUS WITH SYMBOL OF NEITH

CONCLUSION

The original Earth Mother Goddess of the Palaeolithic had long faded from view by the early Dynastic Period. Perhaps it is

---

[283] *Magic in the Sign*, Ciampini, 2006:19
[284] *The Great Goddesses of Ancient Egypt*, Lesko, 1999:56

not too fanciful to see vestiges of a Pre-dynastic Mother Goddess in serpent form when we look at Wadjet and Renenutet. Like the *Uraeus* Goddesses the Cobra Goddesses are primarily protective, beneficent and nurturing – unless you are viewed as the enemy of course. Even though they tend to be less aggressive and volatile they have to be treated with caution and respect, as should any deity. Cobra Goddesses tend to be more focused on this life unlike the Snake Gods who are primarily concerned with the afterlife.

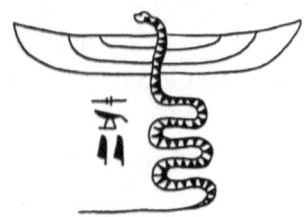

CHAPTER 7

Serpent Gods

"Tell my good name to Nehebkau."[285]

INTRODUCTION

Snake Gods are uncommon and less prominent than the *Uraeus* and Cobra Goddesses, probably because they are associated with afterlife and cosmic roles rather than this life. Like the Goddesses, various Gods can be depicted as a snake to emphasise a particular quality without being a Snake God – that is one whose primary form is that of a snake.

NEHEBKAU

The main Snake God is Nehebkau, an ancient and mostly benign God. His name translates as *"He who harnesses the spirits"*[286] or *"He who collects the spirits"*.[287] The literal translation is *"to make the kas"*. He has no specific epithets except for the generic ones such as Great One.

---

[285] *The Ancient Egyptian Pyramid Texts*, Faulkner, 2007:75 utterance 266
[286] *The Routledge Dictionary of Egyptian Gods and Goddesses*, Hart, 2005:99
[287] *The Tomb of Rameses VI*, Piankoff, 1954:68

Iconography

Nehebkau is depicted in one of three forms. He can be shown as a snake or a snake-headed man. His third form is a composite of these two. He is depicted in composite form on the throne of Sekhmet and in some small faience figurines from the Late Period where he is a snake with human legs. Amulets of Nehebkau can be in the form of a snake with arms but a snake-headed man is the more usual. Sometimes he has a long snake tail, either replacing his legs or as well as.

Aspects

Nehebkau is an afterlife God with a strong connection to the mysteries of rebirth, which are discussed in chapter 12. He is an important and invincible protector in the afterlife and there are a number of spells in the funerary texts for becoming Nehebkau. The deceased identify with him as he can't be harmed by water and is invulnerable to fire. Aligned with Nehebkau the deceased can become immune to being controlled by magic. Nehebkau has an important association with the spine, in particular the neck vertebrae. Some have suggested that this association came about through a pun between his name and the word for neck, *nhbt*. On the Metternich *stele* a spell for a cat who has been poisoned includes "*O thou cat, thy neck is the neck of Nehebkau who is in the Great House, who makes mankind to live by his arms*".[288]

Nehebkau also takes on the role of area and gate guardian in the afterworld. In the *Amduat* Ra says "*O Nehebkau in thy cavern with lifted head, great one, serpent fierce of look, behold. I pass the Impassable Place, I pass to greet Osiris*".[289] He is also present as a protector on the thrones of deities, especially those of Sekhmet. Of critical importance is his control of *ka* energy. At death the *ka* leaves the body. The *ka* energy of the deceased, their vital energy, will have to be replenished before they can continue their journey through the afterlife. Being a chthonic deity Nehebkau will be able to access and control all the energy held in the earth. He was associated with the *kas* of various Gods, especially Atum.

---

[288] *The God Nehebkau*, Shorter, 1935:41-48
[289] *The God Nehebkau*, Shorter, 1935:41-48

The fact that Nehebkau knows the deceased's name and speaks it is very important as speaking their true name enables a person to survive after death. In one spell the deceased asks the deities to make a good report about them to Nehebkau. *"Tell my good name to Re and announce me to Nehebkau, so that my entry may be greeted."*[290] The fact that Nehebkau announces the deceased also acts like a password permitting them to access parts of the afterworld and to come into the presence of certain deities. *"They will raise up this good utterance of yours to Nehebkau when your daughter has spoken to you and Nehebkau will raise up this good utterance of yours to the Two Enneads."*[291] When written a certain way Nehebkau's name can be translated as *"he who appoints the positions"*.[292] As well as giving a person or a deity their *ka* Nehebkau may also allocate their status and roles. This gives him a great deal of power which the deceased are keen to emulate. This role may reflect his importance as a Pre-dynastic God. In the Judgement Hall of the *Book of the Dead* the deceased recite a litany of what misdemeanours they haven't done. Most do not seem to be linked to the deity addressed but the one addressed to Nehebkau specifically refers to this aspect as the deceased says *"I have not made distinctions for myself"*.[293]

In one *Coffin Texts* spell the deceased state that they have departed and returned in the solar barque so that they could give thrones to Nehebkau. Giving thrones to someone is in effect giving them the power associated with kingship. Is the deceased claiming to be as powerful as Ra and able to give power to the deity who gives the same to the deceased? Or does it hint at the reciprocal exchange of energy – the Sun God gives solar energy to Nehebkau who returns chthonic regenerative energy to the Sun God as he goes through his nightly regeneration? Nehebkau provides the essential nourishment for the deceased. *"A meal is given to me by Nehebkau."*[294] Like many afterlife deities Nehebkau is associated with the ferryboat spells. One way of crossing into the afterlife was across the Winding Waterway (the Milky Way) by

---

[290] *The Ancient Egyptian Pyramid Texts*, Faulkner, 2007:72 utterance 263
[291] *The Ancient Egyptian Pyramid Texts*, Faulkner, 2007:252 utterance 609
[292] *The God Nehebkau*, Shorter, 1935:41-48
[293] *An Ancient Egyptian Book of the Dead*, O'Rourke, 2016:104 spell 125
[294] *The Ancient Egyptian Pyramid Texts*, Faulkner, 2007:73 utterance 264

boat. He also appears in some ascension texts.

When the king ascends to the sky *"Nehebkau grasps your hand"*.²⁹⁵ In the *Book of the Dead* there is a spell for transitioning into the afterlife *"for leaving yesterday and coming into today"*.

There are some hints that Nehebkau isn't always benevolent, particularly in the Old Kingdom, but the spells in question are ambiguous. In one *Pyramid Texts* spell Atum appears to control Nehebkau by pressing a fingernail in his spine. *"This here is the fingernail of Atum which is (pressed) on the spine of Nehebkau, and which stilled the turmoil in Unu; fall down, crawl away!"*²⁹⁶ This could be read as Atum repelling Nehebkau but this is strange, especially as Nehebkau was associated with Atum's *ka*. It could be that Atum is connecting with Nehebkau to obtain or channel some of this power. The spine was thought to transmit the life energy throughout the body. There are a number of anti-snake spells which appear to show Nehebkau as the enemy of the deceased. *"Nehebkau burns with the poison. O monster, die!"*²⁹⁷ One long *Coffin Texts* spell against snakes refers to consuming fire being sent against Geb and Nehebkau. Is this spell really attacking these two Gods or is this a way of saying to the snake being targeted that this spell is so strong that even the Gods can't withstand it?

Relationships

In the *Coffin Texts* Nehebkau is described as being the son of the Earth God Geb and the Cobra Goddess Renenutet. This is a suitable ancestry where he inherits his chthonic powers from his father and his serpentine ones from his mother. Serket (Selkis) can also be his mother. She is a Scorpion Goddess with a protective aspect. She is frequently mentioned in spells to counteract venomous bites, especially those of snakes. She has a strong afterlife role and can be depicted as a cobra in the Netherworld Books. The Goddess Nehmataway can also be his consort. She is often cited as a consort of Thoth and was worshipped at his cult centres. Little is known about her but there

---

²⁹⁵ The Ancient Egyptian Pyramid Texts, Faulkner, 2007:280 utterance 667
²⁹⁶ The Ancient Egyptian Pyramid Texts, Faulkner, 2007:54 utterance 229
²⁹⁷ The Ancient Egyptian Pyramid Texts, Faulkner, 2007:313 utterance 727

are a few references which could explain her link to Nehebkau. A Late Period *stele* refers to her as "*Nehmataway, the Eye of Re*".[298] At Hermopolis she was sometimes linked with a local version of Hathor. One myth says that she was given as a consort to Thoth after he had brought the Distant Goddess back to Egypt. In this form she might be one of a pair of Goddesses representing the angry and pacified Eye of Ra. There is reference to Ayet and Nehmataway who are worshipped at Herakleopolis. As an Eye Goddess Nehmataway would also be a *Uraeus* Goddess and thus a suitable consort for a Snake God. The only depictions found show her as a nursing Goddess.

Worship

Given his afterlife role it is unexpected to find that Nehebkau had a cult at Herakleopolis Magna and probably in other places. His feast was celebrated from at least the Middle Kingdom on the first day of the first month of winter. The large number of amulets of Nehebkau that have been found attest to his popularity. He appears to have been venerated in popular religion as a powerful and helpful God. Most of the amulets date to the 3rd Intermediate Period and the earliest to the late New Kingdom, a troubled time when such a God was much needed. He is normally depicted as a snake-headed man on amulets and plaques and frequently holds an offering pot in his raised hands.

Nehebkau's Alter Ego

In the *Pyramid Texts* the snake determinative is not used in Nehebkau's name but he is described as being a snake. By the time of the *Book of the Dead* the snake determinative is common in his name, especially when used in reference to the Sun God. Shorter (1935) asks if this hints at the association between the two aligning Nehebkau with the serpent form of Atum-Ra. As mentioned above, Nehebkau is associated with the *ka* of Atum. He can be seen as symbolising the invincible living power identified with Atum.

---

[298] *Two Overlooked Oracles*, Klotz, 2010:247-254

MEHEN

Iconography

Mehen, the Coiled One, provides protection for Ra during his night-time journey and is usually depicted as a long snake draped over Ra's shrine in the Solar Barque. He is often shown with multiple coils, rather than draped straight over, especially in the Netherworld Books.

4 - MEHEN

In the *Book of Gates* he has a particularly distinct curly form. In one depiction of Mehen in the *Book of Gates* he becomes the *ouroboros* encircling the Sun God, who is shown in scarab form, but he still retains his distinctive curly shape. He also protects Osiris, in the *Amduat* he encloses an enthroned Osiris. Sometimes Mehen takes on different epithets, forms and roles. In the 11th hour of the *Amduat* he is depicted as a very long snake carried on the heads of twelve Gods in front of the Solar Barque. He is referred to as "*World-Encircler of the earth*" and the Gods carry him to the gateway of the eastern horizon in anticipation of sunrise.[299]

---

[299] *The Egyptian Amduat*, Abt & Hornung, 2007:340-341

Mehen is sometimes shown with multiple heads. In the 6th hour of the *Amduat* the corpse of the Sun God is protected by Many-Faced who has five heads.

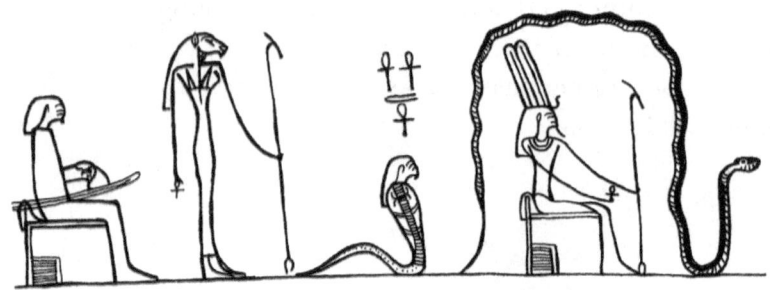

5 - HUMAN-HEADED COBRA & MEHEN

The Development of Mehen's Theology

There is reference to the Coiled Serpent, rather than Mehen, in the *Pyramid Texts*. "*O Lord of the horizon, Foremost of the gods...the King lies down in your coil, the King sits in your circle, the King lives on your life, the King is provided with your peace.*"[300] The earliest mention of Mehen by name occurs in the *Coffin Texts*. The concept of the secrets of Mehen and his paths were introduced during the Middle Kingdom. One illustration to *Coffin Texts* spell 758 shows an enthroned Ra wearing a crown of snakes surrounded by Mehen.[301] By the New Kingdom Mehen is depicted in vignettes for the *Book of the Dead* and the Netherworld Books draped over the shrine of the night barque of the Sun God. His role is obvious and clearly stated; to guide the barque on its journey through the underworld and to protect Ra from his enemies. Hidden below the illustrations is his primary role which is kept secret. (This will be discussed further in chapter 12.) Sometimes Mehen is shown as double-headed. In the New Kingdom the mysterious double-headed aspect of Mehen appears, related

---

[300] *The Ancient Egyptian Pyramid Texts*, Faulkner, 2007:318 utterance 758
[301] *Mehen, Mysteries, and Resurrection from the Coiled Serpent*, Piccione, 1990:43-52

specifically to the birth of the Sun God. This aspect may have been kept secret and revealed only as part of the mysteries of Mehen. He occurs in this form in the *Book of Day* as a circular double-headed *uraeus* coiled around the new-born Sun God who is passed from Nephthys, in the Night Barque, to Isis in the Day Barque. Tyldesley (2010) suggests that the *ouroboros* is an aspect of Mehen whose complex coils form the symbol for eternity as well as defining the boundary which encloses and separates creation from the *nun*. The ouroboros is described in the *Pyramid Texts* "*your tail be on your mouth, O snt-snake*"[302] and its first depiction appears to have been on the gilded shrine of Tutankhamun. Here a snake, named as Mehen, encircles the head and feet of the mummified king.[303]

Aspects

Mehen has three main roles. As previously mentioned, he is a protector especially of the Sun God and those who align themselves with him. He will stay with Ra until sunrise. "*Elevated is the disc of him who disposes of Mehen.*"[304] The coils of Mehen were both protective and deadly. Like a python he could surround and crush to death the enemies of both the Sun God and the deceased. Mehen acts as the mentor of the initiate, or deceased. When the deceased align themselves with Ra in the solar barque they associate themselves with Mehen, who is draped protectively over the Sun God's shrine. "*My brother is the Enveloper during the sailing. I am in his following.*"[305] Another critical role of Mehen is that he enables metamorphosis to take place. Before metamorphosis can progress what is old and worn out has to be dismantled. This is achieved by being immersed in the dissolving and healing waters of the *nun*. But this solution must be contained so that the essential essence of the deity or the deceased can be retained. In the final illustration in the *Book of Gates* the Sun God in his form of Khepri is shown being lifted from the *nun*. Within the coils of Mehen a bubble of the *nun* can be created allowing

---

[302] *The Ancient Egyptian Pyramid Texts*, Faulkner, 2007:129 utterance 393
[303] *Myths & Legends of Ancient Egypt*, Tyldesley, 2010:93
[304] *The Egyptian Book of Gates*, Abt & Hornung, 2014:247
[305] *The Wandering of the Soul*, Piankoff, 1974:30 spell 1109

the old and worn-out Sun God, Osiris and the deceased to regenerate. As a serpent Mehen is a creature from pre-creation, a former inhabitant from the *nun*. Unlike Apophis he has crossed the boundary between the two and now resides in the stabilising earth where he can retain a connection to *maat* as well as the *nun* which allows the new form to be rebuilt. Mehen protects those undergoing transformation but his role is much more important than that of mere guardian. He both symbolises and is the process of dissolution and rejuvenation that the Sun God goes through every night so that he can be reborn at sunrise.

6 - APOPHIS

Worship

There is no direct reference to cults of Mehen or his worship but one object from the New Kingdom appears to be a votive offering to Mehen. It is a large coiled snake, 25cm in diameter, made of dark blue faience. The body of the snake is fully formed so it does not represent a game board. Its skin is patterned and the eyes and mouth have been outlined in black. It may have been designed to assist the resurrection of the deceased by helping them to pass through the body of Mehen.

The Secret Forms of Mehen

Is the Sun God at the centre of the coils another aspect of the Great Serpent? Is it the Creator in his or her original and ultimate serpentine form? Is the wisdom of the snake the path to the centre? In the 8th and 9th hours of the *Amduat* there is reference to the Sun God in his *"mysterious image of the Mehen-serpent"*[306] which could be read that the Sun God is actually Mehen, because he has reverted back to serpent form, or it appears as though he has. Other texts refer to the Sun God being in the image of Mehen. The deceased identifies with the *"weary one who came forth from the Eye"* and is also described as the one who has created the protective fire around Mehen.[307] As befits one who deals with the mysteries of rebirth Mehen is mostly a mystery. Nehebkau is also associated with the *ka* of Atum and the serpent form of Atum-Ra which reinforces the link between these two Serpent Gods and the Creator Sun God.

THE GRECO-ROMAN SNAKE DEITIES OF EDFU

Gaber (2015) has identified a number of Snake Gods from the Greco-Roman temples, especially those of Horus at Edfu and Hathor at Dendera. He suggests that three of them, including one named Aphety (*'3-phty*), were connected with the original mythology of the temple at Edfu before it was rebuilt in the Greco-Roman Period.

The other prominent Snake Gods at Edfu are Hau-hor (*H'w-Hr* meaning the Body of Horus), Khenty-hor (*Hnty-Hr* meaning Foremost of Horus), Iry-denden (*'Iry-dndn* meaning Who Belongs to his Rage) and Sek-hau (*Sk-h'w* meaning He with the Joined Body). Gaber suggests that Sek-hau was a local form of Khnum. Among all the snake deities depicted there is one Goddess, Remet the Beautiful One. Remet is depicted as a snake-headed Goddess wearing Hathor's crown. Her epithet is similar to ones used for Hathor so she may be an aspect of Hathor who had a close association with the Edfu temple as the consort of Horus. A number of these snakes have names relating to Horus so they may be avatars or aspects of Horus. The text and depictions are not easy to interpret. The presence of Remet as an aspect of Hathor may support this interpretation.

All of the Gods have a large number of epithets, especially

---

[306] *The Egyptian Amduat*, Abt & Hornung, 2007:259&286
[307] *Mehen, Mysteries, and Resurrection from the Coiled Serpent*, Piccione, 1990:43-52

Iry-denden. A lot of the epithets are used interchangeably, which suggests a close and special relationship. It also makes interpretation of the various depictions difficult. The names of some of the Gods, such as Nesbety, are used as epithets for Hauhor and Khenty-Hor. If Gaber's conclusion that some of the deities belong to an earlier mythology is correct it could explain some of this confusion. It is possible that the original understanding was lost or misinterpreted or the names changed so much that one God appears later as several individuals. It is surprising though that none of these deities are referenced in the Pharaonic texts (as far as my research has found) apart from the *Sata*-snakes. Alternatively, they could have belonged to a localised serpent cult or one that developed in the Late and Greco-Roman Periods. These Snake Gods are often depicted as two groups of four deities. A number of the epithets are used collectively. Hauhor and Khenty-hor are referred to as *"the W3dd-snakes of Dendera"*.[308] In the Chapel of the Throne of Ra Ptolemy IV (221-205 BCE) is shown worshipping Horus and four snake-headed Gods referred to as the *Sata*-snakes. Other collective epithets are Lords of Might, the Strong *3krw*-snakes, the Great *Hty*-snakes and the *Srfw*-snakes.

These Snake Gods are usually depicted either as crawling snakes or as snake-headed deities. Sometimes they are enthroned and receiving offerings such as meat, bread, beer and water from the various Ptolemies. They appear to have two main functions. They are protectors of the temple and the city. *"Nesbty, who protects the throne of Rē"* and *"the mighty watchers of the Edfu land"*. They also rid the temple of snakes. *"Sk-h'w and 'Iry-dndn are with him (Horus) catching snakes and reptiles in the Throne of the Gods."* In addition they have responsibility for the fertility of the land and through that ensure an abundance of offerings for the temple. *"Lords of the provisions before the Mansions of Horus."*[309] Some of these Snake Gods are found at other Greco-Roman temples. A *stele* found at Karnak shows one of the Ptolemies offering to Aphety. Some of them are connected with the inundation, which will be discussed in the following chapter.

---

[308] *Some Snake Deities from the Temple of Edfu*, Gaber, 2015:1104
[309] *Some Snake Deities from the Temple of Edfu*, Gaber, 2015:1103-1106

GODS WITH OCCASIONAL SNAKE FORM

Amun is associated with Kematef during creation. His name means hidden or invisible. His soul was said to be enshrined in a serpent-shaped sceptre called Kematef *"he who finished his moment"*.[310] Watterson (2003) suggests this might have been his original fetish. One *Coffin Texts* spell refers to Atum coiling up. Hybrid forms of Atum, and other deities, were common during the Late Period as it was thought to increase the magical effectiveness of the image. A small rectangular bronze box dating to the Late Period depicts two identical Gods with the bodies of a rearing cobra and human heads. They are bearded (a sign of divinity) and wear the *Atef* crown (the White Crown with a plume on either side). The cobras' bodies are cross-hatched and there is a ladder design down the front of the hood which has associations with the ascent of the deceased to heaven. The inscription reads *"may Atum give life to Teshnefer"*.[311]

Horus can be associated with the snake. At Dendera Harsomtus (Horus who unites the Two Lands) is depicted sitting on a lotus in both snake and human form. In the *Bremner-Rhind* papyrus he is referred to as the Divine Snake. In the *Book of the Dead* spell 166 refers to Hathor and her son Horus as fiery serpents. A gilded wooden figure of a rearing cobra was found in a chest in the tomb of Tutankhamun (18th dynasty) and represents the Serpent God Netjerankh *"the Living God"*.[312] Little is known about this God but it is assumed that he guided the king on his journey through the afterlife. Similar depictions occur on painted wooden coffins from the end of the Middle Kingdom.

THE OTHER SNAKE GODS

Sometimes there are passing references to snakes who may be Gods but who equally could be demons or other supernatural beings. Many of the snakes referenced and depicted in the funerary texts are given names. Translations vary over time, and the Egyptian names will have altered as well, and it isn't always

---

[310] *The Gods of Ancient Egypt*, Watterson, 2003:130
[311] *The Quest for Immortality: Treasures of Ancient Egypt*, Hornung & Bryan, 2002:192
[312] *The Animal World of the Pharaohs*, Houlihan, 1996:170

easy or possible to connect names. Is it a new individual or a variation on another's name? Denwen is mentioned in a *Pyramid Texts* spell where he has the power to start a fire which could destroy the Gods.[313] It is not clear if he is actually a god or just a demon.

THE GRECO-ROMAN PERIOD

There had been contact between the Greeks and Egyptians for many centuries before the Alexandrian conquest. During the early Ptolemaic there was a fusion of Egyptian and Greek deities and symbolism in areas with a strong Greek influence. This was encouraged by the Ptolemies as it was seen as producing a unifying, and controllable, religious system. This produced some hybrid deities who took a snake form. Particularly in Alexandria, tombs were decorated in a distinctive hybrid style.

Agathos Daimon

In Alexandria there was a cult of Agathos Daimon, the Good Spirit of the city. His Greek name was Zeus Ktesios, the protector of the home, who was also depicted in snake form. Agathos Daimon may have coalesced with Shay, the God of destiny. He personified the life-span and prosperity allocated to each individual. By the Late Period he was popular as a protector of homes and harvests. The legend says that the snake embodying the Agathos Daimon died as a result of building work during the founding of the city of Alexandria. Alexander (332-323 BCE) created a temple to this snake and the cult soon became popular in domestic religion. He is depicted as a snake, often with a beard, who wears the Double Crown or the cow-horn sun disc. The snake's body is treated in a naturalistic style and is usually shown rearing with his body coiling under him in a figure of eight. The snake is either the straight bodied Asclepian snake or a cobra with a small hood and horizontal banding.[314] The Agathos Daimon can be shown with the *caduceus* and an ear of wheat representing his healing and his harvest aspects. In the Roman Period he was

---

[313] *The Routledge Dictionary of Egyptian Gods and Goddesses*, Hart, 2005:52
[314] *The Roman Uraeus*, Hardwick, 2017:254-257

depicted on *stelae* and coins as a bearded snake and was often accompanied by Isis in the form of a cobra. He was later incorporated into state religion coinciding with the Period when Serapis and Isis began to be depicted with the body of a snake. Many Alexandrian coins show the Agathos Daimon on the reverse and those minted during the reign of Hadrian (117-138 CE) suggest the start of the synchronising the Agathos Daimon and Serapis.[315]

Serapis

The God Serapis was deliberately created by Ptolemy I (305-285 BCE) as a new consort for Isis because he wanted a pair of deities who would be popular with both Greeks and Egyptians. Osiris and the Apis Bull were merged with their Greek equivalents of Dionysus and the chthonic Zeus-Hades. Serapis is usually depicted as a Greek God, but during the Roman Period he is sometimes synchronised with the Agathos Daimon and shown, alongside Isis, as a snake with a man's head – in the Greek style and with a beard. This emphasised his function of the Agathos Daimon. In this form he had a similar role to Renenutet as the protector of harvest and the bringer of fertility to the fields.

Anubis

Normally depicted as a jackal or jackal-headed man, the funerary God Anubis is sometimes depicted in serpent form in the Greco-Roman Period. The *Jumilhac* papyrus tells how Anubis takes the form of a snake and used flint knives against the enemy. In a tomb decoration from Alexandria Anubis is depicted as a Roman legionary but with the lower body of a snake.[316] This composite image appears to be a unique depiction of him.

Dionysus

Dionysus was honoured in Alexandria and was popular with the early Ptolemies. A marble *stele* from Naukratis depicts

---

[315] *Romanising Oriental Gods*, Alvar, 2008:58
[316] *Visualising the Afterlife in the Tombs of Greco-Roman Egypt*, Venit, 2016:71

Dionysus with the lower part of a snake. His torso merges into the snake's body whose tail is coiled into a figure-of-eight. He is depicted in Hellenistic fashion with a bunch of grapes in his hand but wears a complex crown composed of the *atef*-crown, ram's horns and either ostrich feathers or *uraei* – the details are not fine enough to discern. This type of crown is seen in other Greco-Roman Period depictions of deities. Standing next to him on a ledge is a child, probably Harpokrates. In Egypt Dionysus was equated to Osiris (they both are dying Vegetation Gods) which would explain the Horus child and his association with Isis in a sandstone relief. Here they are depicted in snake form as the Agathos Daimon. They are shown with the body and hood of the cobra and human heads, done in the Hellenistic style.[317] The entrance to a tomb at Kom el-Shoqafa is flanked by two rearing Agathos Daimon snakes. They both wear an Egyptian crown but in their coils hold Greek sacred objects. One has the *thyrus*, a staff associated with Dionysus, and the other the *caduceus*, the staff of Hermes.[318] Both Gods are associated with the afterlife so can easily be depicted as snakes.

Shena

There was a local cult of Shena in Naukratis in the Ptolemaic Period. His epithet was *"the one who repels"*.[319] A sarcophagus of the Egyptian priest Panehemise from this Period gives him the title *"prophet of the snake Shena in Naukratis"*.[320]

Chnoubis (Chnouph)

Chnoubis was a lion-headed snake popular in magic and often depicted on magical gemstones. He was a combination of the Egyptian Creator God Khnum, the serpent Kneph and the star *Kmn*.[321] Plutarch mentions the worship of Kneph at Thebes, who

---

[317] *A Snake-Legged Dionysus from Egypt, and Other Divine Snakes*, Bailey, 2007:263-270
[318] *Visualising the Afterlife in the Tombs of Greco-Roman Egypt*, Venit, 2016:69
[319] *Sunken Cities Egypt's Lost Worlds*, Goddio & Masson-Berghoff, 2016:68
[320] *Sunken Cities Egypt's Lost Worlds*, Goddio & Masson-Berghoff, 2016:245
[321] *The Greek Magical Papyri in Translation Volume I*, Betz, 1996:333

is thought to have originated from Amun as Kematef. Kneph occurs in a number of spells in the Greek Magical Papyri.

GEB AND THE SNAKES

Geb is the Earth God, the son of Shu and Tefnut and the consort of the Sky Goddess Nut. He is not depicted as a snake but as the Earth God he was responsible for all the dangerous snakes who lived on and under the earth. One *Coffin Texts* spell refers to snakes on the back of Geb. In the *Book of the Heavenly Cow*, before he departs to heaven, Ra tells Geb to warn the snakes not to abuse their magic. *"Take heed because of your snakes which are in you! See, they feared me when I was there. Also you have become acquainted with their magical power…you are to draw up notices with respect to each mound for your snakes that are there, saying 'beware of disturbing anything!'…Now as for their habitation, it is what will exist in this land forever."*[322] Snakes may be dangerous but if Ra was the Creator then snakes were part of his creation and thus were due respect. This is seen in one spell in the *Book of the Dead* where the deceased explains that they are there to look after *"the earth-snakes of Re"*.[323] If people had treated the snakes with respect during their life the snakes would be more likely to assist them in the afterlife. *"The snakes will permit N to follow Re into his bark. A bowl will be offered to them on earth by N."*[324]

CONCLUSION

In theory any God can take a snake form because the *bas* of the Gods reside in snakes. They usually adopt the snake form to emphasise a specific aspect or affiliation. There is reference to the *"first serpent form of Thoth"* which alludes to his role as the original Creator.[325] In the myth of Horus at Edfu the defeated Seth *"turned himself into a roaring serpent and entered the ground…and was seen no more"*[326] to align him with Apophis.

---

[322] *The Literature of Ancient Egypt*, Simpson, 2003:294
[323] *The Ancient Egyptian Book of the Dead*, Faulkner, 1989:139 spell 149
[324] *The Egyptian Book of the Dead*, Faulkner & Goelet, 2008:126 spell 168
[325] *Thoth or the Hermes of Egypt*, Boylan, 1922:171
[326] *The Myth of Horus at Edfu – I*, Fairman, 1935:26-36

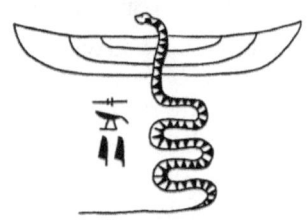

CHAPTER 8

Serpents of Fire, Earth and Water

"Hail, serpent and stout lion, natural sources of fire."[327]

INTRODUCTION

The Egyptians may not have viewed the elements as we do, but their symbolism and roles align the snake with three out of the four elements; fire, earth and water. The role of air is absent, Aeilan's flying snakes excepted. As the Egyptians used the feather as the symbol for breath and air it was largely birds which took over the symbolism of air. Although there are astral snakes these do not have an air element. The Egyptians, quite correctly, differentiated between the atmosphere, the realm of Shu, and the sky above, the realm of Nut. The close link between felines and snakes will also be examined in this chapter.

SERPENTS OF FIRE

The *uraeus* is the ultimate fiery elemental and has already been discussed in detail.

---

[327] *The Greek Magical Papyri in Translation Volume I*, Betz, 1996:56

SERPENTS OF EARTH

Snakes are an obvious chthonic symbol living on and in the earth, and this is largely seen in their afterlife aspects. A deeper level of symbolism is also present. As mentioned previously, Kematef can be viewed as creating Irta as the Earth Serpent and Hathor or Mut as the primeval *uraeus*. Splitting the androgynous Creator Serpent gave us the fiery *uraeus* and the earthbound snakes. The two are connected not only by their common origin but also by a mineral which was considered to be imbued with special powers which linked the earth with fire and the heavens – flint.

FLINT

Flint is a form of quartz found as nodules within chalk and limestone. It was an important tool-making resource as it can be knapped to produce sharp cutting edges. Flint, along with fossils, iron pyrites and meteorites, was thought to originate in the heavens. This was partly because they were often found on the surface as if they had just fallen from the sky, which in the case of meteorites is correct. They have an unusual texture compared to many other rocks and minerals with a glassy or waxy appearance. Flint varies in colouring but is often bi-coloured which was considered a symbol of duality and of liminal objects. It was associated with snakes because it is found in the deserts and mountains, a common habitat of snakes. More significantly, flint appears to emerge from a different type of rock in the same way as a snake emerges from cracks in the rocks. Flint produces a spark when struck and the accompanying smell of burning gives it a direct link with fire and through that with the Solar Eye, the Sun God and the *Uraeus* Goddess. Fire also connects it with the burning pain of snake bite. Its natural tendency to shatter and produce very sharp cutting edges aligns it to the fangs of the snake.

Minerals, especially flint, were believed to be created by the Eye of Ra or the Eye of Horus. Flint was particularly common in the Eastern Desert which was associated with sunrise as well as heat and danger. The deities were said to extract their power from the Eastern Desert. Until the Bronze Age (about the early Dynastic period) flint was used to produce tools and weapons. Its great antiquity as a raw material gave it power and significance. A flint knife was considered a suitable weapon for deities to use, especially against snakes. Apophis is described as flinty. *"Three cubits from his foreside are flint."* Using a flint knife to attack Apophis is appropriate as it is fighting like with like. *"Re triumphs over Apopis…and the flint knife shall be stuck fast in his head."*[328] Flint nodules of unusual shapes were collected around Deir el-Medina. One with a snake shape was found in a chapel with a *stele* dedicated to Thoth. It is believed to be an offering to the Cobra Goddess Meretseger.[329] The papyrus of Nu refers to the flint snake and uses the phrase *"of light colour, shiny, spitting flint"*.[330] Tomb paintings show *uraei* spitting fire. Graves-Brown (2003) says the spittle of those in the tomb of Sety I (19th dynasty) resembles Old Kingdom depictions of spalls (splinters of rocks) produced when flint knives are sharpened. Flint was also heated to improve its flaking ability and the heated fragments could be considered as being spat out by the main stone. Like the snake, flint is also associated with lions as they are both found in mountains and deserts and associated with the Sun God and the Solar Eye. The claws of lions were equated to flint knives and either word could be used for both. Sekhmet was said to use a flint knife. As with the *Distant Goddess* flint was found in the desert and brought back to the settled lands where it was transformed.

SERPENTS AND FELINES

As mentioned previously, there is a noticeable link between snakes and lions. Like the snake, the feline deities are both solar and chthonic. Lions were considered solar creatures for a number of reasons. They lived in the hot desert regions and their coat was pale yellow. According to Horapollo it was because *"its mane*

---

[328] The Spitting Goddess and the Stoney Eye: Divinity and Flint in Pharaonic Egypt, Graves-Brown, 2003:62
[329] Emergent Flints, Graves-Brown, 2006:48
[330] The Spitting Goddess and the Stoney Eye: Divinity and Flint in Pharaonic Egypt, Graves-Brown, 2003:58

radiates from about it, in imitation of the sun".[331] Eyes are always significant and the lion's eyes are yellow like the sun. Like all felines they can see in near darkness and a reflective layer at the back of their eyes makes them shine at night. This was believed to be the reflection of the sun as the Sun God traversed the underworld. It is normally the lioness, the Feline Goddess, who is associated with the Sun God as his Eye and Daughter. As such she represents fire and energy. The two main Lion Gods, Aker and Ruty, possesses a different energy – that of the earth. Aker is a very ancient Pre-dynastic God with a funerary role. He was depicted as the front parts of two lions and was a guardian to the deceased and of the eastern and western horizons. Ruty was similar, his name means Twin or Double Lion (who are sometimes associated with Shu and Tefnut) and he was also associated with the east and west horizons. The *Coffin Texts* describe him as being older than Atum. The lion can easily be equated with the earth. On a visual level a lion walking through a dry, dusty land will take on the colour of the soil and could be perceived as the earth taking animal form. Like the snakes of the afterworld and Nehebkau, the lion is thus chthonic unlike the lioness.

In both the myth of the *Destruction of Mankind* and the *Distant Goddess* the *uraeus* leaves her place on the brow of Ra and descends to earth. Here she transforms into a lioness who rampages across the land. This informs us that when the *Uraeus* Goddess manifests on earth she takes the form of a lioness. One reason may be that the *uraeus* represents the focused energy of the sun – its heat and light emanating from one point in the sky whilst seemingly never leaving the solar disc. On earth the nature of the solar energy changes becoming more diffuse. The lioness represents this energy, now disconnected from its source, still dangerous but able to spread across the land and able to do so during the hours of darkness.

Snakes often adorn the thrones of Sekhmet and the other Feline Goddesses. Shorter (1932) made a study of two Late Period statuettes of an enthroned Sekhmet. They are small and

---

[331] *The Hieroglyphics of Horapollo*, Horapollo & Boas, 1950:56

the thrones are highly decorated with a significant number of snakes. One has a particularly high percentage of snakes, including Nehebkau, who make up 55% of all figures with Nehebkau making up half of the deities represented. On the second throne snakes, including Nehebkau, make up 34% of all figures. Nehebkau appears five times on the first throne and four on the second. The snakes are shown in a variety of forms. There are double-headed headed ones, some with their heads pointing inwards others outwards. Snakes stand erect on their tails and some have wings. Then there are natural shapes; coiled and on the ground. Three snakes are shown lying on sledges. This may have afterlife symbolism as sledges were used to drag the coffin. Two of the snakes are shown with cross-bars forming the *djed* symbol. The *djed* represents the backbone of Osiris which is associated with stability and the earth. Given the snake's association with the spine this increases the symbolism of both the snake and the *djed*. The *djed* emphasises the stability and chthonic aspects of the snake as well as its life-giving ones. There is also a *uraeus*, a four coiled snake and a normal snake.[332]

Nehebkau is depicted as a snake, sometimes with human arms and or legs. On one throne there is a standing snake with a human torso. He is depicted with the divine beard but there is no inscription to identify him. He may be Nehebkau or another, possibly unknown, Snake God. Nehebkau has no known mythological connection with Sekhmet. Is it Nehebkau's control of *ka* energy which is significant? He may provide the healing and grounding energy to help restore and replenish the vital *ka* energy of the weakened patient. He, and the other snakes, may be present to balance or complement Sekhmet's fiery energy with their chthonic energy. Or they may be there to ground or channel her energy. If the statues were intended as votive offerings related to healing the snakes may be present to enhance the healing power. Snakes are often present to provide protection but does Sekhmet really need additional protection? They are unlikely to be the enemies of Ra subdued by Sekhmet but they may be there to bring additional *heka* to the statue. Nehebkau is sometimes associated with the *ka* of Atum so was this alluding to the Solar

---

[332] *Two Statuettes of the Goddess Sekhmet-Ubastet*, Shorter, 1932:121-124

Eye and the Sun God?

In some depictions of Sekhmet, such as on the Metternich *stele*, she stands on the back of a double-headed snake and holds a head in each hand. The original interpretation was that she was subduing it but this is open to interpretation. She may be working with the snake using its chthonic energy to compliment her own *sekhem*. The snake may represent her energy. A snake is a good way to depict the flow or presence of energy. As such it could be her energy flowing around her – her aura. Her feline energy is being transformed into serpentine energy or combining with it to provide an all-enveloping energy source. The double heads could represent the duality of both Sekhmet and the snake or their combined energies, being both protective and healing as well as dangerous and deadly. The snakes held by Sekhmet might have allusions to time and her control over time and hence fate. Whatever the interpretation the close bond between serpent and feline is clear.

Other Solar Eye Goddesses such as Tefnut and Wadjet are depicted as both a lioness and a *uraeus*. There is a Late Period hollow cast bronze figure of Wadjet as a lioness-headed Goddess with Horus as her son. It contained the mummified bodies of mongoose. Tefnut is depicted as a lioness with her brother Shu to form the Double Lion Ruty. She is also shown as a lioness-headed cobra and as the *uraeus*. The game of the Coiled Serpent, *mehen*, is covered in detail in chapter 12. It is significant that the board takes the form of a snake while the gaming pieces are in the form of lions and lionesses.

Why the Close Bond?

Lions and snakes, both as deities and symbols, not only have a close connection but can appear interchangeable. This stems from their common mythical origin. In the beginning Kematef created the female *uraeus* serpents and the earth serpents. The Creator Serpent split into male and female and earth and fire. If that was all there would be no need for the close feline connection. Solar religion was important and their priests powerful and this cannot be ignored in the development of this dual symbolism. It is significant that when the *Uraeus* Goddess descends to earth she becomes a Feline Goddess; the divine serpent manifesting on earth as the divine lioness. This is also seen in a reference to Ruty in the *Book of Two Ways*. "*Shu and Ruty, Shu to the sky, Ruty to earth.*"[333] The cosmic Shu becomes part of the Double Lion, along with Tefnut, when he manifests on earth. Energy becomes matter, serpent becomes lion. Cats will attack snakes, which gives them a link with snakes even though at an adversarial level. The Egyptians believed that similar-sounding words suggested a link between the two entities concerned. The fact that cats can hiss like snakes will have linked the two creatures at a profound level. Although many deities fight against Apophis in the funerary texts Ra never fights except when he takes the form of the Great Cat in the *Book of the Dead*.

WATER SNAKES

There are snakes which live in, or hunt in, water. Even on land snakes can appear to flow like water and rapidly disappear down crevasses or into the sand. For the Egyptians the most important natural event was the annual inundation, without it there would be no crops and little water. It was personified by the God Hapi. He doesn't take a serpent form but the inundation does have serpentine connections. As the waters flooded the fields it drove the snakes, and their prey, onto higher ground where the settlements were located. Aelian reported that snakes leave their holes near the Nile "*some thirty days beforehand to districts further away from the Nile*".[334] The Egyptians believed that water originated from the *nun*, the primordial ocean, which was inhabited (if that is the correct term for a place of non-being) by Cosmic Snakes. The mythical source of the Nile and the inundation was a cave at Elephantine, the place where the water was believed to flow in from the *nun*. A large snake lived at the bottom of this cave. He guarded this essential portal and regulated the rise and fall of the Nile. In the *Book of the Dead* the 14th mound in the Field of Rushes is associated with the

---

[333] *The Ancient Egyptian Book of Two Ways*, Lesko, 1977:112, spell 1103
[334] *On the Characteristics of Animals Volume III*, Aelian & Scholfield, 1957:353

inundation. *"The snake which belongs to it is in the caverns of Elephantine."*335 A scene at the temple of Isis at Philae depicts the source of the Nile inundation. Hapi holds two jars overflowing with water. He crouches in a cave surrounded by a large snake. In some Greco-Roman temple reliefs the name *Caverns of the Inundation* are written using the hieroglyph of a pair of snakes spitting water into a container. Although Isis was increasingly associated with the inundation in the Late and Greco-Roman Period snakes become more important in this role.

ASTRAL SNAKES AND THE INUNDATION

From a detailed study of scenes on the walls of the temple of Horus at Edfu, as well as the astronomical ceilings of other Greco-Roman temples, Kakosy (1967) concludes that astral snakes were strongly associated with the inundation during the Greco-Roman Period. The zodiac was introduced to Egypt in the Late and Ptolemaic Periods and with it came a renewed interest in the influence of the stars. Astronomical ceilings depicting the zodiac became popular in Greco-Roman temples and tombs. Prior to this the Egyptians divided the year into 36 groups of 10 days, called *decans*. Each *decan* rose at dawn for ten consecutive days. Astral *genii* (guardian spirits) were associated with the *decans*. A snake called Senen (*Snn*) is listed as one such *genie*. Another snake, Pecher-hor (*Phr-hr*), might also have been one of the *genie* of the decans. In one scene at Edfu Horus is depicted standing in front of three snakes who are described as *"the protecting serpent genius of the nome of Edfu"*. On a pedestal above the other snakes is Iry-denden. Senen is in a rectangular frame and he stands up on his tail while the third lies on a pedestal.

Pecher-hor is the main snake associated with the inundation. He is depicted with his tail positioned below his raised head. His body coils to form three circles and he is often depicted with a vulture's head. The vulture is normally associated with the feminine and in particular the Goddess Nekhbet of Upper Egypt. This may allude to the southern origins of the inundation. In some depictions Pecher-hor has the head of a bird but the species

---

335 *The Ancient Egyptian Book of the Dead*, Faulkner, 1989:145 spell 149

can't be determined. It may still be a vulture but might be a hawk given the strong presence of Horus. The bird head may also hint at his heavenly rather than chthonic nature. At Edfu Horus is shown in front of "*Phr-hr whose seat is raised*" who is the God who "*brings the Nile and makes grow the fresh vegetation*". At the temple of Isis at Philae there is an inscription describing the king as the son of Sothis and the heir of Pecher-hor which closely connects Pecher-hor with the star of the inundation. It is possible that the Nile serpent Pecher-hor was present in domestic religion and was absorbed into the state religion during the Ptolemaic Period as a consequence of the increasing interest in the zodiac. He became an important part of the seasonal cycle with his influence needed to ensure that the waters rose. The water bringing snakes were often depicted in groups surrounded by stars emphasising their astral connections. Their names are written with a star determinative indicating that they are astral beings. Texts at Edfu relating to Horus frequently include references to the inundation. In one scene at the temple of Edfu, Ptolemy IV offers water to Horus and three Snake Gods, including Iry-denden. "*The 'h'-nfr snake of Edfu together with the gods who cause the land to grow in the cities and the nomes.*"[336] Two scenes relating to the inundation are very similar. In one Pecher-hor sits on a high pedestal beneath which are a rearing cobra, a baboon and a mummified man. These are described as the Gods "*who open the year and bring forth the Nile from his cavern*". Another scene on a lintel depicts rows of figures comprising of a snake, a baboon, a mummiform man, three recumbent figures and Pecher-hor. They are described as the "*gods of the New Year who draw forth the Nile from his cavern*".[337]

A Roman zodiac at Esna depicts Nut holding the hieroglyph sign for sky, a plinth with downward-pointing peaks at each end. Above this is Pecher-hor in his characteristic pose with the head of a vulture. Above him are two intertwined ram-headed snakes which may or may not be related to the scene. The nature of the ceiling makes it hard to work out relationships between the illustrations. The ram-headed snakes hint at a link with the Sun God, in his ram-headed form his *ba* is emphasised. The zodiac at

---

[336] *Some Snake Deities from the Temple of Edfu*, Gaber, 2015:1104
[337] *The Astral Snakes of the Nile*, Kakosy, 1967: 255-260

Athribis also contains a number of snakes. There are depictions of two human-headed (or hawk-headed, the detail is unclear) rearing cobras, a group of five and then four rearing snakes and a looped snake with its head and tail held high. A snake, in the form of Senen at Edfu, is placed in a rectangle above the sign of Leo. An unnamed snake, with the posture of Pecher-hor at Edfu occurs on one of the zodiacs at Dendera. He is placed in a rectangle between the constellations of Leo and Virgo. In the Late Period the constellation of Leo was associated with the Nile inundation. Plutarch (46-119 CE) reported that the inundation occurred *"When first the Sun doth with the Lion join"*.[338] The solar energy of the lion, or more accurately for Egypt the lioness, combined with the water energy of the astral snakes to bring the inundation. Alternatively the fire of the *uraeus* serpent combines with the water bringing snakes. The constellation of Leo also suggests Ruty or Aker as the Lion Gods of Earth. Kakosy's theory is that these astral snakes were part of esoteric wisdom and that the union of heaven and earth were referenced. This does reflect the strong link between snakes and felines with the female energy of the *uraeus* and lioness combining with the male energy of the chthonic lions and snakes.

CONCLUSION

The elemental nature of snakes pervades all three realms. Some can be seen as deities, others as lesser supernatural beings. Even the snakes of the natural world can be considered elemental in their connection to the earth and water. Their influence in the natural cycles, such as the inundation, formed the essential background to life in Egypt whilst on a day to day level it was their *heka* and healing powers which were of great importance to the people of Egypt, including protection against the snakes themselves.

---

[338] *Plutarch: Concerning the Mysteries of Isis and Osiris*, Mead, 2002:219

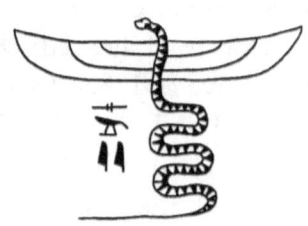

CHAPTER 9

Magic and Healing

"Protect me against…snakes in their caverns. Make them for me as immobile as the pebbles in the desert and the potsherds in the alley. Remove for me the biting poison which has penetrated into the body."[339]

HEKA

Magic was very often directed against snakes but they have strong magic of their own. In the *Book of the Heavenly Cow* Ra tells Geb to watch over the snakes because *"you have become acquainted with their magical power"*.[340] *Heka* is a magical energy which came into being either at the moment of creation or in the instant leading up to it. This energy is one of the elements which bind the created universe together. It flows *"swifter than light"* through all of creation in both the human and divine spheres.[341] A fundamental tenet of Egyptian magic was that *heka*, and other energies, could be transferred into and through an inanimate object. The magician can capture, contain and divert this energy once they have acquired the necessary skill and knowledge. Spirit and matter are all woven from the same substance and threads from this link all of creation. Magic is effective when the magician locates the right thread. In particular the magician needs to know

---

[339] *Egyptian Magic*, Raven, 2012:95
[340] *The Literature of Ancient Egypt*, Simpson, 2003:294
[341] *Magic and Mystery in Ancient Egypt*, Jacq, 2002:17

the real names of objects, people and deities. These contain the residual magic from creation as the spoken word was used to create everything. Knowledge of the true name of a person or object gives you power over them. The sounds of the word contain powerful energy. Naming is an act of creation and to speak the name reveals the true essence of that person or thing. This magical energy is personified as the God Heka. His name means *"who propels the ka"*.[342]

Visualising and depicting *heka* is done in a number of ways but the snake is a very useful form to use. *"The spells of Thoth twist about their faces tail to head among them."* One of the many spells against Apophis states *"their magic enters into you…it has swallowed you by means of the magic of their mouths"*.[343] The magic enters his body like poison, it engulfs him like a snake swallowing its prey. The root of the word for 'remedy' is that of the verb 'to encircle'. The ability of snakes to encircle and engulf demonstrates their magical powers; be they healing, protecting or restricting.

ISIS AND THE NAME OF RA

Isis was always Great of Magic and she had the most *heka* of any Goddess. The one thing she didn't know was the secret name of Ra. The story of how she obtained it is given in the *Turin* papyrus. Ra is ageing and we are told that he dribbled as he walked. The *heka* contained in his words would have been present in his saliva. Clay, although a common material, contained magical potential because the God Khmun used it to create a person's double on his wheel. Isis creates a model of a snake using mud and Ra's saliva. She then animates the clay snake and leaves it at a crossroad on a path she knows Ra uses. He doesn't see the snake, a symptom of his declining powers, and is bitten by it. Ra admits *"I was bitten by a serpent I did not see"*.[344] Only something containing part of Ra's *heka* would have been strong enough to fatally poison him. *"The noble serpent bit him, and the fire of life went forth from him completely."*[345] Ra cries out in agony but none

---

[342] *Egyptian Magic*, Raven, 2012:19
[343] *The Mechanics of Ancient Egyptian Magical Practice*, Ritner, 1993:33
[344] *The Wisdom of Ancient Egypt*, Kaster, 1993:64
[345] *The Wisdom of Ancient Egypt*, Kaster, 1993:62

of the other deities are able to help him. Isis came forward and said that she could save him but to do so she needed his true name. Ra gives her a long list of his epithets but not his true name. This contains all his magical powers, hence his understandable reluctance to share it. Isis insists *"tell me your name, divine father! A person can only relieve if one speaks a conjuration using his name"*.[346] Finally Ra gives in and tells her his true name. Isis then uses it in an incantation to remove the poison. *"Spew forth, poison...I send forth the powerful poison to fall upon the ground...Ra lives and the poison dies!"*[347]

THE MAGICIANS

The Creator *"made for them magic, as a weapon to resist the events that happen"*.[348] As such, magic was there to be used. It was neither good nor bad, only the intent of the magician could determine this. Magic was viewed by the Egyptians in the same way as we view science; something difficult for the layman to understand but which could be studied and applied by those with the knowledge and skill. Magic was normally used to control things which weren't understood or which couldn't be controlled by other means. In the Pharaonic Period magic was used to maintain or restore *maat*, by its use in healing or to protect Egypt. The belief in and use of magic spanned all social classes. It was combined with healing and was considered an important part of the process especially for conditions which were difficult to treat. Whilst there was inevitably some anti-social magic during this time it was during the Greco-Roman Period that anti-social magic came to predominate. The magicians seek to align themselves with the time of the deities and the actions told of in the myths. On a statue of Ramesses III (20th dynasty) the magician claims to have learnt his magic by listening to Horus. *"I have lain down in the bosom of Horus, and thus I have heard what he was saying, while he held in his hand a viper of one cubit, as evil as a viper of a dozen cubits!...I now slay*

---

[346] *Egyptian Magic*, Raven, 2012:21
[347] *The Wisdom of Ancient Egypt*, Kaster, 1993:65
[348] *The Tale of Sinuhe and Other Ancient Egyptian Poems*, Parkinson, 1998:226

a horned viper of one cubit, I being Horus instructed in words."[349]

THE SERPENT WAND

The snake as a symbol of magic was emphasised by the use of serpent-shaped wands. The magician priests' serpent wands were referred to as *weret-hekau*, great of magic, the same name as given to the Cobra Goddess Weret-hekau – Great of Magic. The wand can be viewed as a stiff snake, possibly paralysed by the magician. This allows its energy to be accurately channelled. Excavations of a Middle Kingdom tomb uncovered a chest containing magical papyri and a statuette of a woman wearing a lion mask. She is a priestess or magician and holds either two cobras or two serpent wands. Alongside were amuletic knives which depict Bes and Bestet (both protective dwarf deities) holding bronze serpent wands and snakes. Included in this cache was a bronze serpent wand. The body of the snake wand is coiled and the cobra's hood is extended, the middle section is flattened for ease of use. The wand is short at 16cm. Incised lines depict a cobra's markings. It is now held in the Manchester Museum. Also dating from the 13th dynasty are two bronze snake wands now in the Museum of Fine Arts (Boston). These are longer, 57cm, and they have two heads. Markings are incised on the body and heads but there is nothing to suggest that it is a pair of entwined cobras. It may allude to the power and symbolism of the Two Ladies or two *uraei* or it may provide the power equivalent of two wands but in a form which is easier to handle. Multiple-headed snakes are common in the Netherworld books and mythological papyri. A bronze wand from 18th dynasty Thebes, now in the British Museum (London), is much longer at 164 cm. The snake's body is stiff and outstretched unlike the previous examples and the head is positioned at right-angles to the body. It is similar to the wands held by the masked woman in the above-mentioned statue. Another example is a Late Period bronze wand now held in the Louvre (Paris). This is 70cm in length with an extended undulating tail. The central rib of the hood is made of raised

---

[349] *Gods and Men in Egypt 3000 BCE to 395 CE*, Dunand & Zivie-Coche, 2004:127-128

bronze rather than just being incised.[350]

There are many depictions of deities, demons and magicians holding snake wands. The God Heka is depicted holding two stiff snakes crossed over his chest. There are a few depictions of him dating to the 3rd Intermediate Period where he holds four snakes. The double wands of Heka and double-headed snakes were particularly popular in the 21st dynasty. Perhaps in the chaotic times of the 3rd Intermediate Period there was a great need for magical power to be available at twice its normal strength. In some texts at the temple of Isis at Philae a person holding a snake wand is used as an ideogram for the word *dsr* – to watch over or sanctify.[351] In the tomb chapel of Nebamun one painting shows him hunting in the marshes with his wife and daughter.[352] His throw-stick, normally used for fowling, has been replaced by a snake. Wetlands were very symbolic and could be equated to creation arising from the *nun*. Flocks of wild birds represented the forces of chaos and fowling was seen as symbolic of the fight against chaos. The snake, or snake wand, that Nebamun holds gives him the power of *heka* to fight these enemies of the Sun God. The *was*-sceptre symbolises divine power, prosperity and wellbeing. The head is curved in the form of a canine. The base of the *was*-sceptre is forked and it may have derived from a staff used to pin down snakes. The sceptre is often in a serpentine form. This enables the person wielding it to control both the snake and its power.

APOTROPAIC WANDS

Apotropaic wands (designed to repel evil rather than to focus magical energy) first appear in the Middle Kingdom and begin to be decorated during the 12th dynasty. They are often found in pairs. They were used to draw circles of protection about living and sleeping areas to guard against demons, snakes and anything else dangerous or unpleasant. They often show wear on one side

---

[350] *And Each Staff Transformed into a Snake: The Serpent Wand in Ancient Egypt*, Ritner, 2006:207-209
[351] *And Each Staff Transformed into a Snake: The Serpent Wand in Ancient Egypt*, Ritner, 2006:217
[352] *The Painted Tomb-Chapel of Nebamun*, Parkinson, 2008:8

as a result. Protective creatures carved onto them often hold stiff snakes or snake wands. It is not easy to distinguish, and you are probably not meant to as this is an illustration of *heka*. A line of deities and creatures are sometimes shown alternatively holding snakes and knives. "*The snake is in my hand and cannot bite me.*"[353] This is correct, but only if held by someone who knows what they are doing. By holding a poisonous snake the deity or magician demonstrates their mastery over it. They render it harmless to themselves but it still is a dangerous weapon. Most of the figures on these wands are related to the solar myths and include felines and Bes but there are also creatures such as snakes and turtles who were associated with Apophis and Seth. Their presence was used to fight evil with evil.

PROTECTIVE SNAKES

One early example of magical serpent protection on a large scale is seen on the 3rd dynasty Netjerikhet *stele* from Saqqara. It is from the pyramid complex of Djoser and consists of two fragments of a limestone relief. In the central column are twelve vertical compartments which contain alternating recumbent jackals and lions. Hawass suggests that they are lionesses given the way the tail is carved. This suggests Anubis (or Wepwawet who was another jackal funerary God) and one of the Feline Goddesses protecting the king in the afterlife. On the other hand they may just be protective lions. On either the side of each fragment are two undulating snakes. They dominate the composition both by their size and the fact that they are carved in deep relief, they must have been an important part of the design. Crosshatching gives the impression of skin. Their eyes are clearly defined and their tongues are protruding. Snakes depicted in a similar way can be seen in the open court of the Djoser complex. Hawass suggests that they were part of a door jamb, possibly from a false door that the *ba* of the deceased king would use.[354] Reader (2017) suggests that a pair of such stones were set up at the entrance to a shrine and were linked to the cult of Ra. Royal

---

[353] *And Each Staff Transformed into a Snake: The Serpent Wand in Ancient Egypt*, Ritner, 2006:213
[354] *A Fragmentary Monument of Djoser from Saqqara*, Hawass, 1994:45-56

annals refer to "*Ra in the senut-shrine*".³⁵⁵ As well as being protective the snakes may have represented the rejuvenating power of the earth transmitted to the king in a similar way that Mehen both protects the Sun God in the afterworld and enables his rebirth. They do look similar in style to the snakes guarding the gates of the underworld in the much later *Book of Gates*. A number of *stele* with prominent snake decoration are known such as from 18th dynasty Athribis and on the Festival Wall of Osorkon II (22nd dynasty) in Bubastis.

In terms of state religion the *Uraeus* Goddess is the ultimate protector invoked in temple rituals. Four is the number of completeness and totality as well as indicating all-round protection. A protective ritual for the *Per-ankh* (the temple scriptorium which was used as a library and centre of learning) included burying clay figures of Osiris in four containers. These had protective snakes at each of their four corners. The use of four *uraei* aligns with the four cardinal points and thus produces a perimeter of protection in all directions. Fourfold repetition of a spell or ritual would have the same effect. The *Salt* papyrus contains a ritual to "*preserve life in Egypt*". It references four *uraei* called Mistress of the Slaughter Block, She Whose Terror is Great in Raging, Mistress of Crying and She Whose Burning is Painful. An Edfu text gives a ritual to protect the bedroom of the king. "*I have surrounded your house with the Noble Ladies*" which refers to the lamps used. Another ritual to protect the king includes an invocation to four cobras who are allocated to the cardinal points around the king. Two are the *w3d.ty*-snakes of Horus the others are the *ntr.ty*-snakes of Horus. It ends asking them to save the king from everything evil. Part of a Ptolemaic temple ritual for the *Protection of the House* includes "*the protection of the Great Fiery Cobra who is before Sekhmet in the year of the great trembling*".³⁵⁶ Rituals are inscribed on the walls of the temple of Edfu. In one New Year's Day ritual the *uraeus* is urged to protect the king from the terrors of the year such as plagues and demons. A relief at Edfu depicts four *sata*-snakes being presented to the king by Horus and the texts refer to adoration of and submission to the king from all

---

³⁵⁵ *The Netjerikhet Stela and the Early Dynastic Cult of Ra*, Reader, 2017:421-435
³⁵⁶ *O. Gardiner 363: A Spell Against Night Terrors*, Ritner, 1990:25-41

directions.

Protective snake magic was needed by ordinary people as well. They were at risk from dangerous creatures, robbers and demons. The Egyptians seemed to have been plagued by nightmares given the many incantations against them. Nightmares were believed to be sent by demons. One spell from the *Leiden* papyrus contains the phrase *"the earth is nesret, the sky is nesret, men and gods are nesret"*.[357] This summons a conflagration which engulfs the demons who are causing the nightmares. The word *nesret* is seldom used until the New Kingdom. Its rise coincides with the use of clay figurines of cobras which were used in houses to ward off demons and diseases. The Cairo Calendar refers to the *"great nesret which is in your house"* but it is not known if this refers to the actual figurines or is symbolic of the protective power of the Uraeus Goddess.[358] *"As for that night of reckoning the robber, it is the night of the fiery cobra and of sacrifices."*[359]

Excavations at a number of New Kingdom domestic sites have produced small clay figurines of rearing cobras. They are roughly shaped and about 14cm in height. Their eyes are made from pellets of clay and in some the head is pinched and raised or dented to suggest a solar disc. Traces of colour survive; red, yellow or black and red. Ones from Amarna are often blue. A bowl or offering stand is often incorporated in front of them and some have what appear to be small snakes at the base. At Amarna pottery bowls with clay cobras inside were found alongside freestanding cobra figurines. After the Amarna Period the majority of such cobra figurines found come from sites in the Delta and along the Mediterranean coast – from near Libya to the Levant. They are found in both domestic and military sites. The location of the finds along the coast suggests that they were used by the military and their families who were posted around these areas. One explanation is that they were votive offerings associated with Renenutet. Another explanation is that they were used in association with protective spells. Rameside texts say that the best weapon to use against the nightmare-inducing demons

---

[357] *Playing with Fire*, Smethills, 2014:12-16
[358] *Playing with Fire*, Smethills, 2014:12-16
[359] *O. Gardiner 363: A Spell Against Night Terrors*, Ritner, 1990:25-41

was fire. One such spell was said over *"four uraei made of pure clay and fire in their mouth. One is placed in each corner of each room in which a man or woman is sleeping"*.[360] The bowls on the base could have been used for incense to create this fire but there is no evidence of this in any of the excavated objects. This wouldn't have been a safe practise anyway and the reference to fire probably alludes to that coming out of the mouths of the *uraei*. "*One in the act of striking*" is used in reference to four *uraei* to be made of pure clay.[361]

"*He has enchanted the four noble ladies whose flames are in their mouths and whose blaze is behind them in order to repel every male enemy, every female enemy, every dead man, every dead woman…they shall not come against him by night or by day or at any time.*"[362] These four cobras are aligned with Tefnut, Mehyt, Sekhmet and Nephthys in some of the rituals. They could also be viewed as Hathor *Quadrifons*, Hathor of the Four Faces. Some Hathor Head pillars have her face on four sides which symbolises all-round protection. In the Hall of the Magicians at Edfu is an invocation to Hathor *Quadrifons*. Around this are four protective *uraei* who have their own hymn. This all-encompassing protection of Hathor could be reproduced in people's houses by using four clay cobras. Once the run of nightmares had finished there was no reason why the clay cobras couldn't be used for other purposes until they were needed again. They could act as votive offerings to Renenutet, or another Goddess, and stand as protectors against scorpions.

PROTECTION AGAINST SNAKES

A statue of Rameses III (20th dynasty) was found in the eastern desert, its inscription said it was set up to protect travellers from poisonous animals, especially snakes. "*Biting one, you will not bite at all.*"[363] Given the number of snakes the ordinary people would have encountered there must have been domestic spells which they used themselves. They couldn't have relied upon professionals, many couldn't have afforded to, and faced

---

[360] *Playing with Fire*, Szpakowska, 2003:113-122
[361] *O. Gardiner 363: A Spell Against Night Terrors*, Ritner, 1990:25-41
[362] *O. Gardiner 363: A Spell Against Night Terrors*, Ritner, 1990:25-41
[363] *Ancient Egyptian Magical Texts*, Borghouts, 1978:92

with the imminent threat of a snake it wouldn't have been feasible to summon help. One incantation to a snake addresses *"you who are in the hole, who are at the opening of the hole, who are upon the road"*. The speaker identifies with various deities to intimidate the snake. *"He is Thoth – you will not shoot your poison at him."*[364] Some of the anti-snakes spells from the funerary texts could well have been used as, or adapted from, anti-snake spells in real life. They are short and to the point. *"Turn around, slide into the earth"*.[365] Variations of these spells may have been recited by individuals if they came across a snake. There is a lot of sense in such an action. Stopping and standing still whilst reciting even a short spell gives a startled snake time to retreat and will stop the person thrashing about in panic and further aggravating the snake.

The mineral serpentine has a snakelike pattern and was common in the eastern desert. Because of its appearance it was used from the Pre-dynastic in magical *stele* and amulets used to ward off snakes and scorpions. Snake holes were blocked up by dried fish, lumps of natron or an onion. As with vampires, it was believed that garlic kept the snakes and scorpions away because of its smell. Roasted garlic was sometimes used to treat snake bite. Whilst using garlic to *"close the mouth of any snake, any female snake"* the following words were to be recited while pulverising it and mixing it with beer. *"No male snake, female snake, scorpion, reptile, male dead or female dead will enter this house."*[366] A number of spells differentiate between male and female snakes. The reason for this isn't obvious and the gender of a snake isn't easy to discern. Perhaps they were seen to have different characteristics that needed addressing, or it was merely a way of giving the spell more strength by giving the magic more specific instructions. Aelian reports that *"if a man burn the feathers of a Vulture...he will have no difficulty in inducing snakes to quit their dens and lurking-places"*.[367]

People were more vulnerable at night and when sleeping. Headrests were covered in protective carvings such as Bes eating snakes. Bes was also engraved on water storage vessels to prevent

---

[364] *Ancient Egyptian Magical Texts*, Borghouts, 1978:94
[365] *The Ancient Egyptian Pyramid Texts*, Faulkner, 2007:54 utterance 227
[366] *Ancient Egyptian Magical Texts*, Borghouts, 1978:83
[367] *On the Characteristics of Animals Volume I*, Aelian & Scholfield, 1957:65

contamination by snakes. There was a widespread belief that snakes spat into food and water. According to Omm Sety writing in the 1970's that belief was still present. *"I shared a drinking jar with a cobra for more than three years while working in the Temple of Sety I at Abydos. No ill effects were suffered by either side."*[368]

DREAMS

Dream interpretation was popular in Egypt. A papyrus from the 19th dynasty says that dreaming of a snake is good and means food. This alludes to Renenutet and her role as Goddess of the harvest and grain supply. Dreaming of being bitten by a snake means that there are magic spells against you. The dream *stele* of Tanutamani (25th dynasty) describes how the king dreamt that he had a snake on each hand. Not surprisingly this was interpreted as *"to you belongs the land of the South. Seize for yourself Lower Egypt. The Two Goddesses appear in glory on your head"*.[369] Shortly after this prophetic dream the king launched a campaign to Elephantine.

GREEK MAGIC

Snake magic and mythology were used in Greek magical spells, which merged Egyptian symbolism with the Greek deities, often misunderstanding or ignoring the original symbolism. Their Moon Goddess Selene was often invoked as lunar influences were considered particularly magical. One prayer addressed to Selene accompanying the spell includes the reference *"who shake your locks of fearful serpents on your brow…with poisonous rows of serpents down the back"*. This sounds like a Goddess *"multitudinous of uraei"*. Another prayer to Selene to accompany any spell describes her as having *"hair of serpents, serpent-girded"*.[370] This may also have been influenced by crowns of *uraei* as may have been a love spell addressed to Kore who is *"girt with fiery serpents"*.[371] The concept of the *Uraeus* Goddess was lost, probably because the Egyptian priests didn't disclose anything of real significance to the Greeks.

---

[368] *Omm Sety's Living Egypt*, Hansen, 2008:147
[369] *On Puns and Divination*, Noegel, 2006:101
[370] *The Greek Magical Papyri in Translation Volume I*, Betz, 1996:91-92
[371] *The Greek Magical Papyri in Translation Volume I*, Betz, 1996:65

"A *snake, being the son of Atoum, is that which lies in the uraeus diadem at my head.*"[372] The use of the *ouroboros* was common. A spell to acquire an assistant involved wearing a stone that was engraved with a lion-faced Heliorus (a combination of Helios and Horus) holding a globe and a whip. This was encircled by the *ouroboros*.[373] A ring for success was made with jasper which had been engraved with "*a snake in a circle with its tail in its mouth*". Inside this circle was engraved "*the snake Selene having two stars on the two horns*" (of the crescent moon).[374] There are a number of drawings in the papyri of a lion-headed man holding a snake entwined staff and "*around all his left hand let an asp be entwined*".[375]

Divination was a lucrative trade for the magicians and many deities were invoked. One invokes a "*serpent-faced*" God who was later dismissed with an offering of snake skin.[376] Another such spell references "*a serpent of eternity…I am the serpent who came from the Nun…the rearing uraeus of real gold*".[377] Depictions of snake-headed Goddesses are referenced in one very long spell which addresses the Seven Fates of Heaven who are described as having the face of a cobra.[378] This may be a combination of the Seven Hathors and Renenutet, all of whom were strongly associated with fate. A reference to Seth and Apophis occurs in a prayer to Typhon, who was aligned with Seth. "*I am he who closed heaven's double gates and put to sleep the serpent which must not be seen.*"[379]

MEDICINE IN EGYPT

Although anathema to the medicinal profession today magic and religious belief were an integral part of Egyptian medicine. When so little was known about the cause and curing of ailments the value of the placebo effect can't be underestimated. Reciting spells and retelling myths was an important part of healing magic. The healer and the patient could act out a situation where the

---

[372] *The Greek Magical Papyri in Translation Volume I*, Betz, 1996:211
[373] *The Greek Magical Papyri in Translation Volume I*, Betz, 1996:7
[374] *The Greek Magical Papyri in Translation Volume I*, Betz, 1996:161
[375] *The Greek Magical Papyri in Translation Volume I*, Betz, 1996:75
[376] *The Greek Magical Papyri in Translation Volume I*, Betz, 1996:159
[377] *The Greek Magical Papyri in Translation Volume I*, Betz, 1996:210
[378] *The Greek Magical Papyri in Translation Volume I*, Betz, 1996:51
[379] *The Greek Magical Papyri in Translation Volume I*, Betz, 1996:41

outcome was known and positive. Magic was used more when the condition was hard to diagnose or cure. Physicians were professionally trained and many were attached to temples.

The *Brooklyn Snake* papyrus dates to the Late Period. It lists 38 snakes, each is accurately described along with the symptoms of the bite. It is detailed enough to allow the physician to identify the species of snake solely from the look of the bite and the symptoms. It also indicates which can be treated and gives remedies for treatment and antidotes. Each serpent is considered a manifestation of a particular God. The horned viper was a manifestation of Horus and, somewhat surprisingly, the cobra was a manifestation of Seth.[380] The majority of healing spells only document the magical element, namely the spells themselves. It was assumed that the healer knew how to dress wounds and remove poison. The *Leiden* papyrus does contain details of treatments such as cutting open the wound and trying to remove the poison and then cleaning the wound. Some healers would have specialised in the treatment of snakebite and may well have claimed special powers, as in this spell where the magician states that he belongs to a specific tribe *"those who speak with the snakes, who kill vipers"*.[381] The Greeks commented upon snakebite and its treatment in Egypt. *"The poison of serpents is a thing to be dreaded, but that of the Asp is far worse"*[382] said Aelian. *"The bite of the Viper and of other snakes is not without countering remedies…but the bite of the Asp alone, I am told, cannot be cured and is beyond help."*[383] (The asp is the cobra.) He then goes on to say, a few pages later, that some victims do eventually recover providing that the correct remedial action is taken. Not all snakebite is fatal and some bites are dry, that is without any poison being injected.

HEALING DEITIES

Any deity could be petitioned for healing although there were some who were considered more effective healers or more likely to respond to the petitioner. Some were specialists in areas which

---

[380] *Hieroglyphics: The writings of Ancient Egypt*, Betro, 1996:113
[381] *Ancient Egyptian Magical Texts*, Borghouts, 1978:20
[382] *On the Characteristics of Animals Volume I*, Aelian & Scholfield, 1957:123
[383] *On the Characteristics of Animals Volume I*, Aelian & Scholfield, 1957:73

reflected their roles in the myths. The Horus child was brought up in the marshes and was always at risk of being bitten and stung by snakes, scorpions and other creatures. He was a mischievous child who was always getting into trouble. These tales were a common reference in healing spells. As a result of his childhood adventures Horus was also a renowned healer. Diodorus said that Horus *"was taught both medicine and divination by his mother Isis"*.[384] Shed is a Child God whose name means Saviour. Like the Horus child he was a protector against dangerous creatures. He appears in the 18th dynasty and was later merged with the Horus child. Isis was a great healer, she needed to be when bringing up Horus. Her father, Geb, was said to have taught her how to exercise power over snakes. He taught her how to *"close up the mouth of every snake"*.[385] In one spell Isis says she is *"a knowing one in her town, who dispels a poisonous snake with her oral powers"*.[386] The story of Isis obtaining the secret name of Ra is used in a 19th dynasty healing spell. It was recited over images of Atum, Horus and Isis and was written on linen. *"It is a complete destruction of the poison – successful a million times."*[387]

Even Isis is not infallible. She used the secret name of Ra to halt the Solar Barque when she found Horus dying after being stung by Seth who had disguised himself as a scorpion. She was unable to cure him, probably because the venom came from Seth rather than a natural scorpion. *"Darkness reigned, and light disappeared...the seasons were no longer distinct, forms and shadows were confused."*[388] By halting the Solar Barque she suspended time and imperilled creation to force the deities to come to her aid. Time is critical when treating venom so by suspending time she stopped the venom from spreading and the condition of Horus from deteriorating further until she got expert help. This help arrived in the form of Thoth who was renowned for his healing ability. He was one of the few deities, along with Isis and Horus, who were referred to as *sunu* the word used for physicians. In the Nubian temples of Dendur and Dakka Thoth is depicted enthroned

---

[384] *The Historical Library of Diodorus Siculus*, Diodorus Siculus & Booth, 1814:31
[385] *Magic and Mystery in Ancient Egypt*, Jacq, 2002:91
[386] *Dancing for Hathor: Women in Ancient Egypt*, Graves-Brown, 2010:80
[387] *The Wisdom of Ancient Egypt*, Kaster, 1993:65
[388] *The Gods of Egypt*, Traunecker, 2001:39

holding an *ankh* and a snake encircled staff. He holds a similar staff as Thoth of Pnubs in the temple of Isis at Philae. It was this that evolved into the Rod of Asclepius, a serpent entwined around a staff, which became associated with healing and medicine. In the Greco-Roman Period Thoth the Healer was sometimes equated with Asclepius the Greek God of healing and medicine. Coins depicting Hygiea, the daughter of Asclepius, often show her feeding a snake.

Serket the Scorpion Goddess controlled the breath of life and she was one of the four Goddesses who protected the mummified body and the vital organs. She was benevolent and her power was invoked to drive away snakes and scorpions and to heal anyone who had been bitten or stung. "*Words spoken by Selkis…the noble and the powerful one, who came forth from the primeval water, the noble serpent, great of awe, who heals every snake bite.*"[389] There were people who specialised in the removal of snakes and scorpions. They were referred to as the "*Master of Selket*".[390] There is reference to them accompanying mining expeditions to protect the workers. One spell addresses an unidentified Goddess. "*Hail to thee, O She upon whose head are seven serpents, She to whom the seventy-seven hearts are entrusted in the evening and the night!*" The spell then threatens various Gods, stating that they will not be able to manifest if the patient is not cured. It continues "*as the sun shall rise, as the disk shall shine, as the services shall be performed in every temple, so shall he be better than he was*".[391]

HEALING STATUES

Healing statues, known as *cippi*, became popular in the 18th dynasty and their use continued into the Roman Period. Their peak of popularity was in the Late Period, this may have been a reflection of the uncertainty of the times helped by a decline in the availability of trained professionals due to a lack of funding for temple training centres. Alternatively it could just have been the most fashionable treatment. They are covered with apotropaic

---

[389] *The Canopic Box of NS-'3-RWD (BM EA 8539)*, Ouda, 2017:127-138
[390] *Egyptian Magic*, Raven, 2012:31
[391] *The Wisdom of Ancient Egypt*, Kaster, 1993:149

illustrations and healing spells. No two *cippi* are alike as they were personalised to order but there were many popular themes. Many are known as Horus *cippi* because they depict the Horus child. He was considered a vanquisher of snakes from the Old Kingdom. In the *Pyramid Texts* various spells describe him trampling on snakes and escaping from them. "*The sandal of Horus is what tramples the nhi-snake underfoot.*"[392] He was depicted naked, this is rare in Egyptian depictions of deities. Nakedness was probably seen as apotropaic as well as being a reflection of his youthful power. Water was poured over the *cippi*, it absorbed the magical power of the inscriptions and illustrations and was then used to treat snake bites and scorpion stings. Djedhor from Arthribis was a benefactor of his city. He said that he "*carried out rituals for those in his city in order to save them from the poison of every male and female viper and every kind of snake*". His statue shows him holding a Horus *cippi* and gives biographical information. A basin at its base shows that the statue was intended to be used for cures. It would have been sited in a public place and was designed to "*save everyone thereby from the poison of every male and female viper and all snakes*".[393]

The *cippi* are covered with illustrations and on many snakes predominate. On the *cippi* of Hor, for example, about 70% of the figures depicted are snakes and this excludes snakes held as wands. The snakes are present in such high numbers for two reasons. They are shown being defeated which will weaken the effect of their poison. Horus and Bes hold snakes, and other dangerous animals such as scorpions and lions, to demonstrate their control over them. Many deities or supernatural beings stand on or trample snakes – such as a bull, Taweret and other Hippo Goddesses and Amun. The God Onuris-Shu spears a snake as do various Falcon Gods. Snakes are also present because they are in the myths which the healing spells refer to. In addition they were able to reverse the effects of the venom. The creature or deity who caused the problem has the ability to resolve it. The snake's venom can thus be used as an antidote or to generate immunity. The Egyptians weren't the only ones with this belief. The Greeks and Romans wore snake ring amulets for the same reason.

---

[392] *The Ancient Egyptian Pyramid Texts*, Faulkner, 2007:125 utterance 378
[393] *Djedhor the Saviour Statue Base OI 10589*, Sherman, 1981:82-102

The *cippi* of Hor depicts Isis nursing Horus in the marshes. She is flanked by two snakes while two *uraei*, wearing the Red and White Crowns, form an arch above her. In another vignette she is shown enthroned above a huge snake and is described as Isis Great of Magic. A child wearing a sun disc sits on a crocodile while a huge snake forms a vault above him. *"The child was bitten by the Holy-headed serpent. Silence, my son. I am your mother. I am who will save you, the Mistress of Magic of the Uraeus of Re."*[394] On another *cippi* there is a cow whose horns are formed from a human-headed snake who has a divine beard and wears the Red Crown. The snake is referred to as Neith, the beard might allude to her androgynous nature, and the cow is the *Ihet* Cow. She is probably Mehet-Weret, a Creator Goddesses who rose out of the primeval waters.

Feline imagery is also important. On one *cippi* a lioness-headed Goddess, either Tefnut or Sekhmet, holds a huge snake. She wears the hieroglyph for flame as a crown. *"Mistress of Flame who defeats all the reptiles which are in the sky, in the earth and in the water."*[395] Another depicts a cobra around a papyrus stalk wearing the White Crown who is described as Sekhmet from Bubastis. Tefnut is depicted as a lioness-headed cobra with outstretched wings who wears a sun disc. The Lunar God Khonsu, depicted as a baboon, offers the *wedjat* eye to a lioness-headed cobra who sits on a plinth at the top of a flight of stairs. She is referred to as Sekhmet-Bastet-Tefnut. This image is seen elsewhere when Thoth, in his baboon form, presents a *wedjat* eye to a cobra seated on the top of a flight of stairs. One spell from the *cippi* of Psammetik-Seneb concerns Ra fighting Apophis having transformed himself into a large mongoose of 46 cubits (24m). Ra then *"came and expelled all bad harms and all impurities and poisons of all male serpents and all female serpents…that are in the limb of any man and any animal who are under my fingers"*.[396] The *cippi* of Djedkhonsuiufankh calls upon Shed. *"I am Shed, victorious over*

---

[394] *Egyptian Healing Statues in Three Museums in Italy (Turin, Florence, Naples)*, Kakosy, 1967:81
[395] *Egyptian Healing Statues in Three Museums in Italy (Turin, Florence, Naples)*, Kakosy, 1967:143
[396] *Egyptian Healing Statues in Three Museums in Italy (Turin, Florence, Naples)*, Kakosy, 1967:45

*Magu who closes all the snakes who bite. Who are against me in the heaven, on earth, in the water and in the desert forever."*397 Magu might be a form of Seth. *"Turn back you serpent. Remove the venom...flow out you enemy."*398

TREATING SNAKEBITE

Prevention was better than cure, hence the number of spells for warding off snakes. It was impossible to completely avoid snakes though. There is a general spell against pain, whether caused by snakebite or not. *"Kill the two h3h3-snakes, O Lower Egyptian Crown snake...the Treader is for the Death-snake and the Wanderer he is for the king...Gladness is free from panic; the cobra is free from Dep."*399 In one spell Ra speaks. *"It is at the voice of my daughter Isis that I have come – see, a smooth bull-snake has bitten! Break out, poison, retire from all the limbs of the sufferer."*400 Being able to identify the snake, either from the symptoms or a description given by witnesses, gives the magician greater power as they know its name. It also helps the physician as they can select the most appropriate treatment.

One long spell describes how the Horus child trod on a snake while playing. *"I trod on the tail of the nbsty-snake...it wound itself around my toe. Its poison came up to me like the rush of the flood."* Horus explains that he was playing in the valley with the *"children of the team"* in the *iniw*-plants (wild mint). This level of detail suggests that it was designed to be tailored to the patient's specific situation. Isis calls to Neith and Serket and says *"may you flow out, O poison, acting in your ignorance"*.401 Had the snake known that it was Horus it might not have bitten him. It was an accident which may make the poison more amenable to being treated. If the snake was set against the victim with the intent to harm then the healer has to fight malevolent magic as well. *"My magical powers are against my enemies, to render the influence of the poison of the nh3-hr snakes*

---

397 *Egyptian Healing Statues in Three Museums in Italy (Turin, Florence, Naples)*, Kakosy, 1967:157
398 *Egyptian Healing Statues in Three Museums in Italy (Turin, Florence, Naples)*, Kakosy, 1967:163
399 *Ancient Egyptian Magical Texts*, Borghouts, 1978:36
400 *Ancient Egyptian Magical Texts*, Borghouts, 1978:71
401 *Magical and Medical Papyri of the New Kingdom*, Leitz, 1999:19

*harmless."*402 Another spell says *"Horus sleeps, unaware of what the cobras, who are in their holes, had done against him"*. Are they referred to as *"in their holes"* so as not to call them? Serket replies *"have no fear...I have spat out the poison"*.403 Animals also needed protection and healing from snakebite. A relief from the Old Kingdom depicts the king performing a ritual to protect all the cattle in Egypt from snakebite. There are spells to conjure poison from a cat. *"Your claws are saved from the poison of any biting snake."*404 Persistence is sometimes needed in medicine. One spell addressed to a snake ends *"if it does not glide away I shall indeed repeat this spell"*.405

CHILDBIRTH

Clay models of beds have been found at Deir el-Medina. These are thought to be birth amulets, designed to ensure a safe delivery for both the mother and child. They are also depicted on *ostraca* with the same function. Images of Bes and snakes are shown on the long edge of the bed. Bes has a strong connection with childbirth. The snake is either red or red and black and is the protective *krht*-snake who is a guardian of fertility.406

MEDICINES AND INGREDIENTS

Kyphi was a common blend of incense, often replicated today. Galen (129-210 CE), a Greek physician, reported that kyphi was used to treat snake-bite. A similar substance was known to the Classical and Islamic writers as *tiryac*. It was said to include snake skin as this was considered an antidote to snakebite. Magical papyri give details of potions used to prevent grey hair. Using sympathetic magic they included parts of black animals such as the fat of a black snake. This was also used to treat baldness.407 Snake's blood mentioned in medicinal recipes is

---

402 *Magical and Medical Papyri of the New Kingdom*, Leitz, 1999:11
403 *Magical and Medical Papyri of the New Kingdom*, Leitz, 1999:28
404 *Ancient Egyptian Magical Texts*, Borghouts, 1978:57
405 *Egyptian Healing Statues in Three Museums in Italy (Turin, Florence, Naples)*, Kakosy, 1967:122
406 *Dancing for Hathor: Women in Ancient Egypt*, Graves-Brown, 2010:64
407 *Sacred Luxuries*, Manniche, 1999:133

thought to be haematite.[408]

CONCLUSION

Having control over a snake neutralised its power over the magician and allowed the magician to use its *heka* for his or her own purposes. Protector deities, especially in the funerary texts, are often shown holding snakes for this reason. Their *heka* meant that snakes were important in healing magic, despite being part of the problem in many cases. The snakes' destructive power is turned into a power used to heal. Magic and healing have strong roots in mythology and stories both at the state level and amongst the ordinary people. It is stories which help us understand and explain events beyond our control or understanding. Stories allow us to glimpse other worlds and shape our understanding and expectations of the deities and the afterlife.

---

[408] *Magic in Ancient Egypt*, Pinch, 2006:80

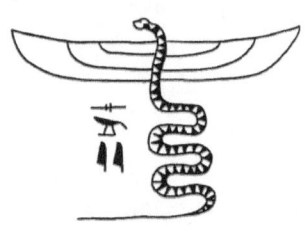

CHAPTER 10

Two Serpent Stories

"I bared my face and found it was a serpent coming my way: the thing was over fifty huge feet long! Its beard hung down a yard! Its flesh was gilt, its eyebrows lapis lazuli."[409]

INTRODUCTION

A reasonable amount of the mythology of Ancient Egypt has survived because it was referenced in spells, funerary texts and inscribed on the walls of Greco-Roman temples. Much will have been lost though. Virtually all the stories told by ordinary people have vanished because they were part of an oral tradition. A few have survived as they were recorded on papyri which have been preserved and this includes the story of the Shipwrecked Sailor. There are also stories about real-life events which capture the public imagination and take on a life of their own persisting and evolving over the centuries.

THE DEATH OF CLEOPATRA

Although there is no doubt that Cleopatra VII (51-30 BCE) killed herself, the method of her death was not witnessed nor are there any written comments from the time. There was never any rumour of her murder. It therefore has the makings of a good

---

[409] *Ancient Egyptian Literature*, Foster, 2001:11

short story. The widely accepted version is that a cobra (Classical sources use the word asp) was smuggled into her room inside a basket of fruit and she forced it to bite her. The choice of a snake was deliberate. Cleopatra saw herself as a reincarnation of Isis and the snake was important in the cult of Isis. Hellenistic statues of Isis often depict her as a snake or with one. Cleopatra often wore the triple *uraeus* on her crown. The cobra was a sacred emblem and as such provided the most appropriate way for an Egyptian Queen to die. Although a Ptolemy Cleopatra thought of herself as both divine and Egyptian. Strabo (63 BCE – 24 CE) is one of the earliest sources after her death and he lived during her lifetime. He reported that she died "*by the bite of an asp…or by applying a poisonous ointment*".[410] The majority of sources mention one snake but four of them say it was two.[411] As there were no eyewitnesses this is conjecture but two would equate to the double *uraeus*. Other Classical writers were contemplating the subject over 150 years later. Galen (129-210 CE) refers to the belief that she poured snake poison into a wound on her arm. Dio Cassius (150-235 CE) states that the only marks on her body were slight pricks on her arm. Plutarch (46-119 CE) reports that her death was sudden and that she was bitten on the arm by a snake hidden in a basket of figs. He also suggested the alternative method of poison.

Aziz (2018) has studied the theories and concludes that death by snakebite was unlikely. A cobra would have been too large to conceal in a basket of figs. There is only a 10-20% chance that the bite would have resulted in her death as most snakebites are dry and don't inject venom.[412] Plutarch reports that Cleopatra experimented with snake venom. If this was true she would have known about the low chance of a fatal bite. Two of her servants were found dead with her. One cobra couldn't have killed three people. Aziz suggests death by cobra bite can be ruled out and had more to do with symbolism and sensationalism. Others also remain unconvinced about the snakebite theory because the bite of a cobra couldn't have been guaranteed to kill Cleopatra. She

---

410 *The Top Ten Myths About Ancient Egypt*, Kriz & Burzacott, 2017:15-25
411 *The Death of Cleopatra VII*, Griffiths, 1961:113-133
412 *An Examination of the Death of Cleopatra and the Serpent in Myth, Magic and Medicine*, Aziz, 2018:29-34

needed to guarantee that her suicide attempt would work given that Caesar's soldiers were, allegedly, at her door. Death by cobra venom would have taken 30 minutes to an hour and would have left physical damage to the body. He suggests that she used a poison which guaranteed a quick death: a mixture of hemlock, wolfs bane and opium.[413] None of the ancient sources suggest that she drank poison, but that she injected it into her bloodstream. Galen was a physician, unlike the other commentators, and he supported this theory. Cobra venom will remain toxic after it has been extracted, a high dose would have killed quickly and it was easy to smuggle in. Pouring it into an open wound is a viable option.

Why does the snakebite story prevail? Initially it was probably to do with the importance of the snake in Egyptian mythology. It was certainly a fitting and symbolic way for Cleopatra to kill herself. Although the Classical writers said that Cleopatra had wounds on her arms Shakespeare had her press the snake to her breast. This necessitated the removal of clothing and the exposing of breasts – making the image far more appealing to both the audience and to later artists. Despite its scientific validity, the Shakespearean version has more erotic appeal guaranteeing that his version is the one which persists.

THE SHIPWRECKED SAILOR

This story survives in the Middle Kingdom *Leningrad* papyrus and it may have been a narrative poem. There were probably many versions of the story and it might derive from a cycle of narratives designed to be told over a series of nights. The complete story is told by Tyldesley (2010), Parkinson (1998), Lichthiem (1975) and Foster (2001). The fact that classical writers knew of and commented on the story shows that it was still in circulation in a similar form over 1,000 years after it was first written down. It is a nested story; the sailor tells one to the captain, the sailor tells his story to the snake then the snake tells his story. Stories of shipwrecks and islands are common motifs as the hero has to leave the everyday life behind. It starts in the

---

[413] *The Top Ten Myths About Ancient Egypt*, Kriz & Burzacott, 2017:15-25

present day in the ordinary world where the official of a failed expedition to Nubia reaches port and contemplates his ruined career. In an attempt to persuade the official to pull himself together and report to his superior the sailor relates what happened to him on a previous trip.

He was with a mining expedition sailing on the Great Green. This was the Egyptian term for the open sea and is probably the Red Sea given the mining context. A storm wrecks their ship and all but the narrator are drowned. He is swept ashore on an island and spends three days either recovering or unconscious. Then he explores the island where he finds birds and fish as well as figs, grapes and vegetables *"as if they were tended"*. It is an island of abundance where *"there was nothing that was not within it"*.[414] After eating a meal he lights a fire, having first made a fire-stick, and gives *"burnt offering to the gods"* to thank them.[415] *"I heard a thunderous noise which I thought was the wave of the sea. The trees were breaking and the ground was shaking."* The audience imagines a natural disaster such as a tsunami, storm or earthquake. The sailor lies down then lifts his head. He sees a giant snake approaching. *"He opened his mouth to me while I was on my belly in his presence."* The snake is 30 cubits in length (15.7m) with a beard over 2 cubits (1m). *"His body was fashioned in gold, his eyebrows in real lapis lazuli."*[416] We are not directly told that he was a God but the audience would immediately know because he wears a beard which is a sign of divinity, as is his body of gold. The snake demands to know who brought him to this island. *"If you delay in telling me who brought you to this island, I will make you know yourself to be ashes."*[417] The terrified sailor can only mumble incoherently. His first mumblings to the snake are rebuffed. *"You speak to me but I do not hear it."* He is picked up by the snake, who takes him back to his home to recover. Then he asks again what brought him to the island. The sailor's first response is *"I am in your presence – I don't know myself"*.[418] He may be showing the expected submission

---

[414] "The Shipwrecked Sailor" Prose or Verse? (Postponing Clauses and Tense-neutral Clauses), Foster, 1988:69-109
[415] Ancient Egyptian Literature, Foster, 2001:10
[416] Writings from Ancient Egypt, Wilkinson, 2016:247
[417] The Tale of Sinuhe and Other Ancient Egyptian Poems, Parkinson, 1998:93
[418] Questions and Answers in Middle Kingdom Dialogues, Worthington, 90:113-121

before a deity but he fails to answer the question. Only when he has given a satisfactory answer is he safe. This emphasises the Egyptians' respect for words and their proper use – the hero is not a warrior but an orator. The sailor recounts his story and in the last sentence answers the snake's question. He was "*brought to this island by a wave of the Great Green*".[419] The snake expresses surprise that the sailor has found his island and tells him that it will soon disappear under the waves never to reappear. He concludes that "*a god has brought you to his island*" as a living mortal could never reach it.[420]

He tells the sailor not to worry and explains that the island is the Island of the Spirit (the Island of the *Ka*). The snake says that in four months a ship will arrive and take him home where he will be reunited with his family. After a long life he will die in his home city. The snake's promise to the sailor that he would die in Egypt would have been of immense comfort to someone who believed that only the properly observed funerary rites would allow him to be reborn in the afterlife. He also adds "*never again shall you see this island which shall turn to waves*".[421] The snake then reciprocates and recounts his own tragic tale about the loss of his own family. "*We totalled five and seventy persons, consisting of my offspring, relatives and friends. I cannot bear to dwell on a small daughter brought to me through prayer. A star fell and they were gone, gone up in flame. It happened when I could not be there...all burned.*"[422] Whilst waiting for his rescuers the sailor asks the snake "*let me relate your Powers to the Sovereign, let me cause that he be acquainted with your greatness*".[423] Although eager to relate his encounter he must first ensure that he is not betraying secret knowledge. He then lists the vast riches which will be offered up to the snake, who laughs when hearing them. "*I am the ruler of Punt; myrrh is mine; that malabathrum you speak of bringing is this island's plenty.*"[424] All the snake asks of the sailor is that he "*give my good name in your city,*

---

[419] Literary Devices in the Story of the Shipwrecked Sailor, Rendsburg, 2000:13-23
[420] Questions and Answers in Middle Kingdom Dialogues, Worthington, 90:113-121
[421] "The Shipwrecked Sailor" Prose or Verse? (Postponing Clauses and Tense-neutral Clauses), Foster, 1988:69-109
[422] Ancient Egyptian Literature, Foster, 2001:13
[423] "The Shipwrecked Sailor" Prose or Verse? (Postponing Clauses and Tense-neutral Clauses), Foster, 1988:69-109
[424] The Tale of Sinuhe and Other Ancient Egyptian Poems, Parkinson, 1998:96

behold, it is what is due me from you". The deities' main desire is to be known. The sailor tells him "*you will be praised in the city before the magistrates of the entire land*".[425] When the rescue boat arrives the snake presents generous gifts to the sailor and, as foretold, the island sinks back into the water. On his return to Egypt the sailor presents the king with his tribute and is duly rewarded. The doomed official fails to hear the message and is unwilling to take comfort from it but asks bitterly "*who gives water to a bird on the morning of sacrifice*".[426]

Over-analysis can spoil a good tale but there are some points worthy of discussion. Although we are told that it is the Island of the Spirit, or *Ka*, a number of commentators have tried to locate it and suggest that the island has a geographical counterpart. In the Rameside Period one of the branches of the delta was called *Ka*. Strabo suggests that it was the "*Island Ophiodes*" – the Island of Snakes. Pliny (23-79 CE) mentions "*an island in the Red Sea called 'Topazos' at a distance of three hundred stadia from the mainland. It is surrounded by fogs, and is often sought by navigators*".[427] 300 stadia is about 55.5 km. Wainwright suggests that it is the Island of Zeberged in the Red Sea.[428] Sand haze is common in the Red Sea, equivalent to the reported fog, as are storms. In the story the island is a place of natural abundance, in reality all these islands mentioned are described as barren. If the listeners knew of the island and the hazards of getting to it, would it have made the story more interesting?

Does the real island act as a portal to another world? Is it a phantom island, an island of the dead and of spirits? Most commentators take the more spiritual interpretation and understand that it is the Island of the Beyond and that is it the sailor's *ka* who talks to the snake while he lies unconscious on the beach. The fact that the sailor sees abundance on an island known to be barren supports the concept of a place that only his *ka* can visit. The island is described by the snake as having "*shores

---

[425] *Literary Devices in the Story of the Shipwrecked Sailor*, Rendsburg, 2000:13-23
[426] *"The Shipwrecked Sailor" Prose or Verse? (Postponing Clauses and Tense-neutral Clauses)*, Foster, 1988:69-109
[427] *Pliny the Elder, the Complete Works*, Pliny, Bosatock & Riley, 2015:26
[428] *Zeberged: The Shipwrecked Sailor's Island*, Wainwright, 1946:31-38

as changing as the shifty waves"⁴²⁹ which alludes to its liminality with undefined edges. Human visitors must have been expected though. Why else would there be cultivated crops? Snakes are not vegetarian, even divine ones. The snake's island could have been Punt as he describes himself as the Lord of Punt. Punt was known as a land of the Gods and a place rich in resources and is thought to have been on the Red Sea coast. Although the Egyptians knew that Punt was a real place, as trading expeditions had brought back riches from there, it was thought of as so remote as to be an almost mythical Land of Beyond. This is the 'a time long ago' and 'in a galaxy far away' setting for the story. Alternatively the island could have been the Field of Reeds (a place in the afterlife) or the primeval mound. The island emerges from the ocean in the same way that the primeval mound emerged from the waters of the *nun*. The sinking island is the reverse of creation and alludes to the destruction of creation when everything returns to the *nun*. As far as the story goes the island exists for the duration of the story and lives on in the minds of the audience, so indeed is an Island of the Spirit.

Who is the divine snake? He is believed to be the Sun God Ra or Atum. In the *Book of the Dead* the deceased addresses Ra as the Great One *"whose island does not exist"*⁴³⁰ which alludes to the Creator at the moment before creation. The snake explains that there were 75 serpents. The Sun God was believed to have 75 aspects, the symbolism behind this number is not known. Does the story allude to the *Litany of Re* in which Ra is invoked 75 times in his various names and forms? If so folklore would be a strange place to find reference to restricted sacred knowledge, unless the *Litany* was known of in some form by ordinary people. Baines (1990) suggests that it is not an allegory but is partly based on esoteric wisdom with the 75 names of the Sun God referenced within a story. The identity of his daughter is not known. Could she be one of the Daughters of the Sun – the *Uraeus* Goddess and his Eye? Some have suggested that she is his other daughter Maat.

The star which destroyed the snake's family might have been a meteorite. We still refer to them as shooting stars. This would

---

⁴²⁹ *Ancient Egyptian Literature*, Foster, 2001:12
⁴³⁰ *An Ancient Egyptian Book of the Dead*, O'Rourke, 2016:100 spell 64

link it to the solar cults. The *benben* stone, considered to be part of the original mound of creation, is thought to have been a piece of meteorite. It was a cult object in the temple of Ra at Heliopolis. The central idea of the snake surviving the end of creation would have been a well-known part of the mythology. At the end of creation only the Sun God in his serpent form will survive hence the loss of the 74 other members of his family or different forms. However, the reference to the end of creation in the *Book of the Dead* names Osiris as the survivor with Atum. Here we have the narrator's journey to the end of creation. If the snake is the Creator then he does not determine his own destiny, although he may have foretold it. It is a physical event, the falling star, which destroys the rest of the family whilst the snake was away and could not save them. The moral, although hardly a comforting one, is that horrible things happen even to the deities. The death of the snakes could also allude to the creation story as described in the Khonsu cosmography. Here the early generations of snakes, such as Irta and the deities of the Ogdoad, finish their work in creation then die. The snake's loss of his family is paralleled by the sailor's loss of the other members of his crew – though this is hardly an equal loss. In the end the sailor is reunited with his family but the snake has to master his grief and be stoic in the face of his loss. Despite his divine power he is helpless. This is perhaps the bleakest and saddest part of the story.

Some have suggested that the story is in part an astronomical metaphor and that the duration of the journeys and the sailor's stay on the island have significance. The dimensions of the ship and the crew numbers may be significant or they may just be to give further detail to the story. We can only speculate. The tale also carries a deviant message. For the Egyptians, received wisdom said that the deities expected offerings and would act favourably if they are given to them despite their apparent lack of need. But the divine snake laughs when the sailor promises offerings and tells him that this is the *"island of the ka. There is not anything that is not in it. It is full of good things"*.[431] If the deity has no need of the offerings are they pointless? What is the purpose of

---

[431] *Some Notes on the Shipwrecked Sailor*, Ignatov, 1994:195-198

giving them if the only beneficiaries are the temple staff and the state through temple taxes? This would have been a comfort to the poorer members of the audience. Fire is important in the story. The snake's family is destroyed by fire. The sailor burns offerings as thanks to the deities who have saved him but is threatened with fire if he fails to answer the snake's question. Burnt offerings are not believed to have been the norm in Egypt. Burning results in a complete destruction of the food so would render it useless and its essence unable to pass into the otherworld for the benefit of the deities and the deceased. Food was normally cooked. New Kingdom depictions of offerings at the Theban Valley Festival show offerings in flames. Is this just to show it cooking or are they literally burnt offerings?

The story can be interpreted in a number of ways; a fairy-tale, a metaphor of the sun's journey or an allegory of an individual's journey. Like any good story it is long-lasting and multi-layered. Some of it we can understand and interpret, probably there is much that we miss completely. There is a lot of wordplay throughout the story with puns, alliteration and so forth which is lost in the translating. The virtues of bravery and self-control are emphasised. The snake delivers a moral message – the sailor can only react to what is happening. He must experience without being able to control the situation. Unlike some other Egyptian stories there is no magic or magicians. If this was primarily a story with a moral for the audience to take away it would have defeated the object if magic had been used. Everyone, including the deities, has to deal with situations that are totally outside of their control. The snake's prophesy that everything will turn out well for the sailor helps him persevere and have faith. Faith and the hope for an improvement in the circumstances are all we have at certain times in our lives. The snake constantly tells the sailor that the most important thing is his family.

The tale is also about the importance of speech, something which was very prominent in Egyptian culture. At the start the sailor tells the official that he should speak "*heart-in-hand, without stammering*".[432] To be effective words must be delivered clearly and

---

[432] *Questions and Answers in Middle Kingdom Dialogues*, Worthington, 90:113-121

confidently. "*The mouth of a man, it can save him; His speech, it can cause the countenance to soften for him.*"[433] The sailor has learned this through his experience with the snake. The sailor is a flawed hero though. He lists all the things which will be sent to the snake but he has no resources to make good his promise. All he could do would be to petition the king to send them. All the snake asks of the sailor is to "*place my good name in your town*".[434] The sailor's boast that the snake will be praised before the people of the city is reversed. He tells the official that it was in fact him who praised, and rewarded by the king. Not only does the sailor omit to do this the name of the snake is never revealed to the audience. They would have appreciated that the name may be secret. It might be better to interpret 'name' in this context as 'reputation'. If the name of the snake was revealed the story would lose some of its mystical character. Or perhaps the audience knew who the snake was without being told.

CONCLUSION

Like divine myths, stories were not just to entertain. They imparted important lessons for this life and the next.

---

[433] *"The Shipwrecked Sailor" Prose or Verse? (Postponing Clauses and Tense-neutral Clauses)*, Foster, 1988:69-109
[434] *Interpreting the Story of the Shipwrecked Sailor*, Baines, 1990:55-72

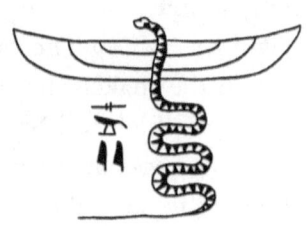

CHAPTER 11

Snakes in the Afterlife

"Mysterious serpents, keepers of the gate, keepers of my way."[435]

INTRODUCTION

In general snakes are found in the afterlife and cosmic realms because they are found on earth and all these places were a reflection of, and connected to, each other. As soon as the Egyptians placed the afterlife in the underground snakes became an integral part of the environment if only because holes, caves and crevasses are part of their natural habitat. As in all realms the serpents act to help and hinder. In their positive aspects they guide, protect and enable rebirth. In their negative role they become a hazard; a destroyer, jailer and tormentor. These roles are fluid. There can be a very narrow line between protector and aggressor – a lot depends on your point of view and whether you are perceived, rightly or wrongly, as a threat. This and the following chapter looks at the various roles of serpent deities and snakes in the afterlife. Because this is such a large and wide-ranging topic I have split it into two chapters by separating the mysteries of rebirth from the process of traversing the afterworld. Obviously this is an artificial split. Everything that happens after death is a mystery and serpents do not like to stay in neat

---

[435] *The Ancient Egyptian Book of Two Ways*, Lesko, 1977:77 spell 1180

compartments for the convenience of the author.

There are many deities encountered in the afterlife. Some, like Ra, Horus and Osiris form the driving or background mythologies of the journey. Others are present to assist Ra, Osiris and the deceased in various ways. The Snake deities are no exception to this. Isis and Nephthys are closely involved with the protection and rebirth of Osiris and the deceased but they are also present as *uraei* emphasising their protective and light-bringing roles. They are shown on the Solar Barque in this form and in the Netherworld texts.

AN OVERVIEW OF THE AFTERLIFE TEXTS

The *Pyramid Texts*, *Coffin Texts* and *Book of the Dead* consist of a series of spells sometimes with accompanying vignettes. There is no overall structure although general themes can be discerned and many spells are duplicated or omitted depending on the sources. The Old Kingdom *Pyramid Texts* are the oldest collection of funerary spells. Designed purely for the king, they were carved on the walls of the pyramids and have no accompanying illustrations. Towards the end of the Period other royals began to use them. They were intended to guide the king through the dangers of the afterlife and enable him to ascend into the divine realm in the sky. The king identifies with Osiris even though he aims to join the Sun God in his barque. The Middle Kingdom saw the development of the *Coffin Texts* which were based in part on spells from the *Pyramid Texts* and which were available to anyone who had the money to buy them. Major changes are seen. Apophis appears for the first time, the deceased have to face judgement and have the chance of reuniting with their loved ones. One set of *Coffin Texts* are known as the *Book of Two Ways*. Painted on the base of the coffin was a map of the underworld which the deceased negotiated with the help of the spells. Gateways and their guardians are introduced. The *Book of the Dead* was developed in the New Kingdom and was mostly written on papyrus. It has accompanying vignettes to some of the spells. Like those of the preceding funerary texts they were viewed as a practical guide to help the deceased. The judgement of the deceased becomes more important. Developed during the Greco-

Roman Period the *Books of Breathing*, as the name describes, place emphasis on the reanimation of the deceased. Some focus on purification, the survival of the corpse and the vindication of the deceased. Others include the gatekeepers and guardians the deceased will encounter. Snakes are much less important in these texts. I refer to all the above texts collectively as the funerary texts to differentiate them from the very different Netherworld texts.

What are known collectively as the Books of the Netherworld (with the exception of the *Enigmatic Book*) consist of illustrations and accompanying text which form a coherent whole describing the journey of the Sun God through the hours of darkness, his battles with Apophis and how he unites with Osiris as part of the rebirth process. They were developed in the New Kingdom in parallel with the emergence of the *Book of the Dead* from the *Coffin Texts*. The Books of the Netherworld were originally painted on tomb walls and were the preserve of royalty. Later they appear on sarcophagus and papyrus. As well as describing the nocturnal journey and renewal of the Sun God these texts also relate to the inner journey of the soul and its transformation. The importance of the soul is emphasised by the depiction of the Sun God in his ram-headed form as the word *ba* also means ram. Hornung (1999) gives a detailed overview of all these books with accompanying illustrations. While snakes appear throughout the funerary texts those in the books of the Netherworld appear more prominent and most references to them have accompanying illustrations. This may reflect the greater emphasis on the mysteries which the snakes represent and also on the hazards of the afterlife which are frequently of serpent form. The earliest Books of the Netherworld, the *Amduat* and the *Book of Gates*, are divided into twelve sections representing the twelve hours of the night which the Sun God has to pass through. The *Book of Gates* is similar in context but, as the name suggests, each hour is divided by gates. The Sun God has lost his entourage in the *Book of Gates*. He relies on the Gods Sia, who personifies the intellect, and Heka. The deceased appear to be confined to specific hours rather than traversing the whole night. The two later books, the *Book of Caverns* and the *Book of Earth*, lose the formal structure and division into hours. Osiris is given more prominence and the battle with Apophis less. On the walls of the sarcophagus hall of the tomb of Rameses VI (20th dynasty) are texts and pictures which also depict the journey of the Sun God. Some are similar to those found in the *Book of Caverns* but the text is fragmentary. The *Enigmatic Book of the Netherworld* is incomplete and little understood. Parts are found on the shrine of Tutankhamun (18th dynasty). The title was given by scholars and refers to the fact that cryptographic hieroglyphs are used so the text is hard to interpret. The emphasis is on the unification of Ra and Osiris.

THE *URAEUS* AND THE *URAEUS* GODDESS

The *uraeus* isn't always on the brow of the deities, many independent ones are found throughout the underworld. Most of the *uraei* have generic epithets so it is not clear if they are independent *uraei* or manifestations of the various *Uraeus* Goddesses. Sometimes one in a group will be named as a Goddess, such as Wadjet. The others may be different manifestations of her to represent her multiplicity. The text does refer to some as living *uraeus*-serpents which might specifically mean the *Uraeus* Goddess rather than the *uraeus*. A number of the *uraei* have specific duties and some will remain in certain sections of the underworld.

The first thing that anyone needs underground is a source of light. Despite the fact that the Sun God is traversing the underworld his Eye is no longer with him. The Eye is the visible sun disc so it cannot be present in the hours of darkness otherwise there would be no darkness. The only explanation is either that it is elsewhere or that it is hidden for safety. In the 4th hour of the *Amduat* we are told that the Sun God has swallowed his Eye, to protect it, until he has passed Apophis. As the visible manifestation of the Sun God the Eye can be equated to creation and is his most important aspect. Without the solar disc there is no light or heat and thus the end of creation. In the underworld its protection is more important than its provision of light. Torches and lamps used by the living may not work in the afterworld and even then only last for a limited duration. There is no supernatural glow coming from the cave walls, for that only exists in Hollywood, so who better to supply light than the *uraeus* serpents who *"illuminate the darkness"*.[436] In the 8th hour of the *Amduat* four *uraeus* serpents sit on the hieroglyph sign for clothing in a cavern called Great of Torches. This is permanently guarded, the fire-spitting *uraei* do not have to leave their positions to carry out their other duty of providing light. In the following hour there are twelve fire-spitting *uraei*, again on the same sign. These spit fire to illuminate the chamber containing Osiris but stop when the Sun God has passed. Once the Sun God has left there is no need for further illumination and Osiris must return to the regenerative darkness to rest. Each *uraeus* is named and as usual their names reflect their characters; such as She with Bright Stars, Mistress of Embers and Mistress of Heat. We are told that they *"stay on their clothes in their own flesh"*.[437] They are not undergoing any transformation. They are always present and they continue in the same form.

Sokar is the Hawk God of the Memphis necropolis. He is often viewed as a manifestation of Osiris. The Cavern of Sokar in the *Amduat* is *"filled with flames of fire from the mouth of Isis"* when she is in her cobra form. Sokar is depicted grasping the wings of a multi-headed snake who is described as the *"multi-coloured serpent"* which hints at the light and life to come.[438] In the 12th hour of the *Amduat*, the hour before sunrise, there are twelve Goddesses who wear fire-spitting cobras around their shoulders. One is called Mistress of Cobras, another Lady of the *Uraeus*-Serpents in the Bark of Millions.[439] The text explains that one of their roles is to *"give release to those in the darkness"* with the flames from their *uraeus* serpents.[440] There is a saying that the darkest hour is just before dawn. It is essential not to give up when success is so close. Their light gives encouragement to the fainthearted.

New clothes were an important symbol of rebirth and the provision of new clothing for the deceased occurs in all afterlife texts. Clothing is also associated with light. At Dendera there is reference to Hathor who *"clothes her lord with her light"*.[441] The

---

[436] *Knowledge for the Afterlife*, Abt & Hornung, 2003:113
[437] *The Egyptian Amduat*, Abt & Hornung, 2007:290
[438] *Knowledge for the Afterlife*, Abt & Hornung, 2003:71
[439] *The Egyptian Amduat*, Abt & Hornung, 2007:360
[440] *The Egyptian Amduat*, Abt & Hornung, 2007:362
[441] *The Enigmatic Netherworld Books and the Solar-Osiran Unity*, Darnell, 2004:134

purified and vindicated deceased cannot start their new life as a being of light in used clothing. One spell in the *Pyramid Texts* refers to the king making his way to these "*linen garments which the uraei guard*".[442] The Cobra Goddess Renenutet is associated with funerary linen providing another link with the guarding *uraei*. The *Book of the Dead* also refers to cobras guarding linen garments in spell 174. As mentioned previously, the hieroglyph for clothing dominates in the 8th hour of the *Amduat*. Fine, new linen was expensive and funerary garments had to be of the finest quality that the relatives could afford. That wasn't the only reason they had to be guarded. They were imbued with the magic of the Goddesses who produced them and were not available to the unjustified deceased or the enemies of Osiris.

The ways of the underworld are dark, confusing and dangerous and guides are essential. A number of deities provide this function, as do the *uraeus* serpents. "*They shall guide you your two uraei.*"[443] In the *Coffin Texts* there is reference to the Guiding Serpent in a spell about the ferryboat, where she and Orion "*set the streams in order*".[444] She appears in another spell where the deceased state that the Gods are with them, the Guiding Serpent is on their brow and also that "*my soul has looked in the flame*".[445] Being that close to the *Uraeus* Goddess is indeed to look into the fire. As the deceased traverse the afterlife they are able to see the divine mysteries invisible to them in life and see the Goddess within her fire and understand how to approach her potentially lethal energy.

With its endless hazards, including the terrifying and deadly snakes throughout the underworld the deceased, as well as the deities, need some powerful protectors. Many snakes are present purely for protection. The *Uraeus Goddess* and the *uraei* are the main protectors of the Sun God, Osiris, Horus and the deceased and they occur throughout the Netherworld texts, usually occurring multiple times within each hour. "*Holy serpents are at his brow, and his uraeus-goddess precedes him.*"[446] Ra is constantly under

---

[442] *The Ancient Egyptian Pyramid Texts*, Faulkner, 2007:61 utterance 249
[443] *The Ancient Egyptian Pyramid Texts*, Faulkner, 2007:317 utterance 748
[444] *The Ancient Egyptian Coffin Texts Volume II*, Faulkner, 2007:42 spell 399
[445] *The Ancient Egyptian Coffin Texts Volume II*, Faulkner, 2007:176 spell 573
[446] *Hymns, Prayers and Songs*, Foster, 1995:16

attack by Apophis and Osiris by his various enemies including certain *ba*-souls, presumably of the unjustified dead. Either they have become malevolent or merely desperately needy and are a risk to the process of rebirth and transformation. Perhaps they are just trying to take some of the regenerative energy for themselves rather than deliberately trying to destroy or harm Osiris. The *ba*-soul is independent of the body and yearns to fly free. Of all the component parts of the person perhaps the *ba*-soul is the most desperate to escape the confines of the underworld. *"The Ba-souls are repulsed and the shadows destroyed when the voice of the Uraeus-serpents is heard."*[447]

One spell for entering into the sun disc includes *"O you who are strong in striking-power, who sit on your coils and who hear the speech of the great ones"*.[448] Those who sit on their coils are the *uraei* who surround the Sun God as the emanations of the sun disc. To enter into the presence of the Sun God the deceased first has to be allowed to pass by his protective and dangerous *uraei*. *"My companion is the serpent which came forth from the god, the uraeus which came forth from Re."*[449] The deceased align themselves with the *uraeus* for protection and guidance. Given her nature this isn't always risk-free so they sometimes assume the role of *"Thoth in the northern sky who appeases the raging fiery cobra"*.[450] In the 9th hour of the *Amduat* twelve fire-spitting *uraei* make a formidable guard. These repel every hostile snake, even those whom Ra *"does not know…neither Akh-spirits nor the dead are able to pass them owing to the mystery of their forms"*. The reference to snakes which Ra, as the Creator, does not know alludes to both the clay snake Isis used against him and the fact that he is not the sole creator. Fortunately for the deceased there are spells which provide them with sufficient knowledge to deal with this particular threat. *"He who knows them sees their forms, and does not perish at their flames."*[451] At the 6th hour of the *Amduat* there are three chests which hold the three-fold burial of the Sun God. These are his forms of Khepri, Ra and Atum representing the rising sun, the midday sun and the

---

[447] The Egyptian Book of Gates, Abt & Hornung, 2014:111
[448] The Ancient Egyptian Coffin Texts Volume III, Faulkner, 2007:106 spell 1000
[449] The Ancient Egyptian Pyramid Texts, Faulkner, 2007:181 utterance spell 505
[450] An Ancient Egyptian Book of the Dead, O'Rourke, 2016:144 spell 71
[451] The Egyptian Amduat, Abt & Hornung, 2007:291

setting sun. They are watched over by three fire-spitting snakes. When Osiris is shown standing in his shrine it often has a frieze of *uraei* protecting him. In one vignette of spell 125 of the *Book of the Dead* Osiris stands with Isis in a shrine with a frieze of *uraei*. "*Him whose ceiling is fire, whose walls are living uraei.*"[452]

OTHER SERPENT PROTECTORS AND GUIDES

Uraei are not the only guardians and guides. One *Pyramid Texts* spell calls a snake to protect or assist the deceased. "*O ttw-snake, where are you going? Attend on me…come here.*"[453] A general protection spell from the *Book of the Dead* has to be recited over a drawing of a two *wedjat* eyes and a snake with two legs. In the 11th hour of the *Book of Gates* is a rearing winged snake.

The text names her as She Who Conducts but she is not depicted as a cobra so isn't a *uraeus*. Her role is to escort the Sun God to the gate of the eastern horizon. The wings hint at her mobility and possible ascension with him, at least in the first instant of his rising. In the 3rd hour of the *Amduat* the Solar Barque is accompanied by three other barques carrying images of the Sun God. On each is a protective standing snake, their names indicate their function. He who Burns with his Face (twice) and He Who Burns with his Eye. On the third barque a hawk-headed God, named as a follower of Horus, stands on an unnamed snake. The 4th hour of the *Amduat* is in the Desert of Sokar, the Imhet. It is guarded by a large snake named as the "*smooth one who shines*" who rests on a human-headed barque.[454] This barque is depicted in the register just below the serpent barque of the Sun God and its human heads wear the divine beard.

---

[452] *Journey Through the Afterlife: Ancient Egyptian Book of the Dead.* Taylor, 2010:207
[453] *The Ancient Egyptian Pyramid Texts*, Faulkner, 2007:126 utterance 383
[454] *The Egyptian Amduat*, Abt & Hornung, 2007:129

7 - REARING WINGED SNAKE

The divine human-headed barque of the snake and the snake barque of the Sun God illustrates the interrelationships and interchangeability between the two deities. The Snake God needs assistance of a more human nature whilst the Sun God requires serpentine assistance. Close by is a two-headed snake named as "*She who adores*" who is the guardian of the path through the Imhet.[455]

The judgement scene from the *Book of the Dead* is often depicted on the outside of coffins. The coffin of Pasenhor shows Osiris sitting in judgement as usual but in front of him a large snake stands on its tail to provide additional protection. The *Greenfield* papyrus contains some spells not found in other versions of the *Book of the Dead*. One depicts an enthroned Osiris above a large snake.[456] Osiris usually needs protection because he is either inert, in his mummified state, or is undergoing or enabling the mysteries of rebirth. His enemies are ever-present with the aim of destroying his corpse so that he can no longer

---

[455] *The Egyptian Amduat*, Abt & Hornung, 2007:131
[456] *Journey Through the Afterlife: Ancient Egyptian Book of the Dead*, Taylor, 2010:307

regenerate. In the *Book of Caverns* the mummy of Osiris is depicted at the deepest part of the afterworld, very close to the dangerous but regenerative *nun*. A snake called *"terrible of face"* encircles the mummy to protect it from the malevolent dead.[457] In another section of the *Book of Caverns* Osiris is protected by the Great Serpent, depicted as an *ouroboros*. There are two long snakes, with a concertina form, placed above and below the coffin of Osiris. Known as the Venomous One and Large Mouth they provide protection for his corpse. In the 5th hour of the *Amduat* the burial mound of Osiris is guarded by a two-headed snake referred to as the Unapproachable. Ra tells him to hide his two heads in the earth and requests that he and his entourage be allowed to pass by in peace. Even he cannot take the guardian snakes for granted; they answer to themselves or to another power. In the 4th hour of the *Book of Gates* Osiris is doubly protected, he stands on a snake while a *uraeus*-serpent, called the Flaming One, stands next to him. In one scene from the *Book of Earth* a long rearing serpent emerges from the ground between two arms. The head of the serpent is bent over a mummiform God emphasising his protective aspects as *"guardian of the corpse of the god"*.[458]

Other deceased deities and humans reside in the afterworld and their corpses need protection for the same reasons as Osiris'. In the 3rd hour of the *Book of Gates* are twelve shrines containing mummies, they are referred to as the Protected Gods. A huge snake called the Flaming One is stretched out above their shrines as their protector. In another section twelve mummified bodies lie on a long bier in the form of a snake, they are described as the Followers of Horus. The snake is Nehep who guards the corpses while their *ba*-souls are in the Field of Rushes. On the walls of the sarcophagus hall of Rameses VI a mummiform God is shown with two standing snakes, one with a human head and arms. They are described as the serpents of Penunty who guard the body.

THE SERPENT BARQUE

When transiting through the dangerous desert regions of the

---

[457] *The Ancient Egyptian Netherworld Books*, Darnell & Darnell, 2018:375
[458] *The Ancient Egyptian Netherworld Books*, Darnell & Darnell, 2018:501

afterworld the Solar Barque is transformed into a serpent. Not only does this give immediate protection but in its serpent form it can easily traverse the dry sandy regions. The fire-breathing Barque also provides light for the journey. Sometimes the *was-sceptre* held by the Sun God is transformed into a snake for additional magical protection. One vignette from the *Coffin Texts* depicts the Field of Reeds and a serpent barque. A similar-looking barque is found in the *Book of The Dead* Field of Reeds. At certain places in the afterworld the Solar Barque has to be towed by various deities. One vignette in the tomb of Rameses VI shows 14 human-headed cobras towing the barque, seven are referred to as She of the Bank and the other seven as She Who Guides.[459]

PROTECTING THE BODY

The deceased are provided with serpentine protection and assistance in the afterlife but the physical corpse still needs protection. To emphasise this, depictions of mummified bodies and coffins are often shown protected by snakes as well as snakes being present on the coffin and other funerary equipment. The 19th dynasty funerary bier of Sennedjem was decorated with snakes to protect his mummified body. One each side of the bier are two long snakes, they are yellow with black markings. One has the head of a jackal, a reference to the Funerary God Anubis. Their heads meet at the centre of the top of the bed, their tails at the base. A 22nd dynasty coffin from Thebes is decorated with figures of Anubis, Sobek, a ram-headed God and a lion-headed God, all of whom hold snakes.

GATE GUARDIANS

"*Serpents of the Beyond, who belong to the doors.*"[460] Access into and out of the afterworld as well as through its various areas is controlled and snakes are some of the guardians who will permit only those with the correct knowledge to enter. "*On your faces, mysterious serpents. Let me pass.*"[461] In the *Book of the Dead* there are

---

[459] *The Ancient Egyptian Netherworld Books*, Darnell & Darnell, 2018:499
[460] *The Wandering of the Soul*, Piankoff, 1974:17 spell 1052
[461] *The Ancient Egyptian Book of Two Ways*, Lesko, 1977:20 spell 1034

seven gates of the underworld and 21 portals blocking the way into the House of Osiris. Vignettes on the seven gates do not show any snakes, although one of the gatekeepers has a snake head. The portals of Osiris are protected by snakes. Their lintels show friezes of *uraei* or one or two undulating snakes. The 6th portal of Osiris is covered with an unknown quantity of snakes.

The Netherworld books describe a place of multiple caverns and areas, relating to the specific hour of the night, all of which are separated by gates or other entrance ways. Snakes guard many of these. They prevent unauthorised access in both directions and ensure that no one can progress to the next hour or section until the appointed time or when they have completed what is expected of them. The right words are essential. *"Whoever knows the enchanting of this serpent will not come near to its flame. Whoever makes an offering to those upon this serpent, his ba-soul; will not be in the fire."*[462] Presumably those of the deceased who do not know the correct spells or forms of address will form the damned, or unfortunates, who prowl the afterworld in the form of the *ba*-souls which appear so threatening to Osiris.

As the name indicates each hour in the *Book of Gates* is separated by clearly defined gates or pylons. All but the 1st gate are crowned with two fire-spitting rearing cobras annotated as *"she light up for Re"*.[463] Each gate has a large snake guardian who stands in front of the gate, the final gate has two. All are named referencing either their role, such as *"Guardian of the Desert"*[464] or their aspects such as *"Bloodsucker"* and *"Whose eyes spew fire"*.[465] All the snake guardians appear to be male which counterbalances the female *uraeus* serpents. Texts on the gates explain that at each gate Sia commands them to *"open your door for Re"*.[466] The door closes after he has passed into the next hour and the inhabitants wail in grief at the passing of the sun. At the final gate they say *"Open is the Earth for Re, sealed is the Earth against Apophis"*.[467] The final gate is depicted with double doors, for extra security. It is vital that no

---

[462] *The Egyptian Book of Gates*, Abt & Hornung, 2014:329
[463] *The Egyptian Book of Gates*, Abt & Hornung, 2014:52
[464] *Sir John Soane's Greatest Treasure*, Taylor, 2017:42
[465] *Sir John Soane's Greatest Treasure*, Taylor, 2017:38
[466] *Sir John Soane's Greatest Treasure*, Taylor, 2017:42
[467] *The Egyptian Book of Gates*, Abt & Hornung, 2014:87

inhabitants of the afterworld can gain access to the world of the living. Isis and Nephthys take the role of the guarding and guiding *uraeus*-serpents who then join the entourage of Ra as he leaves the underworld as the rising sun. *"Then this door is closed. Then the souls of the hidden region lament after this door has slammed."*[468] The reactions of the inhabitants to the passing of the Sun God and the closing of the doors underlines why the doors in the *Book of Gates* are so heavily protected by the snakes – the unfortunate inhabitants of the underworld would follow Ra into the day and the world of the living if they could.

Most of the time Ra, or one of his entourage, orders the snake to open its gate, but even Ra needs to ask permission from some of the snakes who guard the gates and caverns of the afterworld. Perhaps this is because of the importance of the section which is reflected in the higher levels of security and the increasing restriction of access. At these he addresses the snake by name and explains why he needs access. *"O Biter in your Cavern, Terrifying One, the greatest of the Netherworld, bow down, draw back your arm. Behold me; I am entering the land of the beautiful West to attend to Osiris, to greet those who are with him."*[469] It seems strange to ask a snake to withdraw its arm. Some are depicted with human arms but it is more likely that it is a general phrase used when asking permission to pass a guard. In another part of the *Book of Caverns* Ra is welcomed by the snakes who guard the entrance and he tells them *"hide from me while I pass by and show yourself after I have passed by"*.[470] Why should the snakes hide from Ra? Does he not trust them or are they not entitled to be in his presence? Could his passing damage them as they must remain elusive, hidden and barely present?

AREA GUARDIANS

In the *Coffin Texts* it is the paths which are guarded *"Those who are in their baskets are watchful, sitting on their coils...who guard the ways of the Eye of Re-Atum."*[471] Another path in the *Book of Two Ways* is guarded by a snake underneath it. *"That which is beneath it is a spell*

---

[468] *Sir John Soane's Greatest Treasure*, Taylor, 2017:70
[469] *Daily Life of Egyptian Gods*, Meeks & Meeks, 1999:152
[470] *Daily Life of Egyptian Gods*, Meeks & Meeks, 1999:153
[471] *The Ancient Egyptian Coffin Texts Volume I*, Faulkner, 2007:258 spell 334

for passing it. Serpent-face is its name."[472] One of the ramparts in the *Book of Two Ways* is protected by *uraei*. "*The one who is on the high walls...flame...The mouths of their snakes protect it...Broad is the way which does not embrace snakes.*"[473] Faulkner interprets the last phrase to mean that the path the deceased has to follow is the trail of a snake and thus is a narrow one. In the *Amduat* there are also references to snakes who are "*guardians of this path*" or "*belonging to this path*". Paths are sometimes shown as a zig-zag, replicating the movements of a snake.

The *Book of the Dead* has a number of mounds that the deceased have to pass. Spell 149 describes 14 mounds which have to be traversed. The 4th mound is guarded by Thrower of the Two Knives, a 70 cubits (36.6 m) long snake. He lives on *akhs* and the deceased. "*Who is that, the one who goes upon his belly, you whose strength is your twin mountains? Look at me, I am gone forth for sure, your strength with me.*" A snake called Rerek lives in the 7th mound, he is 6 cubits (3m) in length. The deceased aims a spell at this one. "*You are broken. Your poison is weak in me.*"[474] The serpent Nau, the Slippery One, blocks the way at the 10th mound. The deceased request that the Nau-snake clears the path so that they can pass. An accompanying vignette shows a man or God holding two knives. Directly above him is a snake, possibly a cobra. The 12th mound has cobras, referred to as the Destroyers, upon it. The 14th mound has a snake described as being from the Caverns of Elephantine. Vignettes often show the mounds with a number of horizontal snakes with distinct forked tongues. That of the papyrus of Userhat has six snakes. One is the horned viper while the others are shown with a general undulating form. Four are shown together which may represent the four cardinal points. Spell 168 in the *Book of the Dead* lists the various beings in the mounds of Osiris who will permit the deceased to be with the Sun God and prosper in the afterlife. These include "*the snakes*". At the 11th cavern the deities are described as covered, hidden and secret. They include the Python (female) and the Coiled Serpent (again female) and reference to those who are with the Coiled

---

[472] *The Ancient Egyptian Book of Two Ways*, Lesko, 1977:78 spell 1070-1
[473] *The Ancient Egyptian Book of Two Ways*, Lesko, 1977:31 spell 1139
[474] *An Ancient Egyptian Book of the Dead*, O'Rourke, 2016:92 spell 149

Serpent.[475] It is not clear who these two Serpent Goddesses are. In the papyrus of Nespeher'an is a vignette showing a very long snake coiled in a manner suggestive of intestines. *"O Snh-hr within thy chapel, thou whose lair is a thousand cubits long within thy coils, thou whom no god passes by for fear of thee, grant justification to the Osiris...Nesperhan when he passes by thee."*[476]

In the Netherworld Books there are both static and wandering guardians. There are often references to snakes who don't leave their positions. Both have to be eternally vigilant against the enemies of Osiris *"who carry evil throughout the netherworld"*.[477] Originally the enemies of Osiris were Seth and his followers who murdered Osiris and destroyed his corpse. In later periods the term was widened and encompassed everyone who was deemed an enemy of the king or the state. A number of texts mention what Apophis and the other snakes live on, when it isn't the damned or enemies of Ra and Osiris. There is no obvious source of nourishment, such as sunlight or vegetation, in the underworld and the inhabitants need to feed on something. If they had no other source of energy there is a serious risk that they could turn on Osiris, the deceased or the Sun God as prey hence the need to state the alternate food source.

Roaming the caverns of the *Book of Gates* is a fearsome eight-headed snake, with four heads at each end. He has human legs and is called the Walker or Wanderer. A God called the Divider grasps him in the middle. He may be attempting to control it or to keep the two halves apart. Possibly he is able to weaken it by separating its power thus making it slightly more controllable.

This creature is dangerous and foul-smelling and has access to all of the afterworld unlike many of the snakes who are restricted to one area. This suggests that he is a natural inhabitant of the area, rather than one placed there for a specific purpose. Once again we see the Sun God in a hostile environment which is not of his creating and so is outside of his jurisdiction and control.

---

[475] *The Ancient Egyptian Book of the Dead*, Faulkner, 1989:162 spell 168
[476] *The Funerary Papyrus of Nespeher'an (Pap. Skrine, No. 2)*, Blackman, 1918:24-35
[477] *Daily Life of Egyptian Gods*, Meeks & Meeks, 1999:153

8 - WALKER & DIVIDER

The Egyptians had no concept of an all-powerful Creator who made and could control everything. Even the deities were subject to frightening and uncontrollable experiences. The Egyptians lived in a harsh and unpredictable world and didn't attempt to sugar-coat the divine experience. This barely under control serpent has to be restrained from threatening the Sun God and the blessed dead who accompany him. He is followed by a snake called With Heads. He has eight human heads and eight pairs of legs and he too is held in the middle by a God called the Catcher. At the end of the register are two Gods holding nets which represent the magical forces which they use to protect the Sun God from these two hostile snakes.

It isn't easy to distinguish between ordinary, but deadly, snakes and other supernatural snakes. With such an abundance of snakes how is the deceased to distinguish the good from the bad? In many scenes the depictions of Apophis and some of the more benevolent underworld serpents are identical and some of the epithets, such as Great Serpent, are used for both the *ouroboros* and Apophis. Sometimes the snake has an *ankh* close to its face. Does this hint at its benevolence or merely its divinity as deities are frequently shown with an *ankh*? The afterlife is a confusing and dangerous place. Some of the snakes are a major hazard to the deceased and it isn't clear whether they have a protective role as well or are just dangerous inhabitants. The general guardian snakes and the *uraei* who protect Ra and Osiris and the other deities can pose a serious threat to the deceased. Even though the deceased are not an enemy of Ra or Osiris these serpents still need to be treated with extreme caution.

APOPHIS IN THE FUNERARY TEXTS

Apophis is an ever-present hazard in the underworld. It is close to his natural habitat of the *nun* and he is attracted to the vulnerable Sun God whose passing he can detect. He is absent in the *Pyramid Texts* because they do not deal with the night-time journey of the Sun God. In both the *Coffin Texts* and the *Book of Two Ways* the deceased takes on the role of defeating Apophis often through their own knowledge and skill. At other times they assume the persona of a deity who fights Apophis, such as Horus or Seth. Apophis is either driven off, captured or made impotent. "*I am he who knows how to repulse Apophis, the Retreating One.*"[478] There are a number of similar spells including one where the deceased say that they are bringing the corpse of Apophis with them. Other spells allude to the deceased in the Solar Barque so they can "*rescue Re from Apophis every day*"[479] and to the fact that the deceased has the magical and healing ability to heal the deities injured in the fight. "*I am the abomination of Apophis since I know how to spit on wounds.*"[480] The inference is that Apophis has damaged the Solar Eye, rather like Seth damaging the Eye of Horus. It is never said directly as putting this in writing might have the power to fix in in actuality. Some spells refer to the deceased saving the Solar Barque from the storm of Apophis which is probably a reference to dust storms and high winds which were, and still are, a hazard to shipping on the Nile. During a dust storm it is impossible to see to navigate and high winds make it impossible to control the ship. "*May my eyes be open and may he clear my vision, so that I may not fear Apep the Wanderer, and he will never see Maat or Re.*"[481] The reference to clear vision may also allude to this as well as to the healed Solar and Lunar Eye. It could also refer to some special knowledge or ability that the deceased possess so that they can locate Apophis when others fail to spot him. Apophis will never be able to see *maat* as chaos will never be able to comprehend order.

The threat of Apophis increases in the *Book of the Dead*. As

---

[478] *The Wandering of the Soul*, Piankoff, 1974:25 spell 1089
[479] *The Ancient Egyptian Book of Two Ways*, Lesko, 1977:103 spell 1099
[480] *The Ancient Egyptian Book of Two Ways*, Lesko, 1977:118 spell 1113
[481] *The Ancient Egyptian Coffin Texts Volume III*, Faulkner, 2007:89 spell 957

mentioned earlier, Apophis paralyses the crew using his powerful gaze and then swallows 7 cubits (3.2m) of the waters that the Solar Barque is sailing upon and grounds it. This will have been a familiar image to the Egyptians as grounding on sandbanks was a regular and dangerous hazard to shipping when the Nile fell after the inundation. The sandbank is also referenced in a ferryboat spell but here the objective is to ward off Apophis and navigate over the sandbank. The word sandbank can also be interpreted as vertebrae as there is a pun between the two words. "*O you who sail over this vertebra of Apophis.*"[482] Some interpret the word as coil such as in a spell for passing the "*dangerous coil*" of Apophis.[483] In the Middle Kingdom the word *ts* is used for sandbank as well as for knot. The pun connects this with the spine of Apophis as well as the concept of raised land being created. A series of sandbanks strung along a receding river might have suggested the spine of a giant snake. In the papyrus of Khnememhab a vignette shows the Solar Barque sailing over the water above Apophis and four headless bound captives. Apophis is labelled in red "*Apophis 4*". It is assumed that the captives are the four enemies mentioned in a ritual for destroying Apophis which was said at the four principle times of the day; sunrise, midday, sunset and midnight.[484] The decapitated prisoners symbolise the complete overthrow of the enemy. Another popular illustration from the *Book of The Dead* is spell 40, in which the deceased is shown spearing a snake which is trying to swallow a donkey. The name of the snake, not unexpectedly, is Him who Swallowed an Ass.[485] The snake is Apophis in the form of a python, which in real life can swallow a donkey or a person. The donkey is associated with Seth. It is unusual to see the deceased protecting Seth but in some spells they do identify with Seth and his ability to repel Apophis. If the donkey is Seth then it is essential he is saved for only the power of Seth can save the Solar Barque when Apophis attacks. Seth is a dangerous enemy for Apophis, so he will naturally try and destroy the only God capable of defeating him.

---

[482] *An Ancient Egyptian Book of the Dead*, O'Rourke, 2016:151 spell 99
[483] *The Ancient Egyptian Book of the Dead*, Faulkner, 1989:36 spell 7
[484] *The Papyrus of Khnememhab in University College, London*, Shorter, 1937:34-38
[485] *Journey Through the Afterlife: Ancient Egyptian Book of the Dead*, Taylor, 2010:186

9 - APOPHIS SWALLOWING A DONKEY

One spell is for *"repelling a rerek-snake"* which is used against Apophis. Some of the commands are similar to the general anti-snake spells. He is ordered to *"crawl away…be far removed"*. Many deities are invoked; Maat, Mafdet, Selket, Seth, Hathor and Geb. The defeated and bound snake, whose heart has been cut out by Mafdet, is then cursed. *"You shall not become erect, you shall not copulate…O you whom Re hates."* He is threatened with dismemberment; his face cut away, his bones broken and rather oddly for a snake his limbs cut off. In places the spell appears to be turning into threats against the human enemies of the king and Egypt. This particular diatribe ends with *"the earth-god has condemned you"*.[486] Geb was given jurisdiction over snakes but since Apophis is outside of creation this will have little effect. Despite the intensity of the hate directed against him the Egyptians knew in their hearts that the Chaos Serpent could not be permanently defeated.

---

[486] *The Ancient Egyptian Book of the Dead*, Faulkner, 1989:60-61 spell 39

THE THREAT OF APOPHIS IN THE NETHERWORLD TEXTS

Apophis is particularly prominent on the New Kingdom Netherworld texts from the Valley of the Kings. As in the *Book of the Dead* his sand-bank is a hazard for the Solar Barque. In the *Amduat* the sandbank of Apophis is described as being 440 cubits (230m) in length and breadth which he fills with his coils. Whilst this is a very intimidating length for a snake it is still very human in scale, a size people can understand and visualise. In the *Book of Gates* Seth has to force Apophis to disgorge the water he has swallowed so that the Solar Barque can sail off the sandbank.

Apophis attacks when the Sun God is at his most vulnerable at sunset and sunrise at the western and eastern horizons. These are liminal times and places where the boundaries between worlds are at their thinnest. They are also the times when Ra is weak; in old age when the sun sets and as a newborn child at dawn. Ra is at his weakest during his rejuvenation. This is another appropriate time for Apophis to launch his attack as it occurs at the deepest part of the afterworld when the Solar Barque is closest to the *nun*. Ra has to face Apophis even though he tries to make the Solar Barque "*swerve away from Apophis' path*".[487]

The Netherworld Books tell how his glance can halt the Solar Barque and there is frequent reference to his evil eye. Other texts describe him as blind which may describe a desired condition rather than an actual one. In the *Book of Gates* they say "*darkness for your face*" to Apophis – that is blindness.[488] Ptolemaic texts at Edfu refer to the darkness in his eye. It can also refer to him being deprived of light from Ra so he cannot see; hence the advice from Seth to Ra about closing his eye when approaching Apophis. Much of the journey through the afterworld occurs in the dark as Ra has to swallow the Solar Eye to protect it. In later versions Apophis swallows the Eye and is forced to return it.

Apophis is often depicted chained, staked and pierced by spears. This is a particularly popular illustration in the *Book of Gates*. Apophis is often bound not just to restrain him but to

---

[487] *The Valley of the Kings*, Hornung, 1990:104
[488] *The Evil Eye of Apophis*, Borghouts, 1972:114-150

block and disrupt his powers, especially magical ones, through the use of knot magic. The 10th hour depicts the rejuvenation of the Sun God. Apophis appears at the end of a register as a large coiled snake being attacked by a variety of deities. Geb holds a rope to bind him which is also held by three figures wielding spears. 14 deities spin a powerful net of magic using *"that which is in their hands"*. They generate a powerful force field to catch Apophis. Surrounded by this powerful *heka* he loses his strength and becomes disorientated *"so he cannot find himself"*. [489] The next hour shows the defeat of Apophis. He is fettered at the neck. The chain is held first by Serket, then two figures and a very large fist which emerges from the earth. This probably represents the Earth God, either Geb or Aker. The chain continues to bind four other snakes who are either manifestations of Apophis or his helpers. The text reassures Ra that it is safe for him to continue now that Apophis is restrained. In the final hour the infant Sun God is lifted into the sky while the chained Apophis watches helplessly. In the 6th hour of the *Book of Gates* twelve Gods carry a snake called the Devourer, who has twelve human heads emerging out of him. When Ra calls to them the heads emerge but when he passes the heads return into the body of the snake. Do these heads represent beings that have served Apophis so closely that they have merged with him or are they unfortunate ones who have been absorbed by him. The text refers to Apophis as having no eyes, ears or nose. Are these beings acting as his senses? The emerging head depicted at the head of the snake might also hint at the Devourer integrating their mind as well as their senses.

JAILORS AND TORMENTORS

There is less emphasis on punishing enemies in the earlier funerary texts than in the Netherworld ones but the theme is still present. Enemies of Osiris and Horus are often depicted being burnt because this resulted in a complete destruction of the body and so no chance of rebirth. *"The enemies are slaughtered in order to satisfy the Flame-goddess."* The *uraeus* here is called *wnmyt* 'devouring

---

[489] The Valley of the Kings, Hornung, 1990:105

flame' which puns with the word *wnm* 'eat'.[490] Some vignettes for spell 125 of the *Book of the Dead* show a lake of fire with four baboons and eight *uraei*. The lake is designed to purge the deceased of evil deeds. In later periods there is an increasing emphasis on punishment in the afterlife. The enemies of Ra and Osiris as well as the unjustified deceased are subject to eternal damnation in scenes reminiscent of the medieval Christian hell. This may be a consequence of an increasing fear of losing control. When the king and country are weak the fear and the threat of invasion and civil unrest increases. In the *Book of Caverns* are snakes described as the guardians of the Place of Annihilation. They are told to seize the enemies of Osiris. There are also *uraei* who burn these enemies. One hour in the *Book of Caverns* shows two rearing cobras beneath a cauldron containing bound enemies. This is a Place of Annihilation for the enemies of Osiris. The two Cobra-headed Ones, one male the other female, light the fire under the cauldron and burn the prisoners. In the *Book of Gates* there is a Lake of the *Uraeus*-serpents. Ten cobras upon this lake drive away the damned by hissing and throwing fire. Later twelve more enemies of Osiris are bound and face a giant fire-spitting snake. Horus addresses him. "*Open your mouth, expose your jaws, that you may spit fire on the enemies of my father! That you burn their corpses and cook their souls.*" In another part of the *Book of Gates* there is a fire-breathing snake "*who burns millions*".[491]

THE SONGSTRESS SNAKES

Spell 37 in the *Book of the Dead* is for repelling two Songstress-snakes. They are addressed as the Two Companions and Sisters. These epithets are very similar to those used for Isis and Nephthys but it is unlikely that they would be a threat to the deceased.[492] Perhaps they are the double *uraeus* which is both protective and aggressive. One vignette shows the deceased wielding a knife facing two rearing undulating snakes. He says

---

[490] *The Cannibal Hymn*, Eyre, 2002:173
[491] *The Valley of the Kings*, Hornung, 1990:155-156
[492] *Remarks on Beings Called mrwty or mrwrty in the Coffin Texts*, Bianchi, 1987:206-207

that he has divided them by magic.[493] Does this mean he has physically severed them or has turned them against each other so they don't attack him? The vignette for the same spell on a different papyrus shows the deceased using two spears against one undulating snake who is attacking him. In a different spell the deceased states that the Songstress Serpents are with them. The spell goes on to say *"you shall separate head from head when approaching the Milky Way"*.[494] Is this a reference to the previous spell about dividing the two snakes? Or does it mean that the single *uraeus* becomes a pair? Why should the Songstress Snakes accompany the deceased when an earlier spell is used against them? Is it a way of letting the guardians know that the deceased is aware of the problem? Or are they now his allies in the way that the *uraeus* can be both a threat and a protection?

ANTI-SNAKE SPELLS OF THE FUNERARY TEXTS

As in life, any environment where snakes could be encountered needed to be treated with caution. Some of the snakes were just a natural hazard because they are dangerous creatures. They do not have any supernatural powers nor is the danger personal. Others were demons or supernatural serpents who specifically targeted the deceased. Some were only a risk if you were doing something wrong or were trying to access areas that were restricted. Regardless of the reasons, the deceased needed some strong anti-snake spells. In the *Pyramid Texts*, *Coffin Texts* and *Book of the Dead* there are plenty of such spells. Some sensible precautions weren't even magical. In one *Coffin Texts* spell the deceased say that they know where the snake holes are so they can avoid them. In all three texts there are spells for driving off a snake as well as the more specific ones of not being eaten or bitten. Being bitten might be painful or deadly but being eaten was far more frightening because the destruction of the corpse meant that the deceased could not be reborn as all components of a person have to be reassembled after death before rebirth can occur.

---

[493] *The Ancient Egyptian Book of the Dead*, Faulkner, 1989:58 spell 37
[494] *The Egyptian Book of the Dead*, Faulkner & Goelet, 2008: plate 16 spell 58

A number of deities were invoked in spells against snakes. One long spell in the *Coffin Texts* consists of an amalgam of disconnected phrases from other anti-snake spells, mostly from the *Pyramid Texts*. It references a wide range of snakes trying to cover all eventualities. This includes the bull-snake, the viper in the sky, attacker-snake, necklace-snake and creeping-snake and invokes Atum, Ra and his *uraeus*, Mafdet, Selket and Shu. One spell from the *Book of the Dead* for driving off a snake was carved into a block of stone in the 26th dynasty tomb of Wahibre-akhet. It was probably positioned at the entrance alongside a similar one which had a spell to repel an insect. "*O rerek-snake, take yourself off, for Geb protects me.*"[495] *Rrk* is a common word for snake in the funerary texts. Faulkner suggests that this may be linked to the word meaning '*to get out*' producing the elegantly sounding phrase *pr r.k rrk*.[496] The Earth God Geb was given authority over snakes by Ra so he is often invoked in anti-snake spells, such as "*listen to your father Geb*".[497] Some spells merely allude to Geb as in "*O earth, swallow up what went forth from you*".[498] The deceased are traversing the body of Geb when they travel through the underworld so he is a logical God to call upon. The Horus child was a protector against snakes in life and was invoked the afterlife. He is often referred to as trampling on snakes. In what might seem a sensible precaution to us "*Horus has sandals when he treads down the Lord of the Mountain, the Bull of the Cavern*".[499] The poorer people, especially children, will have had to go barefoot so this emphasis on wearing sandals becomes understandable. Not all snakes were as easy to dispose of even for a God. "*I am Horus who escaped from the snt-snake and ran.*"[500] One spell refers to the snake as "*you whom the vulture tramples*"[501] which may refer to the Vulture Goddess Nekhbet. Thoth is called upon in this brief, panicking spell which sounds as if it could also be used against nightmares. "*Get back, snake which attacks in the night...O Thoth, the night-snake, the night-*

---

[495] *Journey Through the Afterlife: Ancient Egyptian Book of the Dead*, Taylor, 2010:194
[496] *The Ancient Egyptian Coffin Texts Volume III*, Faulkner, 2007:8 spell 369
[497] *The Ancient Egyptian Pyramid Texts*, Faulkner, 2007:127 utterance 385
[498] *The Ancient Egyptian Pyramid Texts*, Faulkner, 2007:53 utterance 226
[499] *The Ancient Egyptian Pyramid Texts*, Faulkner, 2007:89 utterance 299
[500] *The Ancient Egyptian Pyramid Texts*, Faulkner, 2007:128 utterance 388
[501] *The Ancient Egyptian Pyramid Texts*, Faulkner, 2007:314 utterance 732

snake."⁵⁰² He also appears in a spell for *"passing a snake"* in the *Book of Two Ways*. *"The protection of Thoth is my protection from you."*⁵⁰³

Many of the funerary spells are simply commands to the snake with no reference to deities, myths or magic. They include orders such as fall down, turn round, crawl away, be far from me, stand still and sink into earth. *"Fall on your faces, serpents down yonder! Let me pass!"*⁵⁰⁴ Avoidance is an easy option. *"Get back, you hidden snake; hide yourself, do not let me see you…do not come to the place where I am…run away."*⁵⁰⁵ One spell utilises the apotropaic attributes of an amulet made from a plant. *"Pass me by, O zekzek-snake. It is the sema-plant that guards this Osiris."*⁵⁰⁶ Some snakes are addressed by name others by a description. *"You zkzk-snake who are in your hole."*⁵⁰⁷ A number of *Pyramid Texts* spells refer to *"you who are in your n3wt-bush"*.⁵⁰⁸ Is this a shrub which was a popular hiding place for snakes or is it a reference to a myth or an apotropaic plant? Another common description of snakes is *"with raised head"* a snake poised ready to strike, perhaps a cobra. The only one which hints at a threat to the speaker is *"O eye of mine do not look at him"*.⁵⁰⁹ This is an allusion to the hypnotic threat from the snake's evil eye. The spell is against the *hki*-snake and the *hkrt*-snake which may have been thought to poses such hypnotic powers. In any case, avoiding looking at a snake would be a wise precaution in case it was a spitting cobra. A lot of the spells are short and to the point. They read like incantations people would have used in everyday life. A simple, harsh commandment to a snake to go away. *"Fall, O serpent which came forth from the earth! Fall, O flame which came forth from the Abyss! Fall down, crawl away!"*⁵¹⁰ Others are more complex and sound more like a magic spell referencing deities and phrases such as *"the sky is enchanted, the earth is enchanted"*.⁵¹¹

---

502 *The Ancient Egyptian Pyramid Texts*, Faulkner, 2007:314 utterance 733
503 *The Ancient Egyptian Book of Two Ways*, Lesko, 1977:78 spell 1181
504 *The Wandering of the Soul*, Piankoff, 1974:14 spell 1034
505 *The Ancient Egyptian Pyramid Texts*, Faulkner, 2007:88 utterance 293
506 *An Ancient Egyptian Book of the Dead*, O'Rourke, 2016:127 spell 35
507 *The Ancient Egyptian Pyramid Texts*, Faulkner, 2007:84 utterance 276
508 *The Ancient Egyptian Pyramid Texts*, Faulkner, 2007:56 utterance 234
509 *The Ancient Egyptian Pyramid Texts*, Faulkner, 2007:87 utterance 288
510 *The Ancient Egyptian Pyramid Texts*, Faulkner, 2007:55 utterance 233
511 *The Ancient Egyptian Pyramid Texts*, Faulkner, 2007:55 utterance 230

The anti-snake spells so common in the other funerary texts are not found in the Netherworld texts because the emphasis is on the journey of the Sun God through the afterlife rather than that of the deceased who journey alongside the Sun God. The Netherworld is still teeming with snakes though. A number of scenes in the various books show three horizontal snakes which suggests the pervading presence of these creatures. Three was used to show plurality. Many of the snakes have wings or legs and some have suggested that this emphasises their ease of movement in this their natural habitat. In the 5th hour of the *Amduat* is the desert land of Sokar. Like the deserts of Egypt it was infested with snakes.

CONNECTING THE WORLDS

The snake is a good creature to symbolise a physical connection between the words. This is especially significant when linking this world with the afterworld given the way in which snakes can appear and disappear in an instant from the sand and tiny cracks in rocks. The 5th hour of the *Amduat* includes a serpent who is shown with a baboon's head emerging from his head. It is He with the Unapproachable Head who *"transmits the concerns of the living"* to the Sun God.[512] Like the other underworld snakes we are told that he lives on the voices of the Gods. Both the communication role and the presence of the baboon head suggests the God Thoth. He was the messenger of the Sun God as well as being the inventor of speech and writing. He was depicted as a baboon in lunar and scribal contexts. Texts at Dendera refer to him having the form of a serpent. This is an obvious form for him to assume as a secret communicator with the afterworld and the Sun God. The snake can also be seen as metaphor for unconscious or spiritual communication with the divine and the other worlds. The Sun God constantly travels between the two worlds of the living and the dead. For him this is also a journey of transformation from birth to age and back to youth again paralleled in symbolism by the *ouroboros*. Epithets such as *"the old one who becomes young"* are commonly applied to the

---

[512] *The Egyptian Amduat*, Abt & Hornung, 2007:167

Sun God.[513] The wandering of the deities and the deceased through the dangers of the underworld was for one purpose only – that of rebirth. Snakes play a critical role in these ultimate mysteries.

---

[513] *Aspects of rnpy in Ancient Egyptian Texts*, Shoaib, 2012:191-203

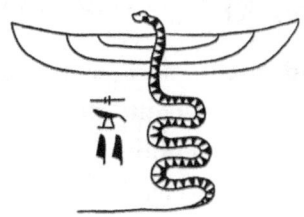

CHAPTER 12

Serpent Mysteries

"I am the serpent Sata whose years are many. I die and I am born again each day. I am the serpent Sata which dwelleth in the uttermost parts of the earth. I die, and I am born again, and I renew myself, and I grow young each day."[514]

INTRODUCTION

Much that appeared mysterious in nature to the Ancient Egyptians was only because they lacked the necessary geographical and scientific knowledge. Natural and cosmic cycles such as the inundation, the daily solar cycle and the passing of time needed to be explained. Some things remain constantly beyond our understanding, what happens after death being the key one. Linked to this are the more spiritual questions. What happens when I die and how can I make the experience and outcome better? How can I become closer to a particular God or Goddess? How can my mind and soul survive the hardships of this life and how do I improve my chances in this life and the afterlife? The mysteries also refer to religious teachings and ceremonies which were disclosed to a select group of initiates to provide answers and insights into such questions.

---

[514] *The Ancient Egyptian Book of the Dead*, Budge & Wilson, 2016:142

THE ROLE OF SNAKES IN THE MYSTERIES

The Netherworld texts place a lot of emphasis on the mysteries. They are less dominant, although still present, in the other funerary texts. Throughout the journey through the afterworld snakes initiate and enable rebirth as well as protecting those undergoing the process. Snakes are not the only deities and supernatural beings involved in the afterlife journey. There are multiple processes and players. I have focused on the role of snakes and picked out dominant themes relating to them. Each individual text has to be studied as a whole to gain an overall appreciation of the journey and the mysteries.

For the Egyptians, the first step was the almost mechanical process of reassembling the component parts of the deceased and enabling them to breathe again. Nehebkau is closely involved in this process. Secondly there is rebirth as a form of escape from the earth, or the physical plane, just as childbirth releases the baby from the confines of the womb. Spells referred to as ascension spells relate to this process. Finally there is the alchemical process of dissolving the old and reforming the deceased into a rejuvenated being of light. In the 6th hour of the *Amduat* there is a snake whose name, Swallower of Forms, describes such a process. Mehen's main role is to be found here. Snakes also perform the critical task of guarding the mysteries of rebirth and time and those undergoing them. *"You guard so that my manifestation can change, you fetter so that my magic power can manifest."*[515]

THE SECRET PATHS OF MEHEN

The role of Mehen is similar in both the funerary and Netherworld texts. This section concentrates mainly on the *Coffin Texts* where he is prominent. As mentioned previously, Mehen is present in the *Pyramid Texts* although he is not mentioned by name. As the solar cults increased in importance after the Old Kingdom so did the nature and role of Mehen. It is possible that Mehen became the focus of the secret knowledge in the 1st Intermediate Period which then emerged as the mysteries of

---

[515] *The Egyptian Book of Gates*, Abt & Hornung, 2014:162

Mehen referred to in the *Coffin Texts*. If the deceased could become as one with Mehen, or at least follow his teachings, then they could progress towards rebirth as they work to protect the Sun God and defeat his enemies. Two *Coffin Texts* spells refer to the mysteries of Mehen. In one the deceased take the role of the guards of those who are trying to illegally obtain the secrets of Mehen. Piccione suggests that these were a system of secret and dramatic rituals used to reveal hidden aspects of various deities where the initiate took on the role of Mehen.[516]

More detailed information on the mysteries seems to be contained in *Coffin Texts* spells 758-760 which describe the paths of Mehen which the deceased, or initiate, must travel if they wish to approach the throne of Ra. The paths are described in detail and as befits the paths of a serpent they are concentric. The spell states that four of these are of fire and they are separated by four dark paths. One vignette of this spell shows four red paths alternating with five black ones. The spells state that the fiery roads protect the sides of Mehen's barque and the sides of his barque protect the roads. The roads of Mehen are also constantly twisting and turning like the serpent they are for Mehen is both the paths and the barque which sails upon them. *"The gates are confused, the bow of the bark of the Coiled One has swung round."*[517] At the centre of the paths sits Ra on his throne of Millions of Years. Mehen will circumnavigate these paths for millions of years – for as long as lasts the sun. Ra's crown is similar in style to the Atef crown but it is made of snakes. The brim of the crown is formed by a double-headed snake which could be Mehen and may allude to his role in the reconciliation of Horus and Seth discussed below. To enter upon these paths and approach the Sun God at their centre the deceased must first show that they have the correct knowledge, as to enter unprepared is a quick way to a second and final death. *"As for him who knows the names of those paths of his, it is he who will go into the Coiled One. As for him who knows this spell, he will never perish."*[518] The deceased are able to name and describe the paths, give their measurements and aspects including

---

[516] Mehen, Mysteries, and Resurrection from the Coiled Serpent, Piccione, 1990:43-52
[517] The Ancient Egyptian Coffin Texts Volume II, Faulkner, 2007:290 spell 758
[518] The Ancient Egyptian Coffin Texts Volume II, Faulkner, 2007:293 spell 760

the dark paths used by the Gods Hu and Sia. Hu personifies divine utterance and the authority of command. The deceased state they are aware of the circuit of Ra, the gates and the enemies they will encounter. There is also reference to a secret path used each day by the She-cat.[519] This is probably Bastet. As one of the Eye Goddesses she will be in close proximity to the Sun God as well as having the characteristically feline desire to wander elsewhere.

Most importantly the deceased know about the secret path *"which is the vertex of Re"*.[520] Vertex can mean the crown or brow which alludes to the *uraeus*. It can also mean the summit or top so could be read as the head of Mehen – after following the circuits of Mehen the deceased reach the end of the trail and the head of Mehen which leads them to the Sun God at the centre. In addition the spell states that the deceased know where the four knots belonging to the celestial cattle are hidden. The alternate translation of knot is vertebrae which may be more appropriate in the context of the celestial cattle. The cervical vertebrae in particular are a significant component of the spine. They are a vulnerable part as this is where decapitation occurs but they are also nodes of power. It is here that the head, which provides the intellect and interprets the senses, is connected to the body. It has been suggested that the spell also alludes to the severed heads of sacrificial bulls. Cattle were of immense cultural and religious importance to the Egyptians from the Pre-dynastic. The spells also reference the backbone being loosened. A flexible spine is connected with movement and life compared to the rigid or disarticulated one of a dead creature.

The main purpose for these spells is to allow the deceased, or initiate, to approach the Sun God and not be put off, turned away or destroyed by the dangers of the approach. Trying to approach the solar deities is not to be taken lightly. It is not that they don't wish to be disturbed but, like the sun, it is in their nature to give off energy which is dangerous to unprotected humans. As this series of spells discloses secret information their inclusion in funerary contexts may have been restricted to those who had

---

[519] *The Ancient Egyptian Coffin Texts Volume II*, Faulkner, 2007:291 spell 759
[520] *The Ancient Egyptian Coffin Texts Volume II*, Faulkner, 2007:291 spell 759

received the necessary initiation. The Mehen mysteries also appear to dissolve gender perception. Here the traditional male and female roles are not always adhered to during rebirth. Enclosure within the coils of Mehen is like being in the womb yet he is male. In the caverns of the 8th hour of the *Amduat* a woman, called the Maiden, holds onto a rearing, coiled Mehen serpent. Next to them are two hieroglyphs for clothing, over the second one are three arrows of Ra, symbols of sunlight. The close connection between the serpent and the Goddess (or the feminine) is seen throughout Egyptian and other cultures. Perhaps female energy is needed to combine with that of Mehen to enable the process of rebirth and rejuvenation. This image of the Maiden holding onto Mehen may depict the earthbound *ka* and male energy combining with the free-flying *ba* and solar-stellar female energy. Or it may hint at a female component within Mehen or his androgyny. In this text Mehen is also referred to as World Encircler who, as Life of the Gods in the 12th hour, gives birth to the Sun God – a feminine role paralleling that of the Sky Goddess Nut.

THE GAME OF MEHEN

Allusion is frequently made to the game of *mehen* in the funerary texts. This game of the coiled serpent was played throughout Egypt in the Pre-dynastic and Old Kingdom. It is the oldest game in Egypt that we have archaeological evidence for. The board is very similar to the paths of Mehen described in the *Coffin Texts*. It is in the form of a spiral body of a snake, usually with the head and tail of a snake, the head being at the centre. A goose head is sometimes carved at the end of the snake's tail alluding either to the primeval Creator Goose or to the Earth God Geb who was also associated with geese. The boards were made of a variety of materials; stone, ivory and faience ones have been found. Traces of paint remain on some examples. The snake's body is divided into segments. Surprisingly, given both the Egyptian's love of precision and the nature of games, the boards vary in much more than size and material. The snake can coil clockwise or anticlockwise and the number of coils in the spiral varies from two to seven. In our culture clockwise and anticlockwise have symbolic significance but perhaps they weren't important to the Egyptians, at least as far as the game was concerned. Or perhaps the game was played differently. We will never know. Of the surviving boards the split is roughly equal. The number of segments which form the playing spaces varies from 29 to 400.[521]

The game was played with counters, usually in the form of lions. Such pieces have been found in graves of the Pre-dynastic through to the 2nd dynasty, a complete set has never been found. Ivory lion and lioness pieces were found at Abu Rawash. A 1st dynasty tomb at Abydos yielded four lion pieces, their bases had been worn smooth suggesting that they were used in daily life by the owner. Throwing sticks have been found but it is not clear if these were used for *mehen*, *senet* or another game. The only complete *mehen* sets are those shown on tomb wall paintings. The earliest one dates to the 3rd dynasty where it is shown with *senet* boards and gaming pieces. One shows 36 marbles, grouped by colour into six sets of six, and six white crouching lion gaming pieces. One painting from the 5th dynasty tomb of a vizier from Saqqara shows four people around the board but it is not possible to tell if all four are playing or if two are observers. It has been suggested that it was a game for two to six players. We do not know the rules. Some have suggested it was a hunting type game which required strategy to win rather than random chance. The gaming pieces were probably moved in a spiral in the squares along the snake's body. Marbles were used on the board and in the grooves of the spiral. Wear to the paint on some of the boards show that marbles were regularly rolled in the grooves. A very small, 10cm in diameter, *mehen* board was found in a Naqada II tomb. It is too small to be of practical use and was either a votive offering or a grave good for use in the afterlife. Other small boards from the same Period have a projecting tab with a hole for a cord which suggests that they were worn as amulets.[522] In some spells the name of Mehen is written with the determinative for the game which gives a link between the game and its religious context. In the *Pyramid Texts* the king is said to

---

[521] *Ancient Egyptians at Play: Board Games Across Borders*, Crist, 2016:15
[522] *Ancient Egypt and Nubia*, Whitehouse, 2009:15

come from the game of *mehen* during his ascension. "*Who has come forth from the mhn-board? When he came around, N came forth from his fiery breath. Just as N has travelled to the Two Skies so N has returned to the Two Lands.*"⁵²³ As the king passes along the coils of the board it reflects his resurrection and ascension. A successful conclusion to the game symbolises escape from Mehen. The *Pyramid Texts* of Queen Neith refer to her resting in the coils of the Snake God Nebakhet, Lord of the Horizon, and compares it to residing in the *mehen* board.⁵²⁴ Nebakhet appears to have been the forerunner of Mehen. "*Just as N resides in your coils, so N sits in your mhn-board.*"⁵²⁵

Texts describe circular travel and exiting on the snake's breath. Some have interpreted this as an ordeal or legal trial for the deceased while others suggest that 'escaping' from the snake is part of the rebirth process. Coming forth from the board is the same as being reborn as Mehen is both the game and the process of rebirth. Spell 172 in the *Book of the Dead* aligns various parts of the body to deities. The teeth are referred to as the "*heads of Mehen where the Two Lords played*". Teeth alludes to the ivory gaming pieces. The Two Lords are Horus and Seth. Many of the boards have a bird's head at the snake's tail, hence the heads of Mehen. The deceased king is told to move his pieces around the *mehen*-board for the same reason. "*Take for yourself your white ivory pieces from the mhn-board. Go around them as an arrow in this name of Arrow.*"⁵²⁶ This also occurs in the Book of Two Ways. "*Who will travel around the mhn-board, whose rank is great, whom Thoth will judge in the early morning?*"⁵²⁷

Playing certain board games could be a way of connecting this world with the afterworld. They are often depicted being played on the tomb walls in the Old Kingdom as part of the rites of Hathor which were celebrated to honour the deceased. Did the

---

[523] *Mehen, Mysteries, and Resurrection from the Coiled Serpent*, Piccione, 1990:43-52
[524] *The Ancient Egyptian Game of the Serpent*, Kendall, 2007:41
[525] *Mehen, Mysteries, and Resurrection from the Coiled Serpent*, Piccione, 1990:43-52
[526] *Mehen, Mysteries, and Resurrection from the Coiled Serpent*, Piccione, 1990:43-52
[527] *Mehen, Mysteries, and Resurrection from the Coiled Serpent*, Piccione, 1990:43-52

game of *mehen* inspire the beliefs around the paths of Mehen in the Middle Kingdom or did the game originate in a preceding theology? We can only speculate. The journey though the *mehen* board is similar to the snake in the 12th hour of the *Amduat* where the Solar Barque and the deceased enter though the tail of Life of the Gods, who is an aspect of Mehen, and exit rejuvenated from his mouth. The game of *mehen* was an allegory of the struggles and dangers awaiting the deceased as they strived to overcome such perils and be reborn. Journeying along the *mehen* board replicates travelling through Mehen, or along the coils of his body, from his tail to his head as part of a process of rebirth or initiation. The game commenced at the moment of death when the deceased arrived at the tail of the serpent. The winner was presumably the one who got to the snake's head first so that they could be reborn. Coming second meant that you were ensnared by Mehen because you didn't know the correct spell or course of action. Piccione concludes that the game was used as an expression of the transformation that took place leading to rebirth. It may also have been used as a teaching aid for initiates as well as being played on a more mundane level in everyday life. The journey is frequently used as a metaphor for spiritual and psychological transformation as well.

The game of *mehen* disappears at the end of the 1st Intermediate Period and Mehen begins to play a more prominent role in the *Coffin Texts* at this time. This is unlikely to be a coincidence or merely that the game had fallen out of fashion. It may have been prohibited or avoided because of its increasingly religious connotations. In the 26th dynasty, after nearly 2,000 years, the game was once again depicted in tomb paintings. There is no evidence that it was played again, because no-one would know the rules, it was probably depicted because there was an interest in art from the Old Kingdom and many of its styles were used in the art of the period. One suggestion for the game's demise is that it was forbidden because incising the squares on the snake's body was tantamount to killing Mehen. Apophis is frequently shown being cut into pieces to destroy his body. This was dangerous magic for the uninitiated to play about with. Kendal believes that the aspects of the game which made it popular might have been the very aspects that made it dangerous in the view of the high priests of Ra. He suggests that it was actually forbidden by the 11th or 12th dynasty. As the mysteries of Mehen were developed there might have been a risk that they could be inadvertently exposed by ordinary people playing and talking about the game. By the New Kingdom Mehen was the patron God of the game of *senet*. This was played on a grid of thirty squares, some of which were marked as good or bad fortune. The objective was to move pieces around the 'S' shaped track. The game often appears in tomb decorations. In depictions of Mehen during this Period he is usually shown as an 'S' shape draped over Ra rather than coiled around him.

REASSEMBLY OF THE DECEASED

As mentioned earlier, the human body consists of a number of components. At death these all disperse and before a person can be reborn, or even start their journey through the afterlife, they all have to be reassembled. One essential funerary ritual was the *Opening of the Mouth* ceremony where the priest would ritually open the mouth of the mummy allowing the deceased to breathe again in the afterlife. In one vignette of this scene in the *Book of the Dead* the adze used to open the mouth has the head of a snake enhancing the magical effectiveness of the ritual. Another critical part of the process of rebirth was reassembling all the component parts of the body. A number of deities were involved with this. "*Set my head in place for me, Nehebkau.*"[528] The Egyptians believed that the spine had magical as well as physical functions in both life and the afterlife. "*Atum establishes for me my head, Nehebkau completes and establishes my vertebrae.*"[529]

Seven was considered a very effective magical number. In the *Coffin Texts* there is reference to the seven creative utterances which brought the world into existence. A transformation spell from the *Book of the Dead* for becoming a phoenix says "*I am the essence of every god, I am the seventh of those seven uraei who came into being*

---

[528] *An Ancient Egyptian Book of the Dead*, O'Rourke, 2016:90 spell 149
[529] *The God Nehebkau*, Shorter, 1935:41-48

in the west".530 The position as the seventh of the seven would have also been powerful through utilising the magic of the number twice. The fact that there are seven neck vertebrae will have added to the importance of this number. One spell in the *Pyramid Texts* states that *"the king is a serpent…who swallowed his seven uraei so that they might become his seven neck-vertebrae"*.531 In the *Pyramid Texts* of Unas there are seven vertical marks under the basket of *uraei* in reference to this spell.532 A number of *Coffin Texts* spells to become Nehebkau (84-86 and 374) reference the swallowing of seven *uraei*. These can be aligned with the seven magical knots of protection. Each vertebra feels like a knot. The magical knot acts as a point where *heka* can form a junction connecting the human and divine worlds. Likewise knots, or vertebrae, in the body provide a point where streams of life energy meet. The common word for knot was *ts* and it is often used in puns with vertebrae and specifically the seven cervical vertebrae. It also puns with words for creating and building. Knots are used to tie things together and hold them in place, just as the vertebrae hold and create the spinal column and with it life. There are many references in the funerary texts to knotting the body back together. Transforming a *uraeus* into a vertebrae involves the absorption of divine solar energy. This invigorating energy, along with the *ka* energy given by Nehebkau, can then move through the snakelike spine directly to the critical neck vertebrae. One long spell, entitled *Protection through Ptah*, makes reference to Nehebkau and also the spine. *"My spine is enduring"* it states then goes on to describe how it is the White Crown *"which twists the n't-snake into my back"*.533 Faulkner's interpretation is that the snake is twisted like a rope which then becomes the deceased's spinal cord.

Another spell refers to the seven *uraei* who give power to the deceased. This can mean both energy and positions of power and status. Nehebkau plays a lesser role in the *Pyramid Texts* but he becomes important in the *Coffin Texts* where he grants *"souls,*

---

530 *The Ancient Egyptian Book of the Dead*, Faulkner, 1989:80 spell 83
531 *The Ancient Egyptian Pyramid Texts*, Faulkner, 2007:100 utterance 318
532 *The Cobra Goddesses of Ancient Egypt*, Johnson, 1990:155
533 *The Ancient Egyptian Coffin Texts Volume II*, Faulkner, 2007:221-222 spell 647

*crownings, doubles and beginnings".*⁵³⁴ He gives the deceased the spiritual energy they need and their status and so starts them on the journey to rebirth. One spell says that he gives power to those who are in their caverns, namely the deceased. They rely on his revitalising *ka*-energy. In one *Coffin Texts* spell Nehebkau is described as taking away powers which suggests that the deceased's *ka* or status could be removed if they were deemed unworthy. The reference to his taking away powers may be a warning. He can remove the vital energy of the unworthy deceased or the enemies of Osiris and Ra. It could also refer to him taking the polluted and decaying energy of the deceased so that it can be replaced with new invigorated energy. Part of a complex scene from texts in the sarcophagus hall of Rameses VI (20th dynasty) shows a mummified God wearing the sun disc. A rearing cobra sits on either side. One is called He Who Assembles Forms which sounds similar to Nehebkau who assembles the *ka*. It is also a rare depiction of a Cobra God, assuming he is a God rather than another supernatural being. The other cobra is called Rich of Forms who has a similar role in the reassembly and regeneration processes. One hymn to Ra at dawn refers to his *uraei* providing his *ka*-energy. "*O hail to these your seven uraeus snakes, who provide your ka-powers.*"⁵³⁵

ESCAPING THE GRASP OF EARTH

The main purpose of the *Pyramid Texts* was to enable the king to be reborn as a star, hence a number of spells dealing with his ascension into the heavens. His ascension can be by a number of means including becoming a snake. Using a ladder was a common means of ascension. The markings formed by the scales on the central portion of the cobra's hood form a series of stacked rectangles and so can appear like a ladder. This suggested a direct link between cobras and the ascension process. One spell to invoke a ladder states "*a serpent is bound for the sky...I ascend to the sky upon the ladder of the god, for I appear as the uraeus which is on the vertex of Seth*".⁵³⁶ During the Old Kingdom Seth wasn't always the villain

---

534 *The Ancient Egyptian Coffin Texts Volume II*, Faulkner, 2007:222 spell 647
535 *Hathor's Alchemy*, Roberts, 2019:20
536 *The Ancient Egyptian Pyramid Texts*, Faulkner, 2007:166 utterance 478

he became in later periods and with Horus helps the deceased ascend to heaven.

Having gone through the necessary metamorphosis, protected by Mehen, the king is reborn and leaves his protective though restrictive embrace. "*I am this one who escaped from the coiled serpent.*" [537] Ascension spells relating to snakes and *uraei* are still common in the *Coffin Texts* but many refer to both descent and ascension, such as the Two Gods who "*as snakes they go down to the earth, and I will go down on their coils; as falcons they ascend to the sky, and I will ascend on their wings*".[538] The Two Gods may be Seth and Horus, falcons allude to Horus. The pair have a close connection to Mehen and to ascension, and are often referred to as the Two Lords. "*If you go up to the sky as snakes, I will go up on your coils; if you go up to the sky as uraei, I will go up on the tops of your heads.*"[539] The descent and ascension may allude to the setting and rising sun whose journey the deceased can participate in. Or it may refer to the communication and exchange of energy between the earth and the heavens. The *Pyramid Texts* have a strong stellar component and you can almost feel the deceased ascend to the stars through the energy of the snake. "*I have ascended in a blast of fire.*"[540] After the Middle Kingdom the theology becomes increasingly earthbound. What was the reason for this change? The *Pyramid Texts* were designed for the king who was semi-divine anyway compared to his mortal, earthbound subjects. But the Sun God faces the same underground journey as the deceased in later funerary texts so the change was probably due to the way the religious culture developed.

EMERGENCE IN THE *BOOK OF EARTH*

The birth of the Sun God as Khepri, and the rising of the sun at dawn, can be viewed as an escape from the earth and the underworld. In the *Book of Earth* (also referred to as the *Creation of the Sun Disc*) a dominant feature is the birth of the sun disc and the effects of sunlight on those in the underworld. The motif

---

[537] *The Ancient Egyptian Pyramid Texts*, Faulkner, 2007:107 utterance 332
[538] *The Ancient Egyptian Coffin Texts Volume I*, Faulkner, 2007:144 spell 167
[539] *The Ancient Egyptian Coffin Texts Volume I*, Faulkner, 2007:150 spell 175
[540] *The Ancient Egyptian Pyramid Texts*, Faulkner, 2007:107 utterance 332

used to depict this emergence is often a pair of arms emerging from the earth or a Goddess who holds the sun disc. Both are accompanied by standing or emerging snakes. A large standing Goddess, the Mysterious One, holds a sun disc and a ram-headed bird in her uplifted hands. Two snakes with human heads and arms rear up to her head to worship the images she is holding. A smaller snake and crocodile stand at her feet. A similar concept is seen on the second shrine of Tutankhamun where large arms emerge from the earth each holding a solar disc and ram-headed bird and accompanied by emerging cows, Goddesses and snakes. The standing snakes emphasise the uplifting regenerative energy as well as depicting movement.

One scene, from the tomb of Rameses VI, has a different form. The sun disc is flanked by two *uraei*, Devourer and Flaming One. From the top of the disc a Hathor Head emerges. (On a Hathor Head the Goddess is shown facing forwards with cow's ears. Her head is normally depicted in this way when it is part of an object such as the capitol of a pillar.) Balancing in a V-shape on the disc is a long snake and the Hathor Head appears to emerge from him. Two Gods hold on to the snake as if pulling him out of the disc. Unfortunately there is no accompanying text other than to name the *uraei*. As a Solar Goddess Hathor can be viewed as the Eye of the Sun, the sun disc, the *uraeus* or the Female Sun. Does this show Hathor as the Daughter of Ra emerging from the disc or does her presence indicate that the Female Sun is being depicted? The snake could be Mehen birthing Hathor and the Gods are assisting the process. Or he could be Apophis who is being restrained so that Hathor can emerge and rise. Vignettes from a later section of the book show a U shaped snake labelled as Apophis with a scarab and *ba*-bird above him. "*Apep foremost of his cavern – Khepri emerges from his coils.*"[541] Another depiction of this process shows both the regeneration of the mummies and the birth of the sun. Six mummies stand beneath the arched coils of two long snakes who appear to represent the regenerative powers of Mehen. Abutting this scene are two pairs of emerging arms cradling the sun disc and two ram-headed Gods. Again there is no accompanying text.

---

[541] *The Ancient Egyptian Netherworld Books*, Darnell & Darnell, 2018:481

DEPICTING REBIRTH AND TIME IN THE AMDUAT

An important part of the mysteries in this text is the uniting of the *ba* of the Sun God with either his corpse or that of Osiris. The 5th hour shows the secret cavern of Sokar. He is a hawk-headed underworld God who is a manifestation of Osiris. His cavern is described as invisible and imperceptible. Sokar stands in the cavern and grasps the wings of a snake who is described as a God with multi-coloured wings. He is shown with three heads with a bearded human head at his tail and is understood to be a form of the Sun God. The three snake heads may indicate his many aspects, three representing plurality, or his three-fold aspect of the Sun God. The bearded human head may emphasise his divinity. The multi-coloured wings allude to his divine light splitting into its component parts and hints at the new light and life that will be generated in the forthcoming hours. This metamorphosis into a snake may be a phase of the regeneration process. The Sun God may have to revert to his original serpent form before he can be reborn in his form of Khepri the Rising Sun.

In the 6th hour the corpse of the Sun God is shown lying down, but not mummiform, at his head is a scarab (representing Khepri) hinting at what is to come. The encircling Mehen is shown with five heads and is described as Many-Faced. One head bites his tail. Elsewhere the three-fold burial of the Sun God (representing his morning, noon and evening aspects) is protected by three fire-spitting snakes. Protection is essential here. The 7th hour is the deepest part of the underworld, close to the regenerative waters of the *nun*. Here the *ba* and the corpse unite and the first spark of new life is kindled. The process is shown underway in the following hour as Osiris sits enthroned with Mehen draped protectively over him. The Sun God sits enthroned on the coils of a snake who is called He who Puts Together. In the 11th hour the Sun God is referred to as Atum. Like Sokar in the 5th hour he grasps the wings of a snake. Here the snake has only one head but walks on two pairs of human legs. He is called the Seer – alluding to what is to come in the next hour. The walking snake shows the progression of the rebirth process.

The Time Serpent appears in the 11th hour of the *Amduat* depicting the birth of the hours. A Goddess called Time squats on the back of a leaping snake called He Who Takes Away the Hours. Around them are ten (sometimes eleven) stars representing the hours which have already elapsed. As in 4th hour of the *Book of Gates* the Time Serpents births and swallows each hour. This scene is drawn with red ink indicating its importance. Timing is critical to the alchemical process and the sun must rise at its appointed time. The huge coiled snake World Encircler appears in the 11th hour where twelve Gods carry him on their heads in front of the solar barque. The text refers to him as the Mehen-Serpent who is being carried to the eastern gate of the horizon in preparation for sunrise. Abt and Hornung suggest that he has to be carried until the 12th hour because when he touches the ground he will enter reality, the material world. The process of rejuvenation and rebirth cannot be allowed to occur prematurely. In the 12th hour, just before the rebirth of the Sun God and sunrise, the reversal of time is depicted. Now referred to as Life of the Gods the serpent lies on the ground in front of the Solar Barque which will be towed through his body. According to one source Life of the Gods is 1,300 cubits long (680m).[542] The symbolism of this number is not known. The text also refers to him as the *"Ka-energy of him who makes the gods live"*.[543] The text explains that the Sun God proceeds *"in the spine of this mysterious image...he enters its tail, and he comes out from its mouth, born in his manifestation of Khepri"*.[544] The Gods who tow the barque are given names reflecting their age, such as the Elder and the Grey-haired. They enter as elderly Gods but come out rejuvenated, like Ra. Entering the Serpent of Time through the tail depicts the reversal of time which is needed for rejuvenation. Regeneration isn't possible in our unidirectional time-driven world. In this world aging and decay are inevitable and can only be postponed for so long. As regeneration or rebirth reverses the effects of time then it must occur outside of time. The time controlling serpent allows this to happen. Throughout the Netherworld texts there are references to what the deity or creature lives on. Life of the Gods

---

[542] *The Ancient Egyptian Book of Thoth*, Jaznow & Zauzich, 2005:249
[543] *The Egyptian Amduat*, Abt & Hornung, 2007:370
[544] *The Egyptian Amduat*, Abt & Hornung, 2007:367

lives on the voices of the Venerated Ones as they progress through his body. He may also draw on the temporal energy released during the reversal of time.

MYSTERIES IN THE *BOOK OF GATES*

In the 1st hour the Sun God is depicted as a scarab inside the sun disc rather than in his usual ram-headed form. Safely enclosed by Mehen, this foretells of what is to come when Khepri is reborn with the rising sun. The Egyptians believed that depicting an image anchored the magic in reality. The opening scene reminds us that despite the perils to come the sun will rise again. The powerful regenerative force of the snake is shown in a different way in the 6th hour of the *Book of Gates*. It is represented by the snake-shaped bier, Nehep, on which the mummies of the followers of Osiris lie. When the Sun God passes his energy reacts with the serpent energy of Nehep to animate the mummies. The basic formulae is: snake energy + solar energy = life. It also alludes to the relationship between Atum and Nehebkau and the earth-bound *ka* reuniting with the free-flying *ba*.

One unusual depiction of the process of rebirth is found in the 10th hour. Khepri is normally depicted as a scarab but here he takes the form of the Khepri Serpent – an interim stage in his regeneration. It is a composite image. A falcon wearing the Double Crown of Egypt emerges from the central coil of a double-headed *uraeus* serpent. This *uraeus* serpent sits upon a double-headed snake as if on a sledge or barque. This snake has a pair of human legs at each end. The depiction of the Khepri Serpent on the tomb of Queen Tawseret (19th dynasty) is different. The second snake has been replaced by two individual snakes, one at either side of the *uraeus* serpent, each with a pair of human legs. This may be a personal preference by either the artist or the Queen. The human legs may indicate his ability to move around at will. The text says that when Horus of the Netherworld emerges from the Khepri Serpent then the other forms come out of his coils. Horus is involved in the process of rebirth because as the posthumously conceived son of Osiris he can be regarded as Osiris reborn as his own son. The *uraeus* serpent then reunites with Ra giving the Sun God back his guiding and protective *uraei* and reuniting him with his Solar Eye and Daughter. Horus then merges back into the Khepri Serpent. As he is Horus of the Netherworld he will remain in the earth. Similarly, the Khepri Serpent belongs to the earth as he is part of the regenerative process. It is Khepri the Scarab who will leave the underworld as the rising sun.

In the 11th hour is a double bow with three *uraeus* serpents on each side. In the centre is a two-headed God with the head of Horus and Seth. The texts say that this is Mehen of the *Uraeus-*serpents and that the God is His Two Faces. It refers to Mehen carrying His Two Faces as part of Ra's mystery. The reconciled Gods are now one God with a double aspect. In this form the positive and useful aspects of both Gods can be used effectively against Apophis rather than squandering time and energy fighting each other rather than the real enemy. Their opposing characters and energies represent the duality which is essential for rebirth and rejuvenation. The energy flowing between them is like electricity flowing between two terminals changing the substance it flows through. As mentioned before Isis refuses to kill Seth because he is critical in the fight against Apophis. The essential interplay of the powers of Horus and Seth is another reason for her decision. *"It is Mehen of the uraei, he travels through the Netherworld. The bows, they lift up His Two Faces as his mystery."*[545] Is this a secret form or process of Mehen? He is able to take the opposing powers of Horus and Seth and use them in the rebirth of the Sun God.

Mehen isn't usually depicted as a cobra as this is the form that Goddesses take. However, the *uraeus* cobra appears in the 12th hour where eight Goddesses sit enthroned on coiled *uraeus* serpents who are referred to as their Mehen serpents. Perhaps the gender differentiation isn't as important or clear cut as we expect it to be. Regeneration combines both male and female energies.

---

[545] *Mehen, Mysteries, and Resurrection from the Coiled Serpent*, Piccione, 1990:43-52

METAMORPHOSIS IN THE *BOOK OF CAVERNS*

Qereret, *krrt*, is a cavern and the word was originally applied to the burial shaft of tombs. In later periods the word *krrt* was used for the caverns of the underworld. Cavern is a feminine word so in theory the cavern should be a female entity or a Goddess. In other cultures the concept of caves acting as the womb of the Earth Goddess is a familiar one. Out of an enclosed, nurturing darkness comes new life. The Egyptians didn't have an Earth Goddess and a reading of the *Book of Caverns*, or indeed any of the Netherworld books, soon negates this theory. Despite the correlation between the illustrations and text the book is difficult to interpret. There are six regions but they don't relate to the hours of night. The caverns are referred to as places of mystery so it is inevitable that the text is hard to understand. Nehebkau is depicted in the 3rd register draped protectively over seven catfish-headed Gods, who are described as being in his folds. These elemental beings allude to the initial stages of the creation of life, similar perhaps to the snake and frog deities of the Ogdoad. The process of rebirth involves the destruction of the old form and the rebuilding of a new, perhaps having to pass through several stages mimicking the creation or evolution of life, hence the presence of these primeval deities. In one scene from the *Enigmatic Book* a multi-headed Mehen encircles the corpse in an area called the Place of Destruction alluding to the start of the alchemical breakdown before the process of rebirth can start. The presence of the catfish-headed Gods also indicates that a blending of divine energies is about to take place. Referring to the followers of Osiris we are told they "*repose in their coffins, their bodies of mystery to which are united the serpents who are in the earth*".[546]

Snakes are placed around many of the depictions of Osiris emphasising their role in his rebirth and the rejuvenation of the Sun God, as well as for protection. The presence of the sun disc appears to point to the rejuvenating solar energy (similar to that of germination) working together with serpent energy to produce the miraculous rebirth. In the 3rd section an ithyphallic Osiris lies

---

[546] *The Tomb of Rameses VI*, Piankoff, 1954:51

partially enclosed by a snake, the sun disc is positioned over the gap. The text says that the snake *"makes complete"*.[547] Further along he is shown in his sarcophagus next to a ram's head and Eye of the Sun all surrounded by the *ouroboros* alluding to the unity of Ra and Osiris. A crocodile-headed Osiris then stands on a rearing snake which takes the form of a raised dais. This suggests the gradual ascension of Osiris as he changes from his inert state into an intermediate form.

Covering all registers at the start of the 4th section is a large snake standing on its tail. This is the Cavern of the Great One on his Belly. In a separate section, but close to the snake, is the solar disc. At this stage the sun disc is that of the old and fading Sun God. Showing it in a separate section may emphasise that solar and serpent energy are not yet united. The serpent is described as having his head in obscurity and his tail in darkness. Is this snake so long that its tail penetrates the very centre of the earth and his head the upper reaches of the sky? The process of rebirth and resurrection starts in the 5th section as Isis and Nephthys lift up the body of Osiris. At the start of this section is a depiction of the Sky Goddess Nut, over three registers. She lifts the solar disc and the ram-headed Sun God into the heavens. Standing on their tails at either side are two human-headed snakes. They are bearded showing their divinity. This may allude to the serpentine link or a channel from the earth into the heavens. A similar depiction is found in the sarcophagus hall of Rameses VI where a tall Goddess, referred to as the Mysterious One, lifts up the solar disc and a ram-headed bird (the *ba* of the Sun God). On either side a human-headed snake standing on its tail worships these figures. Towards the end of the 5th section in the *Book of Caverns* is a similar scene to that of the 4th section. An ithyphallic Osiris stands next to a large snake standing on its tail next to the sun disc. This time the snake and disc are in one section and the solar disc almost touches the snake illustrating their combined powers and the subsequent effect on Osiris. He has been resurrected and reinvigorated by the combined power of the solar disc and the serpent. Does this represent the female solar energy, as the Eye Goddess, and the male earthly serpent energy?

---

[547] *The Tomb of Rameses VI*, Piankoff, 1954:75

In the final section Osiris is shown rising from the earth within a U-shaped serpent emerging from the earth, his resurrection fuelled by serpentine earth energy. *"Osiris, whom the Great Serpent envelopes…he who is in the serpent, the Coiled One."*[548] This is Mehen his protector and regenerator. In a different register Khepri is depicted pushing the sun disc as he climbs out of a U-shaped snake. Without the text the same meaning could be read into this depiction. However, the text calls the snake the Great Serpent but also the Evil One. Ra says *"I am being born…the great serpent surrounds me, they charm him, they cut his soul"*.[549] It is strange that they would use the same title for the two different serpents. The preamble to the section refers to the punishing of the serpent Evil Face but the text around the serpent refers to the Great Serpent and the birth of Ra. The Sun God is referred to as him whose forms are complete, that is he has completed his metamorphosis and is reborn as Kephri, the young rising sun, *"who issues forth from the serpent"*.[550] One interpretation is that although reference is made to Evil Face he is not depicted but the Great Serpent, Mehen, is. Another depiction shows a ram wearing the solar disc emerging from a mound. Inside the mound is an undulating snake alluding to the regeneration of the Sun God. Is the Great Serpent who has to be dismembered not Apophis but Mehen? Mehen has protected and carried the regenerating Sun God like a mother carrying her developing child. Unless the baby is born both mother and child will die. Is the magic carried out to enable Khepri to be born? Hornung (2003) suggests that the Serpent of Rebirth, World Encircler, Apophis, the *ouroboros* and others are all forms of the mysterious Great Serpent who continually swallows all forms only to rebirth them after they have been renewed within his body. Certainly in many of the illustrations in each section it is impossible to distinguish between these serpents.

Appropriately enough the closing text, although incomplete, says *"obscurity envelopes this serpent"*.[551] Is this the same serpent as that in the 4th section who is described as having his head in

---

[548] *The Tomb of Rameses VI*, Piankoff, 1954:129
[549] *The Tomb of Rameses VI*, Piankoff, 1954:124
[550] *The Tomb of Rameses VI*, Piankoff, 1954:125
[551] *The Tomb of Rameses VI*, Piankoff, 1954:130

obscurity? The phrase *"obscurity envelopes"* occurs a number of times in the *Book of Caverns*. Even those present cannot fully observe or comprehend the process of metamorphosis. The mystery seems to elude the attention of any observers. The text explains that the deities and deceased who are present look at the earth but do not see the Great Serpent. Perhaps they can see only the rays of light from the emerging Sun God. Is the Great Serpent like a star whose light is eclipsed by the sun? Is the Great Serpent the earth itself as he lies hidden in plain sight? Or is the Great Serpent present in the form of energy, or an ethereal substance, that cannot be seen or felt but only intuited through the effects of his presence? *"His acts are unfathomable to those who are in his hole."*[552]

THE POWER OF FIRE

The funerary texts refer to the Island of Fire which is a place at the edge of the universe. This fire is both dangerous and beneficial as it is the seat of creation where the Sun God emerged out of the waters of the *nun*. It also forms a gateway to the other worlds. *"You have acquired all power and nothing has been left behind you in the Island of Fire. You have filled your body with magic."*[553] At the heart of this is the concept that a state of cataclysm is needed to enable the deceased to pass from one state to another. It is the alchemy of the crucible where the created order is broken down in preparation for reconstitution and rebirth. In the 6th hour of the *Book of Gates* is a rearing cobra, displaying a very distinct symbol of Neith. She sits in a circular pit in which water is drawn in red. It has two mummiform guardians. The text says that she is a 'living cobra' which suggests the presence of the *Uraeus* Goddess rather than just her symbol. The water in the pit is described as fire and the Gods of the Earth and the *ba*-souls of the Earth are unable to approach it. This may be because all earthly forms have to be left behind as part of the process, those who are earth-bound cannot participate. The water in this pit belongs to Osiris and there is also the fear is that the *ba*-souls will

---

[552] *The Tomb of Rameses VI*, Piankoff, 1954:56
[553] *The Cannibal Hymn*, Eyre, 2002:82

somehow damage or weaken Osiris. However we are told that the Great God "*breathes by the unapproachable water of this fiery pit*". This pit appears to be a source of energy of some kind as the text says that the power of the pit "*is not in want*".554 The Island of Fire can be seen as a metaphor for the process of transition between one state and another. Here both the destruction of the old forms and creation of the new take place simultaneously. The deceased are not being destructively burnt and with the help of the *uraeus* they are able to overcome the dangers and traumas of this transformation. Neith is the Creator Goddess who made order out of chaos. This may be part of the reason for the presence of the symbol of Neith on the *uraeus* in the midst of the lake of fire.

THE INTERPLAY OF EARTHLY AND COSMIC ENERGIES

The influence of solar and stellar energy and the interplay of the various types of energy are important in all of the Netherworld Books and it is especially prominent in the *Enigmatic Book*. Solar energy can be represented by the sun disc and the *uraeus*, stellar energy by the star hieroglyph and earth energy by snakes and possibly the emerging arms.

The *Book of Gates* displays stellar influences, in the form of Star Deities, indicated by the presence of a star above their heads. This occurs in the last two hours suggesting the need for an increased level of cosmic energy which can propel the sun into the heavens. The earth's energy has restored the Sun God and the deceased but now a different force comes into play. In the 11th hour Star deities help to tow the Solar Barque. In the 12th hour of the *Book of Gates* eight Goddesses sit on tightly coiled *uraei* who are described as their Mehen-serpents. With one hand they hold a star while the other reaches to the head of their Mehen-serpent. They are named as the Goddesses of the First Light, who conduct the Solar Barque. The text gives no further information so their role and meaning can only be speculated on. The star suggests that they are Astral Goddesses. Their serpentine thrones could provide their energy and affirm their divine power. The

---

554 *The Egyptian Book of Gates*, Abt & Hornung, 2014:226-227

stars may symbolise heavenly or cosmic energy which is combined with the earth energy of the snakes and manifest in these Goddesses. As each holds onto both the star and the serpent they act as a conduit which allows both energies to flow and merge connecting that which is above with that of below. It also emphasises the link between the cosmic and the earthly worlds. They also transmit stellar energy to Mehen and the serpents, possibly to replenish them after the regenerative work of the night has been completed.

A similar exchange is shown in a complex composition from the *Book of Earth*. Two pairs of arms emerge from the ground and support a solar disc on top of which stands a God and two fire-spitting cobras. The text explains that the fire of the *uraei* comes from the Great Horizon and that it is received by the "*two mysterious arms*".[555] On either side of the emerging arms are two Goddesses. Their arms are raised and out of them come twelve discs and twelve stars which form a semi-circle around the disc. It looks as if the Goddesses are throwing, or transmitting, them between each other. Both scenes show the cosmic energy needed for regeneration being transferred to the earth. It may also show the generation or the passing of time where the actions of the Goddesses create and then absorb the hours.

The interplay of the different energies is illustrated in many scenes from the *Enigmatic Book*. One scene shows eight seated mummiform Goddesses. At their feet is a solar disc and above their heads a star. A series of dots from the star to their heads indicates light from the star flowing into their heads. The "*Great god casts his light in the corpses of these goddesses*". Four of the Goddesses are named: She Relating to the Beaming, She Relating to the Gleaming, She Relating to the Light and Female Disc.[556] The second section is dominated by depictions of streams of light and energy which emanate from the solar disc, stars and serpents. Six mummiform Gods are shown a number of times. In the first scene they stand next to their *ba*-birds in front of a large *uraeus* cobra. Streams of fire and light from her mouth enter the forehead of the first God. The other Gods receive theirs from

---

[555] *The Ancient Egyptian Netherworld Books*, Darnell & Darnell, 2018:468
[556] *The Ancient Egyptian Netherworld Books*, Darnell & Darnell, 2018:559

stars set above the head of the preceding God. The text explains that the light of Ra is entering their corpses. When the Sun God calls *"your bas ascend towards the one who created you"*.[557] The *ba*-souls, like moths, are irresistibly drawn towards the flames and light of the *uraeus* serpents and the stars. In the next scene the mummies stand next to a large cat. Their disembodied heads float next to them and they stand on an undulating snake, probably Mehen. Light enters their heads and bodies from sun discs and stars above them and from discs in the folds of the snake. This is not the only place where both the solar disc and stars are used to depict the *"light of Ra"*. We now know that the sun is a star but does this suggest that the Egyptians thought of the sun in the same way? Probably not, but it does hint at the lingering influence of the earlier stellar aspects of their religion. The combined energies of Mehen and the sun energises the corpses and begins their regeneration. The cat may be Bastet, the She Cat referenced in the *Coffin Texts* as using the secret paths of Mehen. She represents the Eye of the Sun and the Gods' disembodied heads suggest their consciousness or spirit which is interacting with the divine energy and presence of the Eye.

The next four scenes continue with the theme of the transmission of energies from serpent and sun disc. Light from the solar disc streams into the forehead of the mummies while at their feet are rearing snakes who emit fire from their heads. These snakes are the Heret Snakes of Atum and are all labelled as Mehen. This scene shows the deceased being rejuvenated and their souls reanimated as Mehen's regenerative power combines with the animating solar energy. *"The light of Re having entered their corpses."*[558] Again the text refers to the *ba*-souls yearning for the Sun God. *"When he calls to their ba-souls, they rise up."*[559] Another scene depicting energy involves six Goddesses. Light streams into their mouths from discs near their heads, it then pours out of their hands like water onto the heads of snakes emerging from the ground. Each Goddess has a star and sun disc on their lower body. Darnell suggests that they represent the underworld as the

---

[557] *The Enigmatic Netherworld Books and the Solar-Osiran Unity*, Darnell, 2004:105
[558] *The Ancient Egyptian Netherworld Books*, Darnell & Darnell, 2018:544
[559] *The Ancient Egyptian Netherworld Books*, Darnell & Darnell, 2018:546

regenerative womb for the sun and the deceased, where solar and serpentine energies mingle. It can also be interpreted as solar energy being transmitted to the earth, symbolised by the snake, via the Goddesses who enable life to develop and thrive. The final scene is a complex composition where cows (representing Hathor) lift Goddesses on their elongated horns and long snakes rise up alongside them. This is framed by large outstretched hands. The sun and the deceased rise out of the underworld, aided by serpentine and Goddess energies in a process echoing that of the creation arising from the *nun*.

In the 6th scene the mummified Gods, now crowned, stand in front of a fire-breathing cobra. In front of each one is a star on top of the hieroglyph sign for a sail, used to represent the breath of life. This supports a sun disc out of which emerges the heads of a lion and a cobra. These heads absorb the energy and transmit it to the next pair, forming an undulating stream of energy around the mummies. As in other sections the text refers to the light of Ra animating the deceased.[560] The alternation between feline and serpent represents the interplay of feline and serpent energy and suggests a concept similar to that in modern physics where light can be viewed both as a wave and as a particle. The light purifies, protects, energises and transforms. The alternation of serpent and feline also represents the ebb and flow of energy passing between forms and states. This interplay of serpent and feline energy is also depicted in a vignette of spell 1116 from the *Book of Two Ways* where a snake rears from the back of a lion-headed entity. It is described as *"that spirit who knows how to enter time and open darkness"*.[561]

THE MYSTERIES FOR THE LIVING

The books of the Netherworld are a map and guidebook for the deceased to traverse the afterlife but the Netherworld Books are also esoteric in nature and the sacred knowledge contained within them was known only to a few select initiates. Deeper meanings lie under the surface and are hidden or highlighted

---

[560] *The Enigmatic Netherworld Books and the Solar-Osiran Unity*, Darnell, 2004:132
[561] *The Enigmatic Netherworld Books and the Solar-Osiran Unity*, Darnell, 2004:138

using wordplay and allegory. It is possible that some were used as part of spiritual or magical initiation and development. The focus was on the evolution of the individual's soul as well as the journey of the Sun God. It covers the process of descent, rebirth and ascension to become at one with the deities. In the *Amduat* it says that *"it is good for the dead to have this knowledge, but also for a person on earth, a remedy"*.[562]

The Book of the Amduat

For those who wish to research this in more detail Schweizer (2010) gives a psychological interpretation of the *Book of the Amduat* as do Abt and Hornung (2003). Here the journey of the Sun God through the underworld is symbolic of an inner psychic process of transformation and renewal. Schweizer believes that concepts from the *Amduat* have influenced the much later gnostic, hermetic and alchemical texts. This is a modern interpretation, what it meant to the Egyptians we can never know.

For the living the helpful, if frightening, serpents of the Netherworld Texts have their parallel in the snake-soul. This is part of our subconscious that can connect us to other realms and ancient wisdom normally hidden and far removed from our everyday reality. The protective and guiding snake force rises from the deepest levels of instinct. It communicates in dreams and intuition and guides us on our path when we have lost our way. Sometimes the ego, like the Sun God, has to relinquish some of its control and let the snake-soul guide it. The snakes are the ones who will give direction and assistance to a life which has been stranded in the sandbank of Apophis. Evil and despair exist and we have to acknowledge and deal with them. Encounters with this darkness can't be avoided – indeed they shouldn't if you wish to develop in this life and participate in the miracles of rebirth. The shadow side can be used to protect against these destructive forces just as Seth joins the crew in the Solar Barque and overcomes Apophis. Our snake-soul will awaken, if allowed, when we are overcome by evil and destructive events or by the

---

[562] *Knowledge for the Afterlife*, Abt & Hornung, 2003:9

blackness of our own thoughts and moods. Like the destructive powers of Apophis these cannot be totally conquered but warded off gradually and temporarily overcome. This may not be the most positive of messages but it is the most realistic and beneficial. During the utterly dark and barren periods of our lives we have to rely on the light and advice which comes from our snake-soul. Dark and dangerous periods are an inevitable part of both the outer and inner worlds. If it can do nothing else the snake-soul carries us through such periods like the Sun God on his serpentine barque. The snakes and ropes used to pull the Solar Barque through the underworld can be viewed as our psychic connection to the subconscious and archetypal powers which will aid healing and assist our traversal through the inevitable painful and distressing stretches of our lives.

Hatshepsut (18th dynasty) said *"I rule as far as the realm of the primeval darkness"*.[563] All divine and royal power ends where Apophis reigns but it is the power of the *nun* which is needed for transformation. The sacred mysteries have to be shielded from the everyday world, the light and the effects of the *nun*. This is one of the roles of the snake. Descent into the abyss is risky, especially when taken voluntarily by the living, and there is no guarantee of return or rebirth. Snakes can be dangerous because it is in their nature to be dangerous. Highly complex processes cannot be guaranteed to work precisely, if at all. Mehen acts as an alchemical vessel. He enables the breaking down and reforming and provides a vessel to contain the dissolved components so they don't dissipate before they have been reassembled. The *ourorboros* shows the moment of the uniting of opposites. The old gives way to the new and the Solar Child emerges from the abyss protected by his guiding serpent.

The Book of Thoth

The *Book of Thoth* dates to the Ptolemaic Period but contains sections which are probably older. Its aim was to instruct initiates in a wide range of subjects. Its teachings are often obscure, heavily veiled and with many layers of meaning. In one section

---

[563] *The Sungod's Journey Through the Netherworld*, Schweizer, 2010:34

the disciple says *"bring me to the ferry of the snake"*. This is believed to refer to the Solar Barque which has transformed into a snake to allow it to traverse the deserts of the *Amduat* in the 4th hour.564 A 21st dynasty funerary papyrus has a similar reference. *"Re has initiated him in his boat. He has seen the sacredness of the one who is in his serpent."*565 Although still living, the initiate wishes to journey in the Solar Barque and experience the mysteries of Mehen. Assuming the procedure was concluded satisfactorily, it would allow the still living initiate to see and experience the miraculous transformation and rebirth of the Sun God. In another part of the *Book of Thoth* the disciple says *"behold, I stand up, I being like unto a mummy, I being as a snake"*.566 The mummy is stood up when the ceremony of the Opening of the Mouth performed. This will allow the deceased to breathe again. Has the deceased also assumed the form of a snake? The *ba* of the deities was said to reside in snakes. It can also allude to the rejuvenating energy of the snake flowing through the body and animating it. It could refer to Nehebkau restoring the vital *ka* energy. In terms of the mysteries the initiate is being 'born again' filled with the wisdom and energy of the snake.

The Mysteries of Mehen

The mysteries of Mehen have remained secret so any ideas about them can only be speculation. My understanding is that Mehen is the way. Follow the serpentine path on the Serpent Barque to approach the hidden sun. As we walk along the serpent, which forms the path, he moves. Sometimes this is in the direction of travel, like a moving walkway. At other times it reconfigures and confuses us so we walk, or appear to walk, in the wrong direction. Mehen appears to be a living labyrinth at times where his paths can be followed from his tail to meet with the Sun God at his head. Labyrinths occur in many cultures but I haven't found any evidence of them in Egypt so maybe this is just a visual connection. The main point of a labyrinth is to turn round and walk back out having accomplished the task – be it the

---

564 *The Ancient Egyptian Book of Thoth*, Jaznow & Zauzich, 2005:306
565 *Hathor Rising*, Roberts, 2001:21
566 *The Ancient Egyptian Book of Thoth*, Jaznow & Zauzich, 2005:49

hero or heroine's journey, to slay the Minotaur at the centre or for contemplative and spiritual reasons. The deceased do not make a return journey but exit from Mehen's head. As nothing is known about the Mehen mysteries for the living we do not know how they made the return journey. However, one passage quoted earlier does hint at a return journey. *"Just as N has travelled to the Two Skies so N has returned to the Two Lands."*[567] The initiate follows the paths of Mehen to the Two Skies (diurnal and nocturnal) but returns to the living in the Two Lands of Egypt.

CONCLUSION

It is no surprise that serpents dominate in the mysteries of rebirth in Egypt, what is interesting is the splitting of male and female roles which dissolves the traditional gender roles of other cultures. Here the process of rebirth is carried out by Gods rather than the Mother or Earth Goddess. Nehebkau reassembles and re-energises the deceased while Mehen encloses and enables the alchemical process of rebirth. Time serpents control and reverse time to allow the transformations to take place. It is the *Uraeus* Goddesses who provide the solar energy essential for the rekindling of life. The transfer and interplay of energy is an essential part of all components of the process be it male and female, serpent and feline or earthly and cosmic. Another area where the serpents are essential.

---

[567] *Mehen, Mysteries, and Resurrection from the Coiled Serpent*, Piccione, 1990:43-52

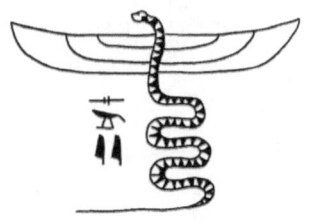

CHAPTER 13

The Eternal Serpent

"I am the Word, which will never be annihilated."[568]

The snake is all-encompassing as both as a symbol and a deity in Ancient Egypt. Its inherent duality is emphasised in its power to both kill and cure as well as protect and destroy. Apophis may well be the nemesis of creation but the protective *uraeus* can also be deadly. A snake's largely undifferentiated body mirrors the way it can blur boundaries especially between male and female roles and energies. The gender of a snake isn't easy to discern. Within the protective coils of Mehen the alchemical process of rebirth occurs as if in the cauldron and womb of the Goddess. A speciality of Egyptian serpents is the easy flowing between snake and feline form and energy as seen by the *Uraeus* Goddess transforming into the Lioness Goddess. Mehen and Nehebkau have a close relationship with the Solar Gods, even being aspects of them.

The serpents of Egypt can be closely entangled in this life; like the bountiful Renenutet or the snakes of the inundation. In the afterlife they are indispensable as protector, guide and light-bringer. Most importantly, they hold the key to sacred knowledge and have great wisdom and power. Creator serpents knew the pre-creation *nun* and created the universe from a current of potential in its non-being. They understand and control time,

---

[568] *Myth and Symbol in Ancient Egypt*, Clark, 1978:77

some can even reverse it. Serpents know how to produce regeneration and rebirth in both deities and humans. Despite its largely chthonic lifestyle the fast-moving and quick-striking snake is ideally suited to both be and to represent energy in its various forms. The earth energy of the Snake Gods reassembles the components of the deceased and revitalises their *kas* while the *Uraeus* Goddess brings invigorating solar energies. There is a constant interchange of energies between the various Serpent deities and also with their feline counterparts. Tension between their contrasting aspects enables energy to flow and transform. At a fundamental level there is only serpentine energy briefly held as matter.

Finally, what of the dragon who personifies many of the aspects of the Egyptian serpents; fire-breathing, water-controlling, dangerous protector and destroyer? Are there no dragons in Egypt? What about the fire-breathing flame-spitting *uraeus*? Or the havoc-wreaking Apophis? Or the winged snakes of Herodotus? What is different is the imagery. A conventionally depicted dragon is immediately recognisable in all cultures. There are snakes with wings and legs in many tomb decorations in Egypt but they persist in looking snake-like rather than dragon-like. Their heads are always snake heads, or those of another creature. They are never depicted with dragon-like heads as they are in cultures from the west of Europe to the east of Asia. Why should this be? Jones (2002) concludes that the visual concept of the dragon comes from the earliest stages of our evolution and was inspired by a combination of the three predators that primates fear the most; the eagle, the leopard and the snake. Interestingly the three predominant animal symbols of the Dynastic Period are the falcon, the lion and the snake so perhaps the Egyptians didn't feel the need to create the composite dragon.

The Serpent encircles all that is. Present before the beginning, serpents will outlast the end. Serpents are always present on our journey should we choose to see them. *"Watch over the Soul! Be helpful, O Fiery One."*[569]

---

[569] *Ancient Egyptian Literature*, Foster, 2001:65

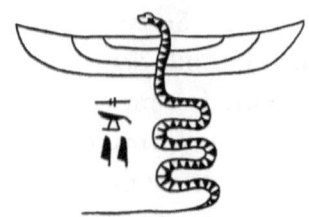

Bibliography

Abdalla, A. (1991) *A Greco-Roman Group Statue of Unusual Character from Dendera*. In *Journal of Egyptian Archaeology*, Vol 77:189-193

Abt, T. & Hornung, E. (2003) *Knowledge for the Afterlife*. Zurich, Living Human Heritage Publications

Abt, T. & Hornung, E. (2007) *The Egyptian Amduat*. Zurich, Living Human Heritage Publications

Abt, T. & Hornung, E. (2014) *The Egyptian Book of Gates*. Zurich, Living Human Heritage Publications

Aelian & Scholfield, A. F. (1957) *On the Characteristics of Animals volume I*. William Heinemann Ltd

Aelian & Scholfield, A. F. (1957) *On the Characteristics of Animals volume III*. William Heinemann Ltd

Allen, J. P. (2005) *The Art of Medicine in Ancient Egypt*. New York, Metropolitan Museum of Art

Alvar, J. (2008) *Romanising Oriental Gods*. Leiden, Brill

Andrews, C. (1994) *Amulets of Ancient Egypt*. London, British Museum Press

Apuleius & Walsh, P. G. (trans.) (1994) *The Golden Ass*. Oxford, Oxford University Press

Assmann, J. (2003) *The Mind of Egypt*. Massachusetts, Harvard University Press

Aziz, S. (2018) *An Examination of the Death of Cleopatra and the Serpent in Myth, Magic and Medicine*. In *Nile Magazine*, Vol 12:29-34

Bailey, D. M. (2007) *A Snake-Legged Dionysus from Egypt, and Other Divine Snakes*. In *Journal of Egyptian Archaeology*, Vol 93:263-270

Baines, J. (1990) *Interpreting the Story of the Shipwrecked Sailor*. In *Journal of Egyptian Archaeology*, Vol 76:55-72

Bakry, H. S. K. (1969) *A Stela from Heliopolis Dedicated to Edjo*. In *Rivista degli studi orientali*, Vol 44:177-180

Bastaway, H. (2018) *The Snake who was God*. In *Nile Magazine*, Vol 12:35-39

Betro, M. C. (1996) *Hieroglyphics: The writings of Ancient Egypt*. New York, Abbeville Press

Betz, H. D. (Ed.) (1996) *The Greek Magical Papyri in Translation. Volume I: Texts*. Chicago, University of Chicago Press

Bianchi, A (1987) *Remarks on Beings Called mrwty or mrwrty in the Coffin Texts*. In *Journal of Egyptian Archaeology*, Vol 73:206-207

Blackman, A. M. (1918) *The Funerary Papyrus of Nespeher'an (Pap. Skrine, No. 2)*. In *Journal of Egyptian Archaeology*, Vol 5:24-35

Blackman, A. M. (1922) *Some Occurrences of the Corn-'Aruseh in Ancient Egyptian Tomb Paintings*. In *Journal of Egyptian Archaeology*, Vol 8:235-240

Bleeker, C. J. (1973) *Hathor and Thoth: Two Key Figures of the Ancient Egyptian Religion*. Leiden, E J Brill

Bleiberg, E., Barbash, Y. & Bruno, L. (2013) *Soulful Creatures. Animal Mummies in Ancient Egypt.* New York, Giles

Bochi, P. A. (1994) *Images of Time in Ancient Egyptian Art.* In *Journal of the American Research Center in Egypt*, Vol 31:55-62

Bomgioanni, A. & Croce, M. S. (ed.) (2003) *The Treasures of Ancient Egypt from the Egyptian Museum in Cairo.* New York, Universe Publishing 2003.

Borghouts, J. F. (1973) *The Evil Eye of Apopis.* In *Journal of Egyptian Archaeology*, Vol 59:114-150

Borghouts, J. F. (1978) *Ancient Egyptian Magical Texts.* Leiden, E J Brill

Bosse-Griffiths, K. (1973) *The Great Enchantress in the Little Golden Shrine of Tutankhamun.* In *Journal of Egyptian Archaeology*, Vol 59:100-108

Bowman, A. K. & Rathbone, D. (1992) *Cities and Administration in Roman Egypt.* In *The Journal of Roman Studies*, 82:107-127

Boylan, P. (1922) *Thoth Or The Hermes Of Egypt.* New York, Kessinger Publishing (Reprints) 1922.

Budge, E. A. W. & Wilson, E. (2016) *The Ancient Egyptian Book of the Dead.* New York, Quatro Publishing

Charlesworth, J. H. (2010) *The Good and Evil Serpent: How a Universal Symbol Became Christianized.* New Haven, Yale University Press

Ciampini, E. M. (2016) *Magic in the Sign.* In Roccati, A. & Swierzowska, A. (2016) *The Wisdom of Thoth.* Oxford, Archaeopress Archaeology

Clark, R. T. (1978) *Myth and Symbol in Ancient Egypt.* London, Thames & Hudson

Conman, J. (2003) *It's about Time: Ancient Egyptian Cosmology.* In *Studien zur Altägyptischen Kultur* 31:33-71

Crist, W. et al. (2016) *Ancient Egyptians at Play: Board Games Across Borders.* London, Bloomsbury Publishing

Cruz-Uribe, E. (1994) *The Khonsu Cosmogony.* In *Journal of the American Research Centre in Egypt*, Vol 31:169-189

Darnell, J. C. & Darnell, C. M. (2018) *The Ancient Egyptian Netherworld Books.* Atlanta, SBL Press

Darnell, J. C. (1997) *The Apotropaic Goddess in the Eye.* In *Studien zur Altägyptischen Kultur*, Vol 24:35-48

Darnell, J. C. (2004) *The Enigmatic Netherworld Books of the Solar-Osiran Unity.* Fribourg, Academic Press

David, R. (2016) *Temple Ritual at Abydos.* London. Egypt Exploration Society

Davis, W. M. (1977) *The Ascension-Myth in the Pyramid Texts.* In *Journal of Near Eastern Studies*, Vol 36:161-179

De Witt, C. (1951) *Le Role et le Sens du Lion dans L'Egypte Ancienne.* Leiden, Brill.

Diodorus Siculus & Booth, G. (1814) *The Historical Library of History of Diodorus Siculus.* London, McDowall

Dunand, F. & Zivie-Coche, C. (2004) *Gods and Men in Egypt 3000 BCE to 395 CE.* Ithaca, Cornell University Press

Eckerman, C. (2012) *A Temple Declaration from Early Roman Egypt.* In *The Bulletin of the American Society of Papyrologists, 49:55-62*

el-Razik, M. A. (1975) *The Dedicatory and Building Texts of Rameses II in Luxor Temple.* In *Journal of Egyptian Archaeology*, Vol 61:125-136

Erman, A. (1995) *Ancient Egyptian Poetry and Prose. New York, Dover Publications*

Eyre, C. (2002) *The Cannibal Hymn.* Liverpool, Liverpool University Press

Fairman, H. W. & Grdseloff, B. (1947) *Texts of Hatshepsut and Sethos I inside Speos Artemidos.* In *Journal of Egyptian Archaeology*, Vol 33:12-33

Fairman, H. W. (1935) *The Myth of Horus of at Edfu – I.* In *Journal of Egyptian Archaeology*, Vol 21:26-36

Faulkner, R. O. & Goelet, O. (2008) *The Egyptian Book of the Dead,* San Francisco, Chronicle Books

Faulkner, R. O. (1934) *Statue of a Serpent Worshiper.* In *Journal of Egyptian Archaeology*, Vol 20:154-156

Faulkner, R. O. (1936) *The Bremner-Rhind Papyrus I.* In *Journal of Egyptian Archaeology*, Vol

22:121-140
Faulkner, R. O. (1937) *The Bremner-Rhind Papyrus II*. In *Journal of Egyptian Archaeology*, Vol 23:10-16
Faulkner, R. O. (1937) *The Bremner-Rhind Papyrus III: The Book of Overthrowing Apep*. In *Journal of Egyptian Archaeology*, Vol 23:166-185
Faulkner, R. O. (1938) *The Bremner-Rhind Papyrus IV*. In *Journal of Egyptian Archaeology*, Vol 24:41-53
Faulkner, R. O. (1958) *An Ancient Egyptian Book of Hours*. Oxford, Griffith Institute
Faulkner, R. O. (1965) *The Admonitions of an Egyptian Sage*. In *Journal of Egyptian Archaeology*, Vol 51:53-62
Faulkner, R. O. (1989) *The Ancient Egyptian Book of the Dead*. London, British Museum Publications
Faulkner, R. O. (2007) *The Ancient Egyptian Coffin Texts*. Oxford, Aris & Phillips
Faulkner, R. O. (2007) *The Ancient Egyptian Pyramid Texts*. Kansas, Digireads.com Publishing
Foreman, W. & Quirke S. (1996) *Hieroglyphs & the Afterlife in Ancient Egypt*. London, Opus Publishing Ltd
Foster, J. L. (1988) *"The Shipwrecked Sailor" Prose or Verse? (Postponing Clauses and Tense-neutral Clauses.)* In *Studien zur Altägyptischen Kultur, Vol 15:69-109*
Foster, J. L. (1995) *Hymns, Prayers and Songs*. Atlanta, Scholars Press
Foster, J. L. (2001) *Ancient Egyptian Literature*. Austin, University of Texas Press
Gaber, A. (2015) *Some Snake Deities from the Temple of Edfu*. In Kousoulis, P. & Lazaridis, N (Ed) (2015) *Proceedings of the Tenth International Congress of Egyptologists volume I*. Leuven, Peeters
Gaber, A. (2017) *The Ten Dead Deities of the Temple of Dendera*. In *Journal of Egyptian Archaeology*, Vol 101:239-262
Gardiner, A. H. (1944) *Horus the Behdedite*. In *Journal of Egyptian Archaeology*, Vol 30:23-60
Gardiner, A. H. (1948) *The First Two Pages of the Worterbuch*. In *Journal of Egyptian Archaeology*, Vol 34:12-18
Germond, P. (1981) *Sekhmet et la Protection du Monde*. Geneva, l'Université de Genève.
Goddio, F. & Masson-Berghoff, A. (Ed.) (2016) *Sunken Cities Egypt's Lost Worlds*. London, Thames & Hudson
Graves-Brown, C. (2006) *Emergent Flints*. In Szpakowska, K. (Ed.) (2006) *Through a Glass Darkly*. Swansea, The Classical Press of Wales
Graves-Brown, C. (2010) *Dancing for Hathor: Women in Ancient Egypt*. London, Continuum
Graves-Brown, C. A. (2005) *The Spitting Goddess and the Stoney Eye: Divinity and Flint in Pharaonic Egypt*. In Piquette, K. & Lowe, S. (2003) *Current Research in Egyptology*. Oxford, Oxbow Books
Griffith, F. L. (1926) *The Teaching of Amenophis the Son of Kanakht. Papyrus B.M. 10474*. In *Journal of Egyptian Archaeology*, Vol 12:191-231
Griffiths, J. G. (1961) *The Death of Cleopatra VII*. In *Journal of Egyptian Archaeology*, Vol 47:113-133
Griffiths, J. G. (1975) *Apuleius of Madauros – The Isis Book*. Leiden, E J Brill
Gunn, B. (1916) *The Religion of the Poor in Ancient Egypt*. In *Journal of Egyptian Archaeology*, Vol 3:81-94
Hansen, N. B. (Ed) (2008) *Omm Sety's Living Egypt*. Chicago, Glyphdoctors
Hardwick, T. (2017) *The Roman Uraeus*. In *Journal of Egyptian Archaeology*, Vol 95:254-257
Hart, G. (2005) *The Routledge Dictionary of Egyptian Gods and Goddesses*. Abingdon, Routledge
Hawass, Z. (1994) *A Fragmentary Monument of Djoser from Saqqara*. In *Journal of Egyptian Archaeology*, Vol 80:45-56
Hayes, W. C. (1938) *A Writing Palette of the Chief Steward Amenhotpe and some Notes on its Owner*. In *Journal of Egyptian Archaeology*, Vol 24:9-24
Hayes, W. C. (1951) *Inscriptions from the Palace of Amenhotep III*. In *Journal of Near Eastern Studies, Vol 10:35-56*
Herodotus & Selincourt, A. (Trans.) (2003) *The Histories*. London, Penguin Books
Horapollo & Boas, G. (1950) *The Hieroglyphics of Horapollo*. New Jersey, Princeton University Press

Hornung, E. & Bryan, B. M. (Eds.) (2002) *The Quest for Immortality: Treasures of Ancient Egypt.* London, Prestel Publishers
Hornung, E. (1990) *The Valley of the Kings.* New York, Timken Publishers
Hornung, E. (1996) *Conceptions of God in Ancient Egypt.* Ithaca, Cornell University Press
Hornung, E. (1999) *The Ancient Egyptian Books of the Afterlife.* Ithaca, Cornell University Press
Houlihan, P. F. (1996) *The Animal World of the Pharaohs.* London, Thames & Hudson
Ignatov, S. (1994) *Some Notes on the Shipwrecked Sailor.* In *Journal of Egyptian Archaeology*, Vol 80:195-198
Jackson, L. (2018) *Sekhmet & Bastet: The Feline Powers of Egypt*, London, Avalonia Books
Jacq, C. (1999) *The Living Wisdom of Ancient Egypt.* London, Simon & Schuster
Jacq, C. (2002) *Magic and Mystery in Ancient Egypt.* London, Souvenir Press
James, T. G. H. (1982) *A Wooden Figure of Wadjet with Two Painted Representations of Amasis.* In *Journal of Egyptian Archaeology*, Vol 68:156-165
Jasnow, R. & Zauzich, K (2005) *The Ancient Egyptian Book of Thoth.* Harrassowitz Verlag 2005.
Johnson, B. (1988) *Lady of the Beasts.* San Francisco, Harper & Row
Johnson, S. B. (1990) *The Cobra Goddesses of Ancient Egypt.* London, Kegan Paul International
Jones, D. E. (2002) *An Instinct for Dragons.* London, Routledge
Kakosy, L. (1967) *Egyptian Healing Statues in Three Museums in Italy (Turin, Florence, Naples).* Turin, Egyptian Museum of Turin
Kakosy, L. (1981) *The Astral Snakes of the Nile.* In *Mitteilungen Des Deutschen Archäologischen Instituts*, Abteilung Kairo 37. 62:255-260
Kaster, J. (1993) *The Wisdom of Ancient Egypt.* New York, Barnes & Noble Books
Kendall, T. (2007) *The Ancient Egyptian Game of the Serpent.* In Finkle, I. (Ed) (2007) *Ancient Board Games in Perspective.* London, British Museum Press
Kerkeslager, A. (2001) *The Apophis Snake on a Coin of Domitian from Alexandria (BMC Alexandria 348; RPC 2, 2756).* In *The Numismatic Chronicle*, Vol 161:287-290
Klotz, D. (2010) *Two Overlooked Oracles.* In *Journal of Egyptian Archaeology*, Vol 96:247-254
Kockelmann, H. (2003) *A Roman Period Demotic Manual of Hymns to Rattawy and Other Deities.* In *Journal of Egyptian Archaeology*, Vol 89:217-229
Kriz, L. & Burzacott, J (2017) *The Top Ten Myths About Ancient Egypt.* In *Nile Magazine*, Vol 7:15-25
Kurth, D. (2004) *The Temple of Edfu.* Cairo, The American University in Cairo Press
Leibovitch, J (1953) *Gods of Agriculture and Welfare in Ancient Egypt.* In *Journal of Near Eastern Studies*, Vol 12:73-113
Leitz, C. (1999) *Magical and Medical Papyri of the New Kingdom.* London, British Museum Press
Lesko, B. S. (1999) *The Great Goddesses of Ancient Egypt.* Norman, University of Oklahoma Press
Lesko, L. H. (1977) *The Ancient Egyptian Book of Two Ways.* California, University of California Publications.
Lichtheim, M. (2006) *Ancient Egyptian Literature Volume I.* California, University of California Press
Lichtheim, M. (2006) *Ancient Egyptian Literature Volume III.* California, University of California Press
Lilleso, E. K. (1975) *Two Wooden Uraei.* In *Journal of Egyptian Archaeology*, Vol 61:137-146
Malek, J. (1993) *The Cat in Ancient Egypt.* London, The British Museum Press
Manniche, L. (1999) *Sacred Luxuries.* Ithaca, Cornell University Press
Manniche, L. (2006) *An Ancient Egyptian Herbal.* London, British Museum Press
Mead, G. R. S. (2002) *Plutarch: Concerning the Mysteries of Isis and Osiris.* Montana, Kessinger Publishing (Reprints)
Meeks, D. & Favard-Meeks, C. (1999) *Daily Life of Egyptian Gods.* London, Pimlico
Morenz, L. D. (2004) *Apophis: On the Origin, Name and Nature of an Ancient Egyptian Anti-God.* In *Journal of Near Eastern Studies*, Vol 63:201-205
Morgan, D. (2008) *Snakes in Myth, Magic and History.* Connecticut, Praeger

Murray, M. A. (1948) *The Serpent Hieroglyph*. In *Journal of Egyptian Archaeology*, Vol 34:117-118

Newberry, P. E. (1948) *Fy 'Cerastes'*. In *Journal of Egyptian Archaeology*, Vol 34:118

Nielsen, N. Gasperini, V. & Mamedow, M. (2016) *Preliminary Report on the First Season of the Tell Nabasha Project, Autumn 2015*. In *Ägypten und Levante / Egypt and the Levant*, Vol 26:65-74

Noblecourt, C. D. (2007) *Gifts from the Pharaohs*. Paris, Flammarion

Noegel, S. B. (2006) *On Puns and Divination*. In Szpakowska, K. (Ed.) (2006) *Through a Glass Darkly*. Swansea, The Classical Press of Wales

O'Roukre, P. F. (2016) *An Ancient Egyptian Book of the Dead*. London, Thames & Hudson

Oakes, L. & Gahlin, L. (2004) *Ancient Egypt*. London, Hermes House

Ouda, A. M. M. (2017) *The Canopic Box of NS-'3-RWD (BM EA 8539)*. In *Journal of Egyptian Archaeology*, Vol 98:127-138

Parkinson, R. (2008) *The Painted Tomb-Chapel of Nebamun*. London, British Museum Press

Parkinson, R. B. (1998) *The Tale of Sinuhe and Other Ancient Egyptian Poems*. Oxford, Oxford University Press

Patch, D. C. (2011) *Dawn of Egyptian Art*. New York, Metropolitan Museum of Art

Piankoff, A. (1954) *The Tomb of Rameses VI*. New York, Pantheon Books.

Piankoff, A. (1964) *The Litany of Re*. New York, Pantheon Books.

Piankoff, A. (1974) *The Wandering of the Soul*. Princeton, Princeton University Press

Piccione, P. A. (1990) *Mehen, Mysteries, and Resurrection from the Coiled Serpent*. In *Journal of the American Research Center in Egypt*, Vol 27:43-52

Pinch, G. (2002) *Egyptian Mythology*. Oxford, Oxford University Press

Pinch, G. (2004) *Egyptian Myth: A Very Short Introduction*. Oxford, Oxford University Press

Pinch, G. (2006) *Magic in Ancient Egypt*. London, British Museum Press

Pliny & Bostock, J. & Riley, H. T. (Trans) (2015) *Pliny the Elder, the Complete Works*. Hastings, Delphi Classics

Raven, M. (2012) *Egyptian Magic*. Cairo, American University in Cairo Press

Reader, C. (2017) *The Netjerikhet Stela and the Early Dynastic Cult of Ra*. In *Journal of Egyptian Archaeology*, Vol 100:421-435

Redford, D. B. (1998) *Report on the 1993 and 1997 Seasons at Tell Qedwa*. In *Journal of the American Research Center in Egypt*, Vol 35:45-60

Rendsburg, G. A. (2000) *Literary Devices in the Story of the Shipwrecked Sailor*. In *Journal of the American Oriental Society*, 120:13-23

Richter, B. A. (2016) *The Theology of Hathor of Dendera*. Atlanta, Lockwood Press

Ritner, K. (1990) *O. Gardiner 363: A Spell Against Night Terrors*. In *Journal of the American Research Center in Egypt*, Vol 27:25-41

Ritner, R. K. (1993) *The Mechanics of Ancient Egyptian Magical Practice*. Chicago, University of Chicago

Ritner, R.K. (2006) *And Each Staff Transformed into a Snake: The Serpent Wand in Ancient Egypt*. In Szpakowska, K. (Ed.) (2006) *Through a Glass Darkly*. Swansea, The Classical Press of Wales

Roberts, A. (2000) *My Heart My Mother*. Rottingdean, Northgate Publishers

Roberts, A. (2001) *Hathor Rising*. Rottingdean, Northgate Publishers

Roberts, A. (2008) *Golden Shrine, Goddess Queen: Egypt's Anointing Mysteries*. Rottingdean, Northgate Publishers

Roberts, A. (2019) *Hathor's Alchemy*. Rottingdean, Northgate Publishers

Robins, G. (1999) *The Names of Hatshepsut as King*. In *Journal of Egyptian Archaeology*, Vol 85:103-112

Roth, A. M. & Roehrig, C. H. (2002) *Magical Bricks and the Bricks of Birth*. In *Journal of Egyptian Archaeology*, Vol 88:121-139

Schweizer, A. (2010) *The Sungod's Journey Through the Netherworld*. Ithaca, Cornell University Press

Sellers, J. B. (1992) *The Death of Gods in Ancient Egypt*. London, Penguin Books

Seton-Williams, M. V. (1969) *The Tell El-fara'in Expedition, 1968*. In *Journal of Egyptian Archaeology*, Vol 55:5-22

Shaw, G. J. (2014) *The Egyptian Myths*. London, Thames & Hudson

Shaw, I. & Nicholson, P. (2008) *The British Museum Dictionary of Ancient Egypt*. London, British Museum Press

Sherman, E. J. (1981) *Djedhor the Saviour Statue Base OI 10589*. In *Journal of Egyptian Archaeology*, Vol 67:82-102

Shoaib, W. (2012) *Aspects of rnpy in Ancient Egyptian Texts*. In *Journal of the American Research Center in Egypt*, Vol 48:191-203

Shorter, A. W. (1932) *Two Statuettes of the Goddess Sekhmet-Ubastet*. In *Journal of Egyptian Archaeology*, Vol 18:121-124

Shorter, A. W. (1935) *The God Nehebkau*. In *Journal of Egyptian Archaeology*, Vol 21:41-48

Shorter, A. W. (1937) *The Papyrus of Khnememhab in University College, London*. In *Journal of Egyptian Archaeology*, Vol 23:34-38

Simpson, W. K. et al (2003) *The Literature of Ancient Egypt*. New Haven, Yale University Press

Smethills, J. (2014) *Playing with Fire*. In *Ancient Egypt*, Vol 15.1:12-16

Smith, M. (2009) *Traversing Eternity*. Oxford, Oxford University Press

Spalinger, A. (2000) *The Destruction of Mankind: A Transitional Literary Text*. In *Studien zur Altägyptischen Kultur*, Vol 28:257-282

Spier, J. Potts, T. & Cole, S. E. (Ed.) (2018) *Beyond the Nile: Egypt and the Classical World*. Los Angeles, J Paul Getty Museum

Stemmler-Harding, S. (2016) *Devil in Disguise – On the Stellar Mythology of Apophis*. In Guilhou, N. (Ed.) *Nut Astrophoros: Papers Presented to Alicia Maravellia*. Oxford, Archaeopress Publishing Ltd

Stewart, H. M. (1971) *A Crossword Hymn to Mut*. In *Journal of Egyptian Archaeology*, Vol 57:87-104

Stutesman, D. (2005) *Snake*. London, Reaktion Books Ltd

Sweeney, D. (1998) *Friendship and Frustration: A Study in Papyri Deir El-Medina IV-VI*. In *Journal of Egyptian Archaeology*, Vol 84:101-122

Szpakowska, K (2003) *Playing with Fire: Initial Observations on the Religious Uses of Clay Cobras from Amarna*. In *Journal of the American Research Centre in Egypt*, Vol 40:113-122

Taylor, J. H. (2017) *Sir John Soane's Greatest Treasure*. London, British Museum Press.

Taylor, J. H. (Ed.) (2010) *Journey Through the Afterlife: Ancient Egyptian Book of the Dead*. London, British Museum Press.

Teeter, E. (2011) *Before the Pyramids*. Chicago, Oriental Institute Museum Publications

Teeter, E. (2011) *Religion and Ritual in Ancient Egypt*. Cambridge, Cambridge University Press

Toye, N. (2017) *A Particular Form of Amun at Deir el-Medina*. In *Journal of Egyptian Archaeology*, Vol 95:257-263

Traunecker, C. (2001) *The Gods of Egypt*. Ithaca, Cornell University Press

Troy, L. *Mut Enthroned*. (1996) In van Dijk, J. (Ed,) (1996) *Essays on Ancient Egypt in Honour of Herman te Velde*. Groningen, Styx Publications

Tyldesley, J (2010) *Myths & Legends of Ancient Egypt*. London, Allen Lane

Venit, M. S. (1997) *The Tomb from Tigrane Pasha Street and the Iconography of Death in Roman Alexandria*. In *American Journal of Archaeology*, Vol 101:701-729

Venit, M. S. (2016) *Visualising the Afterlife in the Tombs of Greco-Roman Egypt*. Cambridge, Cambridge University Press

Vernus, P. (1998) *The Gods of Ancient Egypt*. London, Tauris Parke Books

Wainwright, G. A. (1946) *Zeberged: The Shipwrecked Sailor's Island*. In *Journal of Egyptian Archaeology*, Vol 32:31-38

Watterson, B. (2003) *Gods of Ancient Egypt*. Stroud, Sutton Publishing Ltd

Wente, E. (1990) *Letters from Ancient Egypt*. Atlanta, Scholars Press

Whitehouse, H. (2009) *Ancient Egypt and Nubia*. Oxford, Ashmolean Museum

Wilkinson, R. H. (1994) *Symbol & Magic in Egyptian Art*. London, Thames & Hudson

Wilkinson, R. H. (2000) *The Complete Temples of Ancient Egypt*. London, Thames & Hudson

Wilkinson, R. H. (2003) *The Complete Gods and Goddesses of Ancient Egypt*. London, Thames & Hudson

Wilkinson, R. H. (2011) *Reading Egyptian Art*. London, Thames & Hudson

Wilkinson, T. (2016) *Writings from Ancient Egypt*. London, Penguin Books

Wilkinson, T. A. H. (1999) *Early Dynastic Egypt*. London, Routledge
Wilson, H. (2010) *Snakes*. In *Ancient Egypt*, Vol 10.6:46-47
Worthington, M. (2004) *Question and Answer in Middle Kingdom Dialogues*. In *Journal of Egyptian Archaeology*, Vol 90:113-121
Zabkar, L. V. (1988) *Hymns to Isis in Her Temple at Philae*. Hanover, University Press of New England
Zandee, J. (1960) *Death as an Enemy*. Leiden, Brill

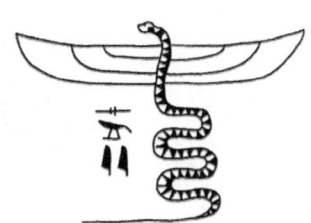

Index

A

Abydos.......51, 70, 74, 75, 76, 85, 87, 93, 142, 194, 221
Agathe Tyche.. 101
Agathos Daimon..........100, 118, 119, 120
Aker...................... 49, 50, 125, 131, 182
Alexandria.... 56, 57, 100, 101, 102, 118, 119, 223, 225
Amarna................................139, 225
Amaunet... 32
Amduat, the.... 25, 28, 36, 43, 50, 51, 54, 64, 66, 107, 111, 112, 114, 115, 164, 165, 166, 167, 168, 169, 170, 171, 175, 181, 187, 190, 193, 196, 202, 203, 214, 216, 220
Amenopet.. 32
Ammut 19, 47
Amun 18, 28, 31, 32, 51, 68, 72, 93, 94, 117, 121, 147, 225
Anubis........................99, 119, 137, 172
Apep.......41, 50, 51, 52, 53, 57, 60, 178, 201, 222
Aphety.. 115, 116
Apollo... 83
Apophis 11, 16, 18, 19, 20, 22, 28, 32, 33, 38, 39, 41, 42, 43, 44, 45, 46, 47, 48, 49, 50, 51, 52, 53, 54, 55, 56, 57, 69, 70, 75, 77, 114, 121, 124, 128, 133, 137, 143, 148, 163, 164, 165, 168, 173, 176, 177, 178, 180, 181, 196, 201, 205, 208, 214, 215, 218, 219, 223, 225
Apuleius......................102, 103, 220, 222

Aqen.. 37
Artemis... 83
Asclepius................................... 19, 146
Athena.. 24
Atum...... 17, 28, 32, 35, 38, 39, 57, 107, 109, 110, 115, 117, 125, 126, 145, 158, 159, 168, 174, 185, 197, 202, 204, 212

B

Bastet....6, 11, 16, 83, 84, 148, 192, 212, 223
Bes 135, 137, 141, 147, 150
Bestet... 135
Biga... 71
Bubastis.. 138, 148

C

Chaos Serpent........................... See Apophis
Chnoubis 120
Cleopatra............152, 153, 154, 220, 222
Cosmic Serpent, the...................... 9, 30, 39
Cosmic Snake 40
Creator Goose, the................................193
Creator Serpent, the...................... 123, 127

D

Deir el-Medina 44, 72, 94, 95, 96, 97, 124, 150, 225
Dendera.... 31, 32, 33, 54, 56, 67, 70, 71, 73, 74, 76, 80, 82, 84, 85, 88, 89, 101, 115, 116, 117, 131, 166, 187, 220, 222, 224

Denwen *118*
Dep *50, 80, 81, 82, 85, 149*
Dionysus *101, 103, 119, 120, 220*
Dja *93, 94*
Djet *25, 34*
Djoser *59, 137, 222*

E

Earth God, the 48, 49, 95, 109, 121, 182, 185, 193
Edfu. 49, 53, 82, 92, 115, 116, 121, 129, 130, 131, 138, 140, 181, 221, 222, 223
Elephantine *49, 128, 142, 175*
Ennead, the *48, 50, 85*
Esna *33, 45, 47, 75, 104, 130*

G

Geb.. 48, 73, 89, 95, 109, 121, 132, 145, 180, 182, 185, 193
Gebel Tarif *23*
Giza *93*
Greek Magical Papyri *17, 56, 120, 121, 122, 142, 143, 220*

H

Ha 49
Hapi *89, 128*
Harpokrates *86, 120*
Harsomtus *32, 117*
Hathor. 6, 11, 26, 31, 32, 33, 48, 53, 56, 61, 62, 65, 66, 67, 68, 69, 70, 71, 73, 74, 75, 76, 77, 79, 80, 82, 84, 85, 89, 98, 101, 110, 115, 117, 123, 140, 145, 150, 166, 180, 195, 199, 201, 213, 216, 220, 222, 224
Hatnub *39*
Hatshepsut *73, 74, 84, 85, 90, 91, 93, 215, 221, 224*
Hauhet *32*
Hau-hor *115, 116*
Heh *32*
Heka *51, 132, 136, 164*
Heliopolis *28, 30, 48, 87, 159, 220*
Herakleopolis *110*
Hercules *24*
Hermes *21, 24, 120, 121, 221, 224*
Hermopolis *30, 31, 110*
Hermouthis *88*
Herodotus *17, 28, 86, 219, 222*

Hibis *57*
Hierakonpolis *82*
Hor *116, 147, 148*
Horapollo *124, 125, 222*
Horus. 16, 17, 26, 27, 32, 38, 48, 49, 53, 57, 60, 62, 63, 66, 68, 74, 76, 81, 82, 83, 89, 92, 100, 115, 116, 117, 120, 121, 123, 127, 129, 130, 134, 138, 143, 144, 145, 147, 148, 149, 163, 167, 169, 171, 178, 182, 185, 191, 195, 200, 204, 205, 221, 222
Horus the Elder *60*
Hu 192
Hygiea *146*

I

Io 102
Irta 31, 32, 33, 34, 123, 159
Iry-denden *115, 116, 129, 130*
Isis 6, 27, 32, 33, 38, 48, 50, 51, 60, 64, 65, 67, 68, 71, 74, 77, 82, 88, 89, 94, 95, 99, 100, 102, 103, 113, 119, 120, 129, 130, 131, 133, 136, 145, 148, 149, 153, 163, 166, 168, 174, 183, 205, 207, 222, 223, 226

K

Karnak..... 30, 32, 38, 51, 72, 89, 90, 93, 98, 116
Kauket *32*
Kebehwet *98*
Keh 32
Kematef.... 31, 33, 45, 117, 121, 123, 127
Khenty-hor *115, 116*
Khepri..... 31, 63, 65, 113, 168, 200, 201, 202, 203, 204, 208
Khnum *33, 45, 47, 115, 120*
Khonsu 30, 31, 32, 34, 68, 148, 159, 221
Kom el-Shoqafa *120*
Kom Ombo *33*

L

Leto *83, 86*

M

Maat *73, 89, 158, 178, 180*
Mafdet *18, 180, 185*
Medinet Habu *32*
Mehen.. 34, 51, 111, 112, 113, 114, 115, 138, 190, 191, 192, 193, 194, 195,

196, 200, 201, 202, 203, 204, 205, 206, 208, 210, 212, 215, 216, 217, 218, 224
Memphis 30, 31, 32, 72, 82, 166
Mercury.................................See Hermes
Meretseger........ 72, 79, 95, 96, 97, 98, 124
Meskhenet 92
Metelis... 28
Metui .... See Time Serpent
Milky Way, the................ 56, 99, 108, 184
Min... 86
Minerva.................................. See Athena
Mo'alla 46
Mut.... 33, 58, 62, 64, 66, 68, 69, 71, 72, 73, 79, 88, 94, 123, 225

N

Naukratis 119, 120
Naunet... 32
Nebakhet... 195
Nebamun 93, 136, 224
Nefertem 83
Nehebkau ... 88, 106, 107, 108, 109, 110, 115, 125, 126, 190, 197, 198, 204, 206, 216, 217, 218, 225
Nehep.. 171, 204
Nehmataway 109
Neith..... 33, 45, 104, 148, 149, 195, 209
Nekhbet..24, 63, 70, 82, 83, 84, 85, 129, 185
Nephthys...27, 33, 64, 67, 102, 113, 140, 163, 174, 183, 207
Nepri 88, 91, 94
Nesbety 116
Nesret 65
Netjerankh... 117
Nile, the 6, 14, 17, 32, 35, 50, 56, 63, 89, 90, 101, 102, 128, 129, 130, 131, 178, 179, 220, 223, 225
Nubia .. 23, 24, 71, 75, 94, 97, 155, 194, 225
Nun.................... 31, 32, 33, 38, 49, 143
Nut 48, 55, 99, 121, 122, 130, 193, 207, 225

O

Ogdoad, the 31, 32, 33, 159, 206
Onuris.. 75, 147
Opening of the Mouth ceremony..... 197, 216
Orion 167

Osiris..27, 28, 34, 36, 38, 48, 60, 64, 70, 73, 81, 82, 87, 88, 95, 103, 107, 111, 114, 119, 120, 126, 131, 138, 159, 163, 164, 166, 167, 169, 170, 171, 173, 174, 175, 176, 177, 182, 186, 199, 202, 204, 206, 207, 208, 209, 223
Ouroboros, the....... 35, 111, 113, 143, 171, 177, 187, 207, 208

P

Pakhet.. 71, 74, 84
Pe 50, 80, 81, 82, 85
Pecher-hor 129, 130
Philae 50, 51, 54, 65, 67, 68, 82, 129, 130, 136, 146, 226
Pliny... 157, 224
Plutarch 120, 131, 153, 223
Pompeii 102
Ptah..............31, 32, 34, 70, 83, 98, 198
Punt 156, 158

Q

Qantir 86

R

Ra 16, 18, 33, 34, 37, 38, 42, 44, 45, 47, 48, 50, 51, 53, 56, 60, 61, 66, 68, 69, 71, 73, 74, 75, 76, 82, 84, 86, 90, 93, 107, 108, 110, 111, 112, 113, 115, 116, 121, 123, 125, 126, 128, 132, 133, 137, 138, 145, 148, 149, 158, 159, 163, 165, 167, 168, 171, 174, 176, 177, 181, 182, 183, 185, 191, 193, 197, 199, 201, 203, 205, 207, 208, 212, 213, 224
Ra-Harakhti 76
Re 31, 39, 44, 45, 50, 53, 61, 65, 67, 68, 74, 76, 77, 85, 87, 99, 108, 110, 116, 121, 124, 148, 158, 168, 173, 174, 178, 180, 192, 212, 216, 224
Red Sea, the.......................... 155, 157, 158
Remet 115
Renenutet.. 19, 72, 77, 79, 87, 88, 89, 90, 91, 92, 93, 94, 95, 99, 102, 103, 105, 109, 119, 139, 140, 142, 143, 167, 218
Ruty 19, 35, 125, 127, 128, 131

S

Saint George 57
Sais 33
Saqqara 137, 194, 222
Sek-hau 115
Sekhmet 6, 11, 26, 49, 54, 60, 68, 69, 70,
  71, 72, 75, 79, 80, 83, 84, 87, 107,
  124, 125, 126, 127, 138, 140, 148,
  222, 223, 225
Selene 142
Selket 33, 146, 180, 185
Selkis .... See Serket
Senen 129, 131
Serapis 100, 102, 103, 119
Serket 109, 146, 149, 182
Seth 44, 47, 48, 49, 52, 57, 68, 121, 137,
  143, 144, 145, 149, 176, 178, 179,
  180, 181, 191, 195, 199, 200, 205,
  214
Shay 92, 100, 118
Shed 145, 148
Shena 120
Shesshes 56
Shu 35, 60, 70, 71, 73, 75, 101, 121,
  122, 125, 127, 128, 147, 185
Sia 164, 173, 192
Sobek 89, 172
Sokar 166, 169, 187, 202
Solar Barque, the... 22, 25, 38, 43, 46, 47,
  48, 49, 50, 51, 54, 55, 57, 111, 145,
  163, 169, 172, 178, 179, 181, 196,
  203, 210, 214, 215, 216
Solar Child, the 215
Solar Eye, the.. 54, 60, 76, 123, 124, 127,
  178, 181, 205
Soped 49
Sothis 49, 90, 130
Speos Artemidos 74, 84, 85, 221
Strabo 153, 157
Sun God, the... 16, 18, 31, 34, 37, 41, 44,
  45, 46, 48, 51, 52, 55, 60, 61, 63,
  83, 108, 110, 111, 112, 113, 114,
  115, 123, 124, 125, 127, 130, 136,
  138, 158, 159, 163, 164, 165, 166,
  167, 168, 169, 170, 172, 174, 175,
  176, 177, 178, 181, 182, 187, 188,
  191, 192, 193, 200, 202, 203, 204,
  205, 206, 207, 208, 209, 210, 212,
  214, 215, 216

T

Tayet 70, 92
Tefnut 35, 60, 70, 75, 101, 121, 125,
  127, 128, 140, 148
Tel Basta 67
Tell el-Fara'in .... See Dep
Tell el-Farkha 59
Thebes.. 28, 68, 75, 93, 97, 120, 135, 172
Thermouthis 88, 89, 93, 99, 100
Thoth..... 6, 17, 21, 26, 31, 50, 61, 73, 74,
  75, 86, 99, 109, 121, 124, 133, 141,
  145, 148, 168, 185, 187, 195, 203,
  215, 216, 220, 221, 223
Time Serpent, the 37, 203
Tutankhamun.. 35, 71, 74, 104, 113, 117,
  165, 201, 221
Typhon 143

U

Uraeus.... 5, 9, 11, 19, 24, 33, 58, 59, 62,
  65, 66, 67, 68, 69, 70, 71, 72, 73,
  74, 75, 76, 77, 79, 80, 84, 87, 103,
  104, 105, 106, 110, 118, 125, 128,
  138, 139, 142, 148, 158, 165, 166,
  167, 183, 205, 209, 217, 218, 219,
  222
Uraeus Goddess, the..... 33, 65, 67, 73, 75,
  76, 77, 79, 123, 165

W

Wadi Maghareh 59
Wadjet 24, 49, 63, 65, 70, 71, 74, 79, 80,
  81, 82, 83, 84, 85, 86, 87, 105, 127,
  165, 223
Wamemty 42
Wepset 71
Wepwawet 137
Weret-Hekau 66, 71, 72, 74, 84
Winding Waterway .... See Milky Way

Z

Zeus 28, 83, 118, 119

OTHER BOOKS BY LESLEY JACKSON

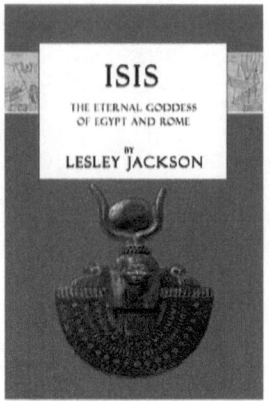

Isis: The Eternal Goddess of Egypt and Rome
ISBN: 978-1-910191-21-7

Sekhmet and Bastet: The Feline Powers of Egypt
ISBN: 978-1-910191-20-0

Hathor: A Reintroduction to an Ancient Egyptian Goddess
ISBN: 978-1-910191-22-4

Thoth: The History of the Ancient Egyptian God of Wisdom
ISBN 978-1-910191-23-1

Available from www.avaloniabooks.co.uk

OTHER BOOKS FROM AVALONIA

Circle for Hekate
Volume I: History & Mythology
by Sorita d'Este
ISBN: 978-1910191071

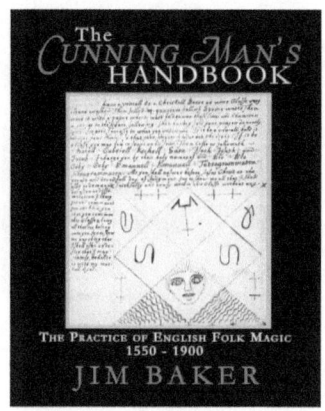

The Cunning Man's Handbook
by Jim Baker
The Practice of English Folk Magic 1550-1900
ISBN: 978-1905297689

Epona: Hidden Goddess of the Celts
by P.D. Mackenzie Cook
ISBN: 978-1905297962

Thracian Magic: Past & Present
by Georgi Mishev
ISBN 978-1905297481

Available from www.avaloniabooks.co.uk

www.ingramcontent.com/pod-product-compliance
Lightning Source LLC
Chambersburg PA
CBHW021808220426
43662CB00006B/228